T0284687

BASTA!

LAND AND THE ZAPATISTA
REBELLION IN CHIAPAS

Basta!

LAND AND THE ZAPATISTA REBELLION IN CHIAPAS

GEORGE A. COLLIER
WITH ELIZABETH LOWERY
QUARATIELLO

THIRD EDITION

FOREWORD BY PETER ROSSET

FOOD FIRST BOOKS
OAKLAND, CALIFORNIA

To David and Lucy and to Stephen, midnight's child

TEXT DESIGN BY COLORED HORSE STUDIOS

TYPESET BY JEFF BRANDENBURG/IMAGECOMP

COVER DESIGN BY AMY EVANS MCCLURE

COVER ART, "BARE BONES #22," BY PHYLLIS PLATTNER

WWW.PHYLLISPLATTNER.COM

Food First Books
398 60th Street
Oakland, California 94618
www.foodfirst.org

Library of Congress Cataloging-in-Publication Data
Collier, George Allen, 1942–
 Basta! : Land and the Zapatista Rebellion in Chiapas / George A. Collier with Elizabeth Lowery Quaratiello ; foreword by Peter Rosset.—3rd ed.
  p.   cm.
 Includes bibliographical references and index.
 ISBN-13: 978-0-935028-97-3 (pbk.)
 ISBN-10: 0-935028-97-8 (pbk.)
 1. Peasantry—Mexico—Chiapas.   2.   Land   reform—Mexico—Chiapas.
3. Agriculture—Economic aspects—Mexico—Chiapas. 4. Chiapas (Mexico)—Rural conditions. 5. Chiapas (Mexico)—Economic conditions. 6. Rural development—Mexico—Chiapas.   I.   Quaratiello, Elizabeth Lowery, 1964–
II. Title.

HD1531.M6C65 2005
333.3'17275—dc22   2005011034

Food First Books are distributed by Perseus Distribution,
387 Park Avenue South, 12th Floor, New York, NY 10016
(800) 343-4499

Printed in Canada
10 9 8 7 6 5 4 3 2 1

CONTENTS

FOREWORD

BY PETER ROSSET

The Zapatista rebellion that began on January 1, 1994, was an event laden with significance for Mexico and for the world. Thus this extraordinary book can be read on various levels. First and foremost, it is a clear and informative history of the uprising and its relationship to that most important of commodities in rural areas: land. It shows why indigenous people and peasants in the Mexican state of Chiapas chose to take up arms. Yet it also takes a remarkable step toward a more nuanced understanding of indigenous and peasant communities than we have had before. It helps us understand how and why the Zapatista Army of National Liberation—the EZLN—is different from previous armed struggles in Mesoamerica and elsewhere. Finally, and perhaps most importantly, it is a poignant case study of how neoliberal economic restructuring reaches into the very heart of communities, enriching the few while impoverishing the many; ultimately turning neighbor against neighbor and leading inexorably toward violent confrontations.

George Collier draws upon more than thirty years of research among the indigenous people of Chiapas to shatter the images held by the Left and the Right, whether they be of "noble savages" holding out against the ravages of capitalism or of "backward Indians" holding back economic development. Taking us inside people's lives, he and Elizabeth Lowery Quaratiello show how the poor in indigenous communities are doubly victimized—first by the relationship between their communities and national or international economies, and second by relatively wealthy leaders inside their own villages who exploit them further in a myriad of ways. Yet Collier and Quaratiello also show how, when given half a chance, peasants and indigenous people can seize upon economic opportunities in dynamic ways that intellectuals of either persuasion had previously claimed were impossible, exposing the myth of the insular community, cut off from the outside world. Without taking this additional step in our understanding of peasant societies, we would be doomed to endlessly repeat the past failures of rural development policies throughout the world.

The rank and file members of the EZLN are refugees from villages where local strongmen, or *caciques*, denied them the right to make a living. Given this anti-leader mentality, it should come as no surprise that Zapatista ideology rejects the vanguardism and top-down organization of previous guerrilla movements. Rather they emphasize communal decision making and stake no claims on state power, instead calling, Gramsci-like, upon Mexican civil society to remake the nation in a form more responsive to the needs of the poor. Collier and Quaratiello show how this uprising, despite coming from largely indigenous communities, reaches out to all of the poor and disenfranchised regardless of their ethnicity, something surprising and perhaps even refreshing in this age of ethnic conflict.

This is a book about the Zapatistas, and about the "indigenous" and "peasant questions" that have troubled Latin America for so long. But it is also a book about people's lives, a book that cuts easily across the geographic and cultural distances that separate readers in the North from Mayan communities in Chiapas. It is in showing ordinary lives, complete with petty and not-so-petty struggles, that the authors are at their best. This book makes it absolutely clear what the economic restructuring of the 1980s has left in its wake, and while their chosen case study is of Chiapas, what they have to say is equally relevant to South Central Los Angeles or any other community that has had its fabric ripped asunder by homegrown or exported neoliberal policies. The growing gulf between rich and poor leads to the desperation and violence of neighbor against neighbor. In Chiapas, at least, a new social grouping has emerged from the desolation, represented by the Zapatistas and their spokesman, Subcomandante Marcos. Perhaps they are showing all of us a path forward, setting aside the ethnic differences that separate us and the verticalism that often stifles popular movements.

PREFACE TO THE THIRD EDITION

In January 1991, Zinacanteco Indians in Chiapas questioned me about the Persian Gulf War. Why had Saddam Hussein and George Bush brought countries on opposite sides of the world into war? Would burning Kuwait oil fields truly pollute the world's skies and seas? Might warfare come to Chiapas?

A different kind of war arose in Chiapas on January 1, 1994, when the Zapatista Army of National Liberation (EZLN) rebelled against the Mexican government in a region that seems remote and exotic to many. But Chiapas and the Persian Gulf are closer than one might think, drawn together by the geopolitics of petroleum that have transformed Mexico's agrarian economy since the OPEC crisis stunned the world in 1972.

Mexico began to produce oil for export in the 1970s, pouring borrowed petrodollars into development that drew people out of the countryside and confronted the country with shortfalls in basic foods and a crisis in agriculture. Subsidies and agrarian reform helped stave off the setbacks in agriculture until 1982, when dropping world oil prices plunged Mexico into a crisis of debt. Austerity and economic restructuring cut support for agrarian programs, and the problems in the countryside worsened. The Zapatista rebellion responds to this crisis.

The Mexican crisis was one that has been felt around the globe in various ways, by people whose jobs have moved offshore in the "free market" economy, by those whose states have cut support for health, welfare, and social services, and by those whose lost livelihoods have forced them into international migration as undocumented and poorly paid workers.

I began studying peasant agriculture in the highlands of Chiapas in the early 1960s and have witnessed many of the changes that oil-led development has brought to the lives and livelihoods of Zinacantecos and other indigenous peasants of the region. This book about the beginnings of the Zapatista rebellion draws on the unusual privilege of my having been able to return to Chiapas repeatedly through more than three decades of dramatic change.

About myself and the perspectives that I bring to this writing, I have the following to say. My values have been shaped by a family firmly committed to New Deal Democratic politics, probably inclining me to sympathy for national states such as Mexico that have embraced responsibilities for popular welfare. Nonetheless, born in 1942, I matured after World War II in the era of cold war that erased much of our consciousness of class and politics. It was when I began to read about Latin American and Iberian history that I decided to study agrarian politics and change.

At the time of Lázaro Cárdenas' 1934–1940 presidency in Mexico, my grandfather, John Collier, Sr., was the commissioner of Indian affairs in the Roosevelt administration and an activist for Indianism (national programs on behalf of indigenous people) in the Americas. I knew him in his elder years as a somewhat eccentric, introspective, yet visionary person whose love of wilderness and solitude, I later realized, stemmed from how he had come to grips with adolescent depression after the suicide and death of his parents. As an anthropologist, I have always been intrigued by, yet distanced from, Indianism, which I understand in historical perspective as partaking of what Renato Rosaldo describes in his *Culture and Truth: The Remaking of Social Analysis* as "imperialist nostalgia." It is not for lack of interest in the contemporary Maya that I take this position; I have mastered Tzotzil as a way of learning from Zinacanteco and other indigenous people of central highland Chiapas about their history, politics, and views of the world. My experience with and understanding of the Maya contribute to my skepticism of those who interpret the Zapatista movement solely as a Maya movement when it has so much in common with the shared concerns of the class of rural poor and the basic rights of all citizens. Since 1994, the Zapatistas have protagonized the cause of indigenous autonomy, but land, health, housing, education, work, and fair prices have always been central to their goals.

I am also wary of idealizations of peasant and indigenous communities. I see such communities as much less egalitarian and more differentiated by class and politics than do many analysts. The appeal to collective sentiments is often combined with maneuvering for personal power. Many of the Mexican indigenous and other peasants I shall talk about have protagonized activism for land, or have challenged the ruling party on behalf of their fellows at one stage of their political careers while taking the side of the national state and exercising its power at another stage. Their rise to power and their exercise of power have as much to do with striving for advantage over one another as with the ways in which the regional or national bourgeoisie gain advantage over them.

My wariness extends to what I sometimes feel has been romantic fetishization of the Zapatista rebellion and of its charismatic spokesperson, Subcomandante Marcos. Indigenous Chiapas involves many who are not part of the rebellion, but whose lives have been caught up in the same forces that precipitated the uprising and have flowed from it. These people all deserve our consideration in understanding what Chiapas means for our world.

I have learned a great deal about Chiapas from the work and insight of colleagues in what began as the Harvard Chiapas Project, led by Evon Z. Vogt, who introduced me and dozens of other students to research in highland Chiapas. Frank and Francesca Cancian, Jane Collier, John Haviland, Lourdes de León, Robert and Mimi Laughlin, Jan and Diane Rus, and Evon and Catherine Vogt have shared their lives and work with me in more ways than I can credit.

Robert Alvarez, Merielle Flood, Daniel Mountjoy, and Ronald Nigh have collaborated in some of my research and writing. Ramón González Ponciano, Aída Hernández Castillo, Gary Gossen, Lourdes de León, June Nash, Thomas Olesen, Stuart Plattner, and Jan Rus have generously shared writing and advice. I am grateful for the research assistance of José Hernández Pérez, María Hernández Pérez, Antonio Pérez Hernández, Namino Glantz, and Apen Ruiz and for the hospitality of Marcy Jacobsen, Janet Marren, and Kippy Nigh. This book has also benefited from comments and suggestions from Federico Besserer, Dan La Botz, Aracely Burguete Cal y Mayor, John Burstein, Frank Cancian, Jane Collier, John Foran, Tim Harding, John Haviland, Lourdes de León, Mimi Laughlin, Robert Laughlin, María Elena Martínez Torres, Bill Maurer, Bridget O'Laughlin, Stuart Plattner, Phyllis Plattner (who provided the cover art as well as years of friendship), Lucía Rayas, Michael Roland, O. P., Jan Rus, and Peter Rosset; and from research material made available by James Breedlove, Dan Rozkuszka, and Teresa Sierra. I also wish to thank staff, student, and faculty colleagues at the Stanford Department of Anthropology and at Wellesley College for opportunities to talk about my analysis of the events in Chiapas. I am also grateful to Alvaro and Sherry Carvajal, and to Bill and Carol Hellums, for their friendship and company during the revisions of the book.

I am very grateful for the assistance of institutions and colleagues in Chiapas. The Instituto Chiapaneco de Cultura (ICC) has generously shared publications of vital research by scholars of the region. I especially appreciate the assistance extended to me by Andrés Fábregas Puig, director general of the ICC, and by Jesús Morales Bermúdez. I thank the Centro de Estudios Universitarios (CEU) and librarian María Elena Fernández Galán for published and unpublished source materials. The Colegio de la Frontera Sur (ECOSUR) has shared library and map resources, and I thank Pablo Farías, José Carlos Fernández Ugalde, Ignacio March, and Manuel Parra for their collegiality and assistance. CIESAS–Sureste, the regional office of Mexico's Centro de Investigaciones y Estudios Superiores en Antropología Social, has also shared their library materials, as has INAREMAC, the Instituto de Asesoría Antropológica para la Región Maya, A.C. I appreciate access to the map collections of Na Bolom and of the Fundación Arqueológica Nuevo Mundo in San Cristóbal de Las Casas.

To the people of Zinacantán, and especially to those of the hamlet of Apas, I owe special thanks for having been welcomed over the years as a guest and researcher.

I am grateful for research support from the National Science Foundation for the study of "Agrarian Change in Southeastern

Mexico" (BNS–8804607), for "Methodological Training for a GIS Application in Cultural Anthropology" (DBS–9221376), and for "Monitoring Rapid Social Change in Southeastern Mexico" (SBR–9601370); from the Consortium of International Earth Sciences Information Network (CIESIN) for the study of "Deforestation, Land Use, and Development in the Greater Mayan Region"; from the Stanford Humanities Center for time to think and write about the changing livelihoods and politics of Zinacantán; from the Center for Latin American Studies for research support in Chiapas during summer 1993 and summer 2004; and from the John D. and Catherine T. MacArthur Foundation, Program on Peace and International Cooperation, for research and writing on "Differentiation, Radicalization, and the Emergence of the Zapatista Rebellion in Chiapas."

The publishers of *BioScience*, *Cultural Survival Quarterly*, *Mexican Studies/Estudios Mexicanos*, and *Research in Economic Anthropology* graciously allowed me to draw upon maps and materials in my previously published work. Chapter Five draws extensively on an essay published as a discussion paper by the United Nations Research Institute for Social Development. Chapter Six is based on an article I wrote for *Dialectical Anthropology* (Kluwer Academic Publishers), and Chapters Seven and Nine, on my 2003 contribution, with Jane Collier, to *The Future of Revolutions* (John Foran, ed., Zed Books). I am grateful for permission to borrow from these previous works and to Food First for the invitation to bring this edition up to date.

Elizabeth Quaratiello and I have collaborated in writing this book, which is based on my research and other scholarly writing. We wish to thank our families for their patience and forbearance in allowing us to bring the work to fruition.

George A. Collier
Stanford, California, August 1994
San Cristóbal de Las Casas, Chiapas, June 1999
San Francisco, California, December 2004

PREFACE TO THE SPANISH EDITION
BY RODOLFO STAVENHAGEN

The Zapatista rebellion broke out in Chiapas in 1994, just as armed guerrilla struggle was thought to have been exhausted as a source for revolutionary change. This social movement coincided with the inauguration of the North American Free Trade Agreement (NAFTA) between Mexico, the United States, and Canada, joining those three countries in a common market. It was the last year of the presidency of Salinas de Gortari, who had promoted the indiscriminate opening of the Mexican economy in pursuit of "modernization," a process that had already ravaged Mexican society with increasing political and social polarization.

Chiapas was the Mexican state that had the highest indices of poverty and the fewest social services. Chiapas had outrageously low life expectancy and was one of the last strongholds of *caciquismo*. It was a place unvisited by modernization and democratization. Yet it was also a region of transformations that penetrated the lives of peasants and of the indigenous people who make up more than 30 percent of the total population and who throughout Mexico have the lowest levels of economic and social development. The transformations began in the 1950s, with the deforesting and colonization of the Lacandon jungle (one of the last primary tropical forest reserves) and the construction of large hydroelectric dams to control turbulent rivers and generate electrical energy for the rest of the country. Then came the discovery and exploitation of vast reserves of petroleum; and finally, at the beginning of the 1980s, the impact of thousands of Guatemalan Indian refugees fleeing military repression in their country.

The indigenous population of Chiapas were thus not marginal to national developments—they suffered their devastating effects firsthand. This was the brew that gave rise to a social movement seeking basic rights, merging older peasant and indigenous demands with new political claims, combining elements surviving from the revolutionary "vanguardism" of the 1960s and 1970s with innovative strands of Christian liberation theology. What occurred in Chiapas beginning in 1994 could have occurred (or can occur) in any state in Mexico. Yet the Zapatista rebellion is also very specific and unique to the process of change that has unfolded in the Chiapas region over a series of decades. Whether or not this uprising can be repeated elsewhere remains to be seen.

The Zapatista rebellion had a profound impact on Mexican society, coming as it did in a year of presidential elections and growing political unrest in all sectors of society. Most sectors of Mexican society expressed sympathy for the goals and objectives of the rebellion (although not necessarily with armed struggle), and the government professed its commitment to finding a peaceful negotiated solution to the problem. Whatever the final outcome of this movement, national and international public opinion rightfully questions the social and economic conditions that gave rise to this uprising, while pondering as well the social and cultural composition of this new popular revolutionary army (men and women), whose presence disproves the myths of political stability, economic progress, and apathy that had more or less taken over national discourse (at least officially).

George Collier, an anthropologist from Stanford University, began to do research on the indigenous communities of Chiapas in the 1960s and has published extensively as a result of his research. Having returned regularly to Chiapas, he has been able study firsthand the diverse transformations that affect the life of the region. He has witnessed ecological and technological changes, migration, the impact of the petroleum economy, the emergence of political, ideological, and religious conflict, deterioration of the environment, increasing poverty, and the accumulating frustrations of local peasant communities upon failure to better their life conditions. He has also been able to observe the growing social and political mobilization of the indigenous peasantry, the emergence of new movements for basic rights, and the questioning of old systems of political power.

In *Basta!* George Collier and his collaborator, Elizabeth Lowery Quaratiello, present a new vision of the great transformations that have affected the indigenous population of the state of Chiapas over the last few decades. This vision is based on detailed and personal knowledge, objective yet at the same time sympathetic to the suffering and deeply held aspirations of the indigenous peasants of the region. This work is not the history of the Zapatista rebellion nor an interpretation of the EZLN and its leaders. It is rather an attempt to frame the social and economic forces indispensable for in-depth understanding of this movement and its place in a broader national and international context.

This book will be required reading for a long time for all those who would like to delve beyond the ephemeral news to reach a deeper understanding of the social movements of our time. George Collier deserves our appreciation.

Rodolfo Stavenhagen, Colegio de México

ABBREVIATIONS

ANCIEZ	Alianza Nacional Campesina Independiente Emiliano Zapata / National Independent Emiliano Zapata Peasant Alliance
ANAGSA	Aseguradora Nacional Agrícola y Ganadero / National Agriculture and Livestock Insurance Program
ARIC–UU	Asociación Rural de Interés Colectivo–Unión de Uniones / Rural Collective Interest Association–Union of Unions
CCRI	Comité Clandestino de Revolución Indígena / Committee of Clandestine Indigenous Revolution
CDLI	Comité de Defensa de la Libertad Indígena / Committee for the Defense of Indigenous Liberty
CEOIC	Consejo Estatal de Organizaciones Indígenas y Campesinas / Chiapas State Indigenous Peasant Council
CIOAC	Central Independiente de Obreros Agrícolas y Campesinos / Independent Confederation of Agricultural Workers and Peasants
CNC	Confederación Nacional Campesina / National Peasant Confederation
CND	Convención Nacional Democrática / National Convention for Democracy
CNDH	Comisión Nacional de Derechos Humanos / National Human Rights Commission
CNPA	Coordinadora Nacional Plan de Ayala / National "Plan de Ayala" Coordinating Committee
CNPI	Consejo Nacional de Pueblos Indígenas / National Council of Indigenous Pueblos
CONAI	Comisión Nacional de Intermediación / National Mediation Commission
CROM	Confederación Regional Obrera Mexicana / Mexican Regional Labor Confederation
CTM	Confederación de Trabajadores de México / Confederation of Mexican Workers
EPR	Ejército Popular Revolucionario / Popular Revolutionary Army
EZLN	Ejército Zapatista de Liberación Nacional / Zapatista National Liberation Army
FDN	Frente Democrático Nacional / National Democratic Front

FIPI	Frente Independiente de Pueblos Indígenas / Indigenous Peoples Independent Front
FZLN	Frente Zapatista de Liberación Nacional / Zapatista National Liberation Front
GATT	General Agreement on Tariffs and Trade
INI	Instituto Nacional Indigenista / National Indianist Institute
INMECAFE	Instituto Mexicano del Café / Mexican Coffee Institute
ISMAM	Indígenas de la Sierra Madre de Motozintla / Indians of the Sierra Madre of Motozintla
LP	Línea Proletaria / Proletarian Line
NAFTA	North American Free Trade Agreement
OCEZ	Organización Campesina Emiliano Zapata / Emiliano Zapata Peasant Organization
OIT	Organización Internacional del Trabajo / International Labor Organization (ILO)
ORIACH	Organización Indígena de los Altos de Chiapas / Indigenous Organization of Highland Chiapas
PAN	Partido Acción Nacional / National Action Party
PP	Política Popular / Popular Politics
PRA	Plan de Rehabilitación Agraria / Agrarian Rehabilitation Plan
PRD	Partido de la Revolución Democrática / Party of the Democratic Revolution
PRI	Partido Revolucionario Institucional / Institutional Revolutionary Party
PRODESCH	Programa de Desarrollo Socioeconómico de los "Altos" de Chiapas / Socioeconomic Development Program for the Highlands of Chiapas
PRONASOL	Programa Nacional de Solidaridad / National Solidarity Program
PST	Partido Socialista de los Trabajadores / Socialist Workers Party
SAM	Sistema Alimentario Mexicano / Mexican Food System
SEDESOL	Secretaría de Desarrollo Social / Ministry of Social Development
SRA	Secretaría de Reforma Agraria / Ministry of Agrarian Reform
UU	Unión de Uniones / Union of Unions
WTO	World Trade Organization

When a housemaid in the Chiapas state capital, Tuxtla Gutiérrez, suddenly quit her job, why had she just used her entire Christmas bonus to buy hundreds of bandages?

Why did a man purchase an itinerant merchant's entire stock of rubber boots in March 1993 at the entrance to Palenque, Chiapas' famous classic Mayan ruin?

What made peasants eking out a precarious existence in the rain forests of eastern Chiapas cite "war" as a threat more dangerous to the world than "poverty," "disease," "deforestation," or "pollution" in a 1992 survey of attitudes about global change?[1]

In the summer of 1993, Tucson writer Leslie Marmon Silko's *Almanac of the Dead,* a novel prognosing Native American rebellion from Chiapas to Arizona, suddenly captured an audience of readers in Chiapas. Was there a special reason for such fascination?

The answers to many such puzzles suggested themselves on January 1, 1994, when the EZLN (the *Ejército Zapatista de Liberación Nacional* or Zapatista Army of National Liberation), equipped with rubber boots, homemade army uniforms, bandanas, ski masks, and weapons ranging from handmade wooden rifles to Uzi machine guns, seized towns in eastern and central Chiapas, proclaiming a revolution on the inaugural day of the North American Free Trade Agreement (NAFTA).

Taking advantage of the New Year's holiday to catch security forces off guard, the Zapatistas—a force of young, disciplined, and mostly indigenous men and women soldiers—ransacked the town halls of Altamirano, Chanal, Huistán, Las Margaritas, Oxchuc, Ocosingo, and San Cristóbal de las Casas—once the colonial seat of government of Chiapas and today an important commercial and tourist center. Some burned district attorney, judicial, and police records (but spared archives in San Cristóbal that a local scholar told them had historic value). Others fanned out into the mountains to seek recruits from among the indigenous and other peasants of the region.

Treating startled tourists and civilians with courtesy, the EZLN pronounced itself in rebellion against the government, the army, and the police. In printed circulars and broadcasts from captured Ocosingo radio station XOECH, the Zapatistas declared:

> *Hoy Decimos Basta!* Today we say enough is enough! To the people of Mexico: Mexican brothers and sisters: We are a product of 500 years of struggle: first against slavery, then during the War of Independence against Spain led by insurgents, then to promulgate our constitution and expel the French empire from our soil, and later [when] the dictatorship of Porfirio Díaz denied us the just application of the Reform laws and the people rebelled and leaders like Villa and Zapata emerged, poor men just like us. We have been denied the most elemental education so that others can use us as cannon fodder and pillage the wealth of our country. They don't care that we have nothing, absolutely nothing, not even a roof over our heads, no land, no work, no health care, no food, and no education. Nor are we able freely and democratically to elect our political representatives, nor is there independence from foreigners, nor is there peace nor justice for ourselves and our children.[2]

Invoking Article 39 of Mexico's 1917 Constitution, which invests national sovereignty and the right to modify government in the people of Mexico, they called on other Mexicans to help them depose the "illegal dictatorship" of President Carlos Salinas de Gortari's government and party. They declared war on the Mexican armed forces and called on international organizations and the Red Cross to monitor under the Geneva Conventions of War. They appealed to other Mexicans to join their insurgency.

Within twenty-four hours, the EZLN launched an attack on the Rancho Nuevo army base about six miles southeast of San Cristóbal and freed 179 prisoners from a nearby penitentiary. They kidnapped Absalón Castellanos Domínguez, governor of Chiapas from 1982–1988, announcing he would be tried summarily and shot for crimes of repression. Instead, he was "sentenced" to a life term of hard peasant labor.

FIGURE 0.1 CHIAPAS AND THE AREA OF ZAPATISTA REBELLION.

The Mexican government quickly moved 12,000 troops and equipment into the region. Within days, and after two pitched battles, the Zapatistas retreated east and southward out of the Chiapas central highlands into rugged and inaccessible strongholds in the tropical forests of the eastern lowlands. Backed by air strikes, federal troops pursued the EZLN in armored vehicles to where roads give way to wilderness.

By that time, journalists from around the world had arrived on the scene to chronicle the Zapatista's exploits and explore their motives, which struck chords of sympathy with the Mexican public. Reporters portrayed the rebels as Maya Indians upset over years of poverty and discrimination as they began to write poignant articles describing the abuses heaped upon the Indians of Mexico's southernmost state. Human rights organizations that had for some time been trying to alert the world to the plight of the region's poor suddenly found an avid audience as they began to document federal army abuses against Zapatista prisoners and civilians caught up in the warfare.

The rebels, disguised with bandanas and ski masks, became instant icons, their images replicated on everything from cloth dolls sold in Mexico's outdoor marketplaces to cartoons in Mexico City's daily newspapers. Zapatista images even appeared on condom wrappers. Guessing the identity of Subcomandante Marcos, the shadowy, green-eyed ideologue and military director of the uprising, suddenly became a popular obsession.

The Mexican government sought at first to paint the Zapatista rank and file as guileless but gullible natives inspired and led by foreign subversives. But public opinion, international scrutiny, and widespread dissension within the ranks of the ruling party itself soon led Salinas de Gortari to acknowledge that the Zapatistas had justifiable grievances based on Chiapas' and Mexico's internal affairs. Salinas fired Interior Minister José Patroncinio González Garrido, who as governor of Chiapas from 1988 to 1993 had been accused of repression and abuses against peasants. The president then declared a unilateral cease-fire on January 12, calling on the Zapatistas to lay down their arms and to negotiate with a specially designated Commission for Peace and Reconciliation.

In the weeks that followed, tensions rose. Citizens seized dozens of town halls in Chiapas and neighboring states to protest that incumbent mayors, most of whom were pawns of the governing party, had stolen office through fraudulent elections. In eastern Chiapas, peasants invaded private ranches. Some landowners fled; others counterattacked with hired gunmen. A broad coalition of peasant and indigenous organizations denounced the government for past neglect and abuse and proclaimed themselves in favor of Zapatista demands for reforms.

Peace talks finally began on February 21 in San Cristóbal de las Casas, under the aegis of the Catholic diocese and noted liberation theologian Bishop Samuel Ruiz García. Salinas designated Manuel Camacho Solís as the government's negotiator, a man respected for the integrity and negotiating skills he had demonstrated as former mayor of Mexico City and as foreign affairs minister. As a gesture of good will, the Zapatistas released hostage and former governor Absalón Castellanos Domínguez. With Subcomandante Marcos as their public relations and military spokesperson, the EZLN's general command, the Committee of Clandestine Indigenous Revolution, made up of eighteen representatives of four Mayan-language ethnic groups, began the talks and demanded attention to thirty-four broad-ranging issues of political, economic, and social reform. Two weeks later, negotiators announced thirty-two tentative accords, and the talks recessed to allow both sides to consult with their constituencies. Mexicans breathed a sigh of relief and hope.

Their optimism proved ephemeral. The uprising had thrown Mexico into crisis, calling into question President Salinas de Gortari's program to restructure and modernize the Mexican economy. Deep fissures in the Mexican political system, papered over during Salinas' regime by a facade of "consensus" building, had revealed themselves to international scrutiny as the highly publicized rebellion evoked public debate over government fraud, corruption, and dereliction of duty to Mexico's peasant and indigenous poor. It became apparent that the government had known about the guerrilla army in Chiapas for over a year. Rumors flew that Salinas had done nothing for fear of jeopardizing U.S. congressional approval of NAFTA, or that hard-liners in the ruling party and in the military had lent support to the rebels in protest against Salinas' policies.

The presidential candidacy of Salinas' hand-picked successor, Luis Donaldo Colosio Murrieta, seemed in jeopardy as speculation flared that Salinas might replace Colosio with peace negotiator Camacho, or that Camacho, whom Salinas had initially passed over in favor of Colosio, might declare a renegade candidacy. For the first time in more than half a century, it began to seem as though Mexico's ruling party, the Institutional Revolutionary Party (PRI), might actually have to relinquish power in the presidential elections slated for August 21, 1994.

On March 22, Camacho declared that he would not run for president, but the next day PRI presidential candidate Luis Donaldo Colosio fell to an assassin's bullet, shocking the nation and provoking charges that the killing had been plotted within the PRI itself.

The violence polarized public debates over the Zapatistas and the government. Although the PRI hastily replaced Colosio with Ernesto Zedillo Ponce de León in the hopes of capitalizing on the reaction against violence, Zedillo, a Yale-trained economist who had been Colosio's election advisor, ran a lackluster campaign. But so did candidates of the opposition parties, Cuauhtémoc Cárdenas of the Party of the Democratic Revolution (PRD) and Diego Fernández de Cevallos of the National Action Party (PAN).

Then, on June 12, the Zapatista rank and file rejected the tentative peace accord their own representatives had negotiated with the government, calling for a national convention to revamp the political system while refusing to lay down their arms. Zedillo deemed the earlier negotiations with the EZLN a failure, blaming Camacho, who then resigned as the government's peace negotiator. As leading Mexicans began to suggest publicly that Mexico might become ungovernable, regardless of the outcome of the August elections, Jorge Carpizo MacGregor, a jurist and former human rights commissioner who had agreed in January to step in as interior minister to oversee the elections, submitted his resignation, asserting that an unnamed party was making fair elections impossible. Salinas persuaded Carpizo to withdraw his resignation, but uncertainties continued to grow as the Zapatistas called for a convention prior to the elections to rewrite Mexico's constitution.

This is a book about the background to the fateful Zapatista rebellion. Despite widespread fascination with the uprising, little is understood about its root causes. I want to look behind the romantic images, instant analyses,[3] and outrage prompted by the rebellion to explore the circumstances and forces—both domestic and international—that created a situation ripe for rebellion.

The region behind the headlines is a complicated one. Chiapas is sometimes described as a picturesque backwater—a quaint stop on the tourist circuit where time has stood still and Maya Indians can be observed performing their age-old crafts and rituals. But beneath the surface seen by the casual visitor, Chiapas is filled with paradoxes that defy easy categorization. In addition to indigenous peasants who weave and wear the traditional *huipul* (tunic) and carry loads on tumplines, there are peasants who dress in jeans and drive trucks. Within even the tiniest Indian hamlets there are wealthy entrepreneurs who own such modern luxury items as televisions and videocassette recorders; poor, marginalized farmworkers; and opportunistic political bosses. The state has plenty of wealthy *ladinos* (nonindigenous Mexicans of the region) who sympathize with the Zapatistas and poor peasants who do not. There are disaffected intellectuals, grassroots organizers, elite colonial families, and ranchers, each with their own political agenda. And in this place where Catholics and Protestants have clashed bitterly, where women are praised for passivity rather than activism, a nonsectarian rebellion has arisen, and mothers, wives, and daughters are among those who make up the ranks of the Zapatista army.

What is it that unites those who took up arms with the Zapatistas? In contrast to some analysts, I posit that it began primarily as a peasant rebellion, not an exclusively Indian rebellion. Although the Zapatistas increasingly have been demanding rights for indigenous peoples, they were first and foremost calling attention to the plight of Mexico's rural poor and peasants, both indigenous and nonindigenous, and their movement built on two decades of peasant organizing in Chiapas. By *peasants*, I mean rural people who produce their own food or who are closely connected to others who produce for subsistence, as contrasted with those who farm commercial crops primarily for sale and profit. In southern Mexico, many peasants, but not all, are *indigenous* people, descendants of those who were conquered and subordinated by the Spanish during the period of colonial rule.[4]

Some may wonder why the rebellion was instigated by indigenous peasants and not by the urban poor or those who toil in the maquiladoras, people who have certainly suffered greatly in recent years. Although there is no clear answer to this question, one possible explanation is that on top of the severe hardships peasants have had to endure during the past decade of economic restructuring, they were also disappointed by a number of broken promises from the government: land reform that never occurred; price supports guaranteed, then taken away; and credits extended, then withdrawn. When, in 1992, the government of President Salinas de Gortari brought land reform—the issue on which his party had originally risen to power— to a halt, he signaled an abrupt end to a traditional government covenant with the peasantry and deprived many peasants not just of the possibility of improving their livelihoods, but of their power as a constituency. The Zapatistas, in their uprising and its aftermath, were trying to reclaim that constituency.

The Zapatista rebellion bears some resemblance to the revolutionary movements of Central America, in that those movements also involved peasants who had no safety net to help cope with marginalization. Mexico's government, however, has been much more stable than any of Central America's regimes and it steadfastly—and successfully—fought off involvement in the geopolitics of the cold war.[5] Until the 1982 debt crisis, Mexico also catered to peasants as a distinct constituency—something most Central American governments never even pretended to do. One of the paradoxes of the rebellion is that the Zapatistas have responded to the adversity of eastern Chiapas more as Mexican nationals than as doctrinaire revolutionaries. While they have been demanding changes for their region and for the rural poor in other areas, they have also been holding Mexico's government responsible for undemocratic politics and

for betraying historic commitments to social welfare when it opened
Mexico up to free trade and foreign investment.

As economic and political forces have transformed peasant farming, indigenous and peasant communities have become less
egalitarian, demarcated by class and by national political affiliation.
My observations are drawn from research I performed as an anthropologist during three decades spent studying agrarian change in
highland Chiapas, including ways in which Mexico's oil boom of the
1970s and the resulting debt crisis of the 1980s redefined the lives and
roles of the region's peasants. Among the indigenous peasants I know,
I saw a gap grow ever wider between the wealthy, who were able to
infuse their farming with cash derived from wage work near oil fields,
on dam projects, and in urban construction projects, and the poor,
who are finding it increasingly impossible to be able to afford to farm
even their own land.

Some peasants in Chiapas have been able to weather the changes
wrought by Mexico's economic restructuring by diversifying their
farming activities, becoming produce and flower merchants, or starting up transport businesses. But many have not. Their successes and
failures have often resulted from and contributed to politics, as I will
show by tracing the rise of local political bosses who used their ties
with the Institutional Revolutionary Party (PRI) to establish
monopolies on small businesses and quell opposition in their towns.
Economic restructuring brought particular suffering to the inhabitants of the eastern part of Chiapas, from which the rebels initially
drew the majority of their members, and where cultural isolation,
political exclusion, and economic depression have combined to leave
people in what is commonly called Mexico's "last frontier" without
hope and without even the most basic necessities of life.

Because the situation of indigenous peasants in Mexico's countryside seems so bleak, the Zapatista rebellion inspired enormous
sympathy from people throughout the world who read about the
uprising in their newspapers and watched reports about it on television. Journalists tended to paint an image of the poor, honest
peasants on one side and the greedy ranchers and corrupt politicians
on the other.

This idealization of indigenous peasants is inaccurate, however, because some of the inequalities in the countryside are the result of stratification within peasant communities, not merely the result of injustices heaped upon them from outside. Understanding indigenous politics in this way necessarily complicates the sympathies one might hold toward peasants, but I view this as salutary. I think we misrepresent peasants if we allow ourselves to view them in simplistic terms—as either the passive victims of the state or as "noble savages" who can reinvigorate modern society with egalitarian and collective values. By acknowledging tensions and differences in peasant communities, we face up to both the virtue and the vice inherent in peasants' exercise of power over one another, and we integrate individual agency into our understanding of peasant communities. We also arrive at an appreciation of why not all peasant and indigenous groups welcomed the Zapatistas. In some highland communities, some people referred to the Zapatistas in native Tzotzil as "troublemakers" or "thieves"—a reference to marauders who roamed the countryside in the 1910–1920 decade of the Mexican Revolution. Others told me that when the Zapatistas fanned into the mountains to look for recruits, a giant snake and a whirlwind—ancestor deities—rose in their paths to block off the entrances to Zinacantán and Chamula, communities whose leaders are loyal to the PRI.

The Zapatista uprising forced a public debate about Mexico's priorities and galvanized many impoverished Mexicans to demand better lives, even as it has to some extent polarized relations among indigenous peoples' organizations in Chiapas. It has also sparked a worldwide movement of protests against what many see as the callous and wrongheaded policies of free-market global financial planners.

SYNOPSIS

This book begins with a broad overview of the social, political, economic, and ethnic history of Chiapas from colonial times to the present day. We trace the development of the state from a logging and coffee-growing center in the nineteenth century to the integral role it plays in Mexico today, providing the country with half of its hydro-electric power and much of its oil, as well as many basic foods such as corn and beans. We look at the bitter history of the indigenous people and their subjugation under the Spanish *conquistadores*, a legacy of injustice that continues to taint present-day relations between indigenous and nonindigenous Mexicans. We examine land distribution and the various means used to effect it during the past century, providing a background against which the current political agitation can be viewed.

Turning to the eastern Chiapas heartland of the Zapatista upris-ing, Chapter Two explores peasant life in this remote tropical wilderness that has become famous as the "jungle headquarters" of the EZLN. Virtually unpeopled until the middle of the twentieth century, eastern Chiapas has been settled by waves of peasants flee-ing land scarcity and religious persecution in the highlands as well as by peasants from other states in Mexico. We chronicle the constant struggle of these settlers who have had to compete with loggers, ranchers, and one another for land and livelihood as deforestation and soil erosion continue to claim more and more of the rain forest. Eastern Chiapas in many ways exemplified the marginalization of the poorest peasants in contemporary Mexico—it is a region com-pletely cut off from government services, political power, and economic opportunity. Without roads, cities, or even small towns, eastern Chiapas was a kind of dumping ground for the marginalized, in which all of the hardships peasants confronted in the highlands were exacerbated. This chapter explores the role that such circum-stances played in fueling the frustrations on which the Zapatistas capitalized.

Chapter Three traces the social history of eastern Chiapas, focus-ing on the cultural and religious factors that may have helped to create a climate in which radical politics were more readily accepted than in other areas of Mexico. We look at the growth of grassroots peasant organizations, study their successes and failures, and investi-gate the ways in which macroeconomic events—such as the collapse of coffee prices in 1989—affected the everyday lives of small farmers in eastern Chiapas. This chapter describes the milieu in which the EZLN grew and gained momentum.

Chapter Four takes a more in-depth look at the effect of macroeconomic trends on indigenous peasant life. We review the development of Mexico's energy economy and examine in detail the negative effects it had on the southern part of the country and the nation as a whole as resources were shifted away from agriculture. In particular, we look at how the oil boom affected indigenous migration and delve into the debates that arose over whether Mexico, flooded with cheap corn from Kansas, needed or could even afford peasants any more. We discuss the events that led up to the 1982 debt crisis and examine the aftermath of the austerity program Mexico was pressured to undertake by the international banking community, paying close attention to the revision of the country's agrarian subsidy system and the ways in which peasants responded to the changes. We take up the theme of peasant-initiated economic restructuring, and the diversification of indigenous economic activities during the oil boom. This restructuring is little known to scholars and policy makers, in part because their analytical frameworks do not embrace the scope of the far-flung enterprises, such as flower retailing, with which many peasants are experimenting, often in new cooperative associations.

Chapter Five looks within communities to explore who profits and who loses from restructuring. We examine how economic distinctions have changed the relationships among women and men, young and old, and within communities. The widening gap between rich and poor has broken down many of the relationships of mutual dependency that once helped poorer citizens, and leaders within communities have begun to shuck off their responsibilities to their poorer constituents.

Chapter Six explores the subtle and not so subtle ways that dissidents were dealt with in the Indian hamlets of Chiapas. We look at how political leaders undermined opponents' recourse to customary law while restricting their access to public funds. We look at the recent phenomenon of expelling dissident "Protestants" from Catholic villages, often for political reasons—an unconstitutional practice, which the government nonetheless tolerated as consistent with native rights to self-determination, a justification that masks the political expedience of supporting indigenous henchmen at the local level. We examine the government's Solidarity Program, which was ostensibly designed to alleviate poverty, but which instead became an instrument for rewarding political loyalty and contributed to the anger and frustration expressed through the Zapatista rebellion.

Chapter Seven explores the implication of the rebellion for Mexico's political future and contains some policy recommendations for how Mexico might capitalize constructively on peasants' demonstrable capacity to embrace and effect change. We look at the organization of the EZLN, examine what politicians might learn from them, and ponder the efficacy of impoverishing huge numbers of people in order to achieve a "modern" economy.

Summarizing developments in Chiapas since 1994, Chapter Eight discusses the Zapatistas' quest for indigenous autonomy. The government has circumscribed the Zapatista movement militarily. But the Zapatistas have focused growing international concern for identity and rights into powerful pressure on the Mexicans to grant indigenous communities the legal right to manage their own affairs in keeping with their customs and culture.

The final chapter turns to the Zapatistas' contribution to the emerging worldwide movement of protests against "neoliberal" free-market global financial planning. Through projects of local and regional autonomy, the Zapatistas are demonstrating how they and others can collaborate in building an alternative global future.

In writing about the causes of the rebellion, I want to raise questions about the social and economic costs of restructuring and suggest that the contributions of small-scale agriculturalists need to be considered when evaluating policies for a nation's fiscal health. Because peasant families often produce only enough food for their own consumption, the product of subsistence farming is not given a value in traditional models of economic analysis. Subsistence crops are neither bought nor sold and are thus often overlooked in calculations of the gross domestic product or income. When economists deride small-scale peasant and indigenous agriculture in Mexico as inefficient and call for its replacement with large-scale agribusinesses, they ignore the fact that such "modern" enterprises often displace as many people as they employ, upsetting the delicate balance between subsistence and marginalization in rural Mexico. Moreover, even those analyses that do focus on small-scale agriculture tend to miss the ways that peasants have restructured their own productive capacity through new microenterprises. In Chiapas, such restructuring has not been acknowledged by politicians and development planners for the potential benefits peasants themselves can contribute to the revitalization of the Mexican economy, if they are supported rather than shunned.

I ✦ CHIAPAS AND MEXICO

The Zapatista uprising caught both Mexicans and Mexico watchers by surprise. Chiapas seemed an unlikely place for a revolution to start. Chiapas peasants had been among the most reliable supporters of the ruling party since the 1930s, and the peasants who took up arms in January 1994 were from the most isolated part of the country. Could their demands for political and economic changes on a national level be taken seriously? When the government made overtures to the EZLN as merely a "political force in formation," Subcomandante Marcos angrily retorted that the indigenous people of Chiapas had been exploited for centuries and had every right to make demands of the Mexican political and economic system:

> Why does the government [refuse to put] national politics on the agenda for negotiation? Are the indigenous people of Chiapas "Mexicans" only for the purpose of being exploited? Do they have no right to speak out on national politics? Does the nation claim Chiapas' petroleum, its electric power, its raw materials, its labor—in effect all of Chiapas' lifeblood—*except indigenous Chiapanecans' opinion* regarding the country's future? What sort of citizens does the government take indigenous Chiapanecans to be? Are they "citizens in formation?" Does the government still treat them as little children, as "adults in formation?"[1]

In light of the region's poverty, racism, and history of exploitation, why hadn't peasants taken up arms long ago? We shall see that in centuries past Chiapas' Indians *did* rebel against oppression and exploitation. But because of land reform after the Revolution they came to see the government as an ally—until the Salinas government brought agrarian reform to a halt.

While its ancient Mayan ruins, colonial towns, and colorful culture have attracted a steady stream of scholars and adventurers, for the most part Chiapas has been little known and visited by the rest of the world. Its mountains, cloud forests, canyons, and jungles are not easily accessible to tourists, and its major cities, small by Mexican standards, rise at the end of long, winding roads. But outsiders have nonetheless exploited its natural resources. The Spanish arrived in the sixteenth century, seeking riches, and were followed by Europeans and North Americans in the nineteenth century who coveted Chiapas' precious mahogany and coffee. Today, Chiapas is almost an internal colony for the rest of Mexico, providing oil, electricity, timber, cattle, corn, sugar, coffee, and beans, but receiving very little in return. Chiapas is aptly described as "a rich land, a poor people."[2]

Chiapas has the highest concentration of indigenous people in Mexico and is one of the country's poorest states. Most of Chiapas' wealth is concentrated in the hands of the small number of ladino ranching families who have dominated Chiapas politics for two centuries. A rise in interest in indigenous peoples has helped to create some tourism and a market for native handicrafts, but endemic racism continues to mar relations between Indians and nonindigenous Mexicans.

Chiapas lags behind the rest of Mexico in almost every way measurable: household income, education, and basic standard of living fall far behind the national average, and infant mortality is much higher. Many indigenous people in Chiapas are illiterate, and only about half of the men and a tiny percentage of the women speak Spanish. According to census figures for the period just prior to the rebellion, only 11 percent of adults earned what the government called moderate incomes of at least $3,450 per year (versus 24 percent nationally); less than 50 percent of households have running water (versus 67 percent nationally); and only 14 percent have televisions (versus 45 percent nationally). It is important to note that most of the development money that has been funneled into Chiapas has been used to build infrastructure such as roads and dams that will help transport products from the state to the rest of Mexico.[3]

With 3 percent of the nation's population, Chiapas produced an astounding 13 percent of the country's corn and 54 percent of Mexico's

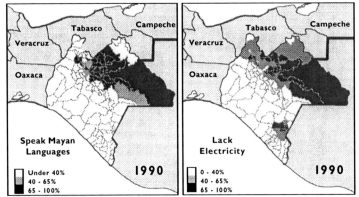

FIGURE 1.1 "A RICH LAND, A POOR PEOPLE." Chiapas produces much of Mexico's hydroelectric power, yet many areas populated by indigenous people remain without electricity or other basic services.

hydroelectric power. It also produced 5 percent of the country's timber, 4 percent of its beans, 13 percent of its gas, and 4 percent of its oil. Ironically, nearly half of Chiapas was without electricity at the time of the rebellion, including most of the regions peopled by Indians (see Figure 1.1).[4]

In addition to food and electricity, Chiapas had for many years supplied Mexico with another vitally important, albeit hard to quantify, resource: political support. Although it is impossible to assess the true numbers involved because of widespread election fraud, the Institutional Revolutionary Party (PRI) had always claimed victory on the basis of overwhelming support from Mexico's rural south. In the 1988 presidential elections, which opposition parties vigorously and effectively contested in northern and metropolitan Mexico, 89.9 percent of Chiapas voters, including impoverished Indian peasants, allegedly turned out for the PRI.

To understand Chiapas' rebellion, we must explore why so stable a regime was challenged by some of its ostensibly strongest supporters. This chapter looks at Chiapas' relationship to Mexico and examines how it came to pass that the national government was able to tap Chiapas' resources and loyalties so effectively, especially in the central and western parts of the state.

THE LEGACY OF CONQUEST

The first town the Zapatistas seized was San Cristóbal de las Casas, a small city surrounded by pine forests in the mountainous highlands of central Chiapas. Once the colonial capital of the region, the city retains many vestiges of its colonial past. Baroque churches stand over Indian markets, and some neighborhoods continue to produce the same goods they manufactured for the Spanish crown. Some of San Cristóbal's elite families pride themselves on being able to trace their ancestry back to the conquistadors who established the city as Ciudad Real in the 1530s; others emphasize the city's association with Bartolomé de las Casas, "the Protector of Indians," who, as Bishop of Chiapas in the sixteenth century, excoriated the conquistadors for their abuse of indigenous peoples. Prior to Mexico's independence from Spain in 1821, Chiapas was governed by the colonial administration of Guatemala, but when Chiapas became part of Mexico in 1824, Ciudad Real was renamed San Cristóbal de las Casas in honor of the bishop.

The city's modern Hotel de Mazariegos, which became a headquarters for journalists following the rebellion, is named after the city's 1528 founder, conquistador Diego de Mazariegos. Up until recently, a bronze statue of de Mazariegos, sword in hand, dominated the courtyard of the beautiful baroque Santo Domingo church and monastery where de las Casas once preached. On October 12, 1992, the Christopher Columbus quincentennial, several hundred Indians marched into San Cristóbal in what may have been a precursor to the Zapatista rebellion. They tore down Diego de Mazariegos' statue, bound it in ropes, and dragged it through the streets of the city as conquistadors once did to punish rebellious Indian subjects.

Chiapas was not easily or quickly conquered by the Spanish. During the 1520s, conquistadors and their native allies from central Mexico launched expeditions into the area. But the region was not completely brought under Spanish dominion until Diego de Mazariegos invaded the highlands, which was peopled with natives who had their own distinct languages and cultures. To the north and east of Ciudad Real, indigenous peoples spoke languages of the Mayan family: Tzotzil, Tzeltal, Chol, Tojolabal. Those to the west and south, especially in the Grijalva River valley, spoke Chiapanec, the language of the kingdom centered in Chiapa de Corzo, or Zoque. Subdued by conquest, Indians were forced to help build Ciudad Real, which became the seat of the colonial administration and the base of the Dominicans and other Catholic friars in Chiapas. Ciudad Real also became home to a growing mestizo population of artisans and tradespeople. The Spanish established ranches in the temperate foothills ringing the highlands and introduced cattle, wheat, pigs, chickens, sugar, and countless other products of Iberian heritage. Indians labored on these ranches as part of the tribute they owed their conquerors, who also demanded tribute goods of cloth and dyes. The colonial overlords resettled some Indians to the highlands as a ready source of labor for the authorities in Ciudad Real. They also conscripted Indians to work on ranches and plantations in the lowlands.[5]

While colonial society thrived in the highlands, it disintegrated in the lowlands, which were largely deforested and alternately humid or torrid by season. Disease and exploitation decimated the native population, who were unable to ward off the Old World diseases of the conquistadors, such as smallpox and measles, or the yellow fever and malaria introduced by African slaves. Entire settlements died out, such as that of Copanaguastla, on the edge of the Grijalva River valley, where Dominican friars had converted Indians to Catholicism and then put them to work cultivating cotton and sugar.[6]

As the indigenous people died—and the Spanish faced a declining labor pool—colonial authorities brought their enterprises in the lowlands to a halt and concentrated on settling natives in the temperate highlands surrounding Ciudad Real, where the milder climate also favored Iberian crops and livestock. In eastern Chiapas, the Spanish organized expeditions to hunt down the Chol-speaking Lacandón Indians and resettle them to the north and west foothills, where they could serve the labor needs of colonial ranchers. Eastern Chiapas came to be known as a depeopled or deserted area.[7]

By the seventeenth and eighteenth centuries, the colonial authorities had organized Indian townships around Ciudad Real to produce certain products. Each town fulfilled its tribute obligation to the Crown by specializing in a product or trade, for example curing hides, making pottery, weaving cloth, or growing tobacco, cochineal, or cacao. Several towns delivered cotton to colonial authorities to pass on to other towns to spin into thread, which was transferred to others to weave into the cloth that authorities sold or traded. The Spanish got rich on the tribute goods and labor of Indians. In addition to the materials mentioned above, indigo and cochineal were shipped to Spain as treasured dyes to compete with the royal purple and red dye-goods that the Florentines had monopolized.[8]

The economic specialization of the Indian townships probably contributed to the collective identities that have come to be associated with them. Each town organized ceremonial life and public expenditures as a corporation under the direction of its native nobility and established public celebrations and civic organizations that continue to distinguish indigenous towns today. Constrained by dress codes that restricted the Indian use of Spanish clothing, each township developed its own style of weaving and embroidery—styles still reflected in ethnic costumes that distinguish highland Indian townships today.

San Cristóbal also retains vestiges of its colonial economic organization. When I first visited the city in 1960, artisanal production was, in large part, still associated with the ladino barrios, as it had been in colonial times. Each barrio had its own church and barrio guilds that were the center of the neighborhoods' economic and ceremonial life. San Antonio was the barrio of the *coheteros* (artisans who manufactured skyrockets, fireworks, and gunpowder). Leatherworking was concentrated along the Calle Real de Guadalupe, and candlemaking, in the barrio of the Merced (whose church was established by the Mercedarian order). The Cerrillo district still specializes in carpentry—much of it undertaken with tools developed by woodworkers of the Renaissance, as illustrated in the notebooks of Leonardo da Vinci. Indigo dye vats are still worked in the Mexicanos barrio, which was originally settled by allies of the Spanish conquistadors from central Mexico. *Cuxtitaleros* (residents of the city's easternmost Cuxtitali ward) specialized in long-distance trade with the remote ranches on the fringes of the highlands. In colonial times, the Spanish and mestizo residents of Ciudad Real also worked as butchers, tailors, blacksmiths, tinsmiths, shoemakers, bakers, potters, goldsmiths, and cigar makers. Women made clothing and cigarettes as specialties, and the town had a hefty complement of lawyers and administrators. Much of this economy, however, relied on the raw materials, food, and fuel obtained from the native hinterlands.

Throughout the colonial period, the Spanish governed Indians as subordinates whom they viewed as less than fully adult. Indians did not even have control over the so-called Indian Republics, which were endowed with communal land and a town center and church, but where everything down to the grid pattern of the streets was decided by the colonists. Indian nobles were given responsibility for their towns, but outside of them they enjoyed little status. In legal matters, the testimony of one Spanish man outweighed the countertestimony of four Indian men, although Indians did have the right to appeal cases to the Crown. Spanish priests at first embraced the challenge of learning native languages so that they could bring a full understanding of church doctrine to the Indians. But they eventually concluded that Indians could not be held fully responsible for backsliding into idolatry, and so exempted them from the Inquisition and limited the sacraments available to them.[9]

Indians who worked the ranches in the outermost reaches of Chiapas' colonial society were generally divorced from the collective identities, protections, and responsibilities of the Indian republics. Colonial ranchers dominated the more remote town centers and held virtually unregulated feudal authority over ranch settlements. On the ranches, Indians generally subsisted as indentured laborers on plots given over to them in return for three or more days per week of labor for the ranch. Ranches were in many ways self-sufficient domains, producing cattle, sugar, and grains for trade, and provisioned occasionally by peddlers from San Cristóbal's Cuxtitali barrio. Owners generally sustained town and ranch homes, circulating between rural and town life by season. Natives on a ranch were beholden to the owner as their *patrón*, who in turn held substantial power over the fates of Indians of his estate. Rosario Castellanos' novel *Balún Canán* (*The Nine Guardians*) evokes a vivid sense of the oppressive life on these remote ranches, based on her childhood experience on a family ranch in the hinterlands of Comitán, where the vestiges of some ranches survive and disputes rage between landowners and the peasants who wish to take over the ranches.[10]

It was at Cancuc, a Tzeltal Indian republic on the fringes of the highlands, that Chiapas' natives mounted the region's first major Indian rebellion in 1712. The rebels rose to protest abuses by colonial Spanish authorities and ladino overlords, including priests who imposed heavy fees for administering sacraments. The uprising began as a cult based on the apparition of the Virgin to natives near Cancuc and quickly spread to nearby Tzeltal and Tzotzil communities.[11] The clergy intervened, claiming that natives were worshipping an idol. Defending their cult, the natives revolted at Cancuc, overpowering local ladinos and forcing them to take indigenous sacraments administered by self-proclaimed native clergy, one of whom declared that

> there was no longer King, tributes, *alcalde mayor* [province governor], nor officials of Ciudad Real because [the native priests] had come to free them from all this; and that there was no longer Bishop nor priest…; and that [Indians] should now enjoy their ancient liberty; and…have only vicars and parish priests of their own who would administer all the sacraments.[12]

Explicitly renouncing the Spanish clergy and inverting the power of ladinos over Indians, the movement, in effect, declared war against the colonial regime. Colonial authorities in Ciudad Real called in troops from Guatemala to crush the rebellion, which had inspired widespread fear of a race war. Cancuc was demoted in status and did not regain its rights as a community until 1989, when President Salinas de Gortari restored it to municipal rank with much fanfare about the reestablishment of native rights.

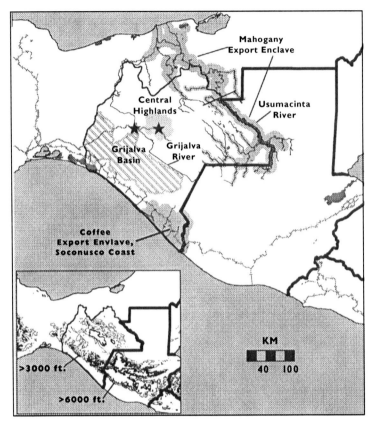

FIGURE 1.2 EXPORT AND DEVELOPMENT IN
NINETEENTH-CENTURY CHIAPAS.

EXPORT ENCLAVES AND
NATIONAL CONSOLIDATION

Chiapas seceded from Guatemala after Independence and joined
Mexico in 1824, but it took nearly a century for the republic to integrate Chiapas and other distant states in economic and political
projects of national scope.[13] The Mexican Republic abolished
Indians' categorically inferior status, but their de facto subordination
continued. In the meantime, European and North American entrepreneurs began to cash in on trade that the Spanish Crown had

formerly monopolized, reorienting it to supply raw materials for new industry and foods for growing cities. In Chiapas, entrepreneurs found two valuable commodities: timber and coffee.

The export of timber and coffee transformed the economic landscape of Chiapas. Indians became virtual debt slaves, working in coffee plantations along Chiapas' western coast and logging the jungles of eastern Chiapas. The central highlands surrounding San Cristóbal de las Casas lost prominence as outsiders began to exploit the lowlands to the east and west. From the nineteenth century onwards, Chiapas was characterized by this new orientation, which created divisions that persist to the present day.[14]

Imagine an invisible line running diagonally through Chiapas from the northwestern corner of the state to the southeastern corner of the state. On the left of this line is the relatively prosperous Soconusco coast, the fertile slopes of the Sierra Madre and the Grijalva River valley, where commercial agriculture established a strong foothold in the nineteenth century. To the east of this line lie the central highlands and the eastern lowlands, peopled largely by Indians. Far in this eastern portion of the state lie the rain forests of the Selva Lacandona (Lacandón jungle), which began to be stripped of old-growth mahogany trees in the 1800s and is now a barely habitable jungle, the heartland of the Zapatista movement. The two sides of Chiapas that this imaginary line represents developed in vastly different ways and have widely divergent political and cultural histories.

The logging business that developed in eastern Chiapas during the nineteenth century was controlled by Europeans and contributed little to Chiapas as a region or to Mexico as a nation. By the 1890s, European-owned logging firms were exploiting the entire drainage of the Usumacinta River and its tributaries for what historian Jan de Vos[15] has characterized as its "green gold," the prized tropical hardwoods of ancient-growth mahogany and cedar. Because both species were widely dispersed throughout the forest with perhaps one or two mature specimens per hectare, the logging firms laid claim to vast tracts along the rivers flowing through the tropical forest. They set up temporary camps along the riverbanks and employed chicle tappers, who gathered tree sap as a base for chewing gum, to scout for preferred timber. After felling an ancient tree, work teams with oxen would haul the trunk to a streambed where cresting flood season waters could carry it downstream. The logging firms then trimmed and shaped giant slabs of wood for shipment to Liverpool or London to auction to furniture manufacturers throughout Europe. Once the coveted trees were harvested from a tract of land, firms relocated their campsites. Indian workers, who were held in virtual servitude through debts to the company stores providing them with food and drink, moved with them. This type of industry, which extracted the desired trees and then moved on, left behind no settlements and no roads, railways, or other productive infrastructure in the eastern lowlands.

The development of coffee plantations in Chiapas' western mountains did contribute to the growth of Chiapas' regional economy. The plantations arose after the California gold rush in the mid-nineteenth century when ships transporting miners around Cape Horn and up the Pacific coast to California provided a way to ship raw materials and foodstuffs to the northern Atlantic ports. Foreign entrepreneurs (primarily Germans) profited from this sudden accessibility to the Atlantic markets by investing in coffee plantations. The steep, fertile slopes of the Sierra Madre by Chiapas' Soconusco coast were ideal for coffee growing, and huge plantations were established.[16]

As a result, the lowland Grijalva River valley, which supplied the coffee plantations with food and draft animals, emerged as a dynamic center of commercial agriculture in the last half of the nineteenth century, and the ranchers who established farms there began to compete with and displace the older oligarchy of the central highlands. This competition sharpened as the two groups took opposite sides in a debate raging between the Mexican Conservatives, who wanted to preserve the prerogatives of the Church and the military, and the Mexican Liberals, who wanted to free up Church lands for entrepreneurial development. As the debate escalated into civil war, the elites of the central highlands, anxious to preserve their control over the highland economy and its native labor, sided with the Conservatives. The lowland ranchers, who coveted the Church-held estates in the Grijalva valley, sided with the Liberals. The Liberals won, and in 1863 the Church was divested of its land, which was put up for sale. The Liberals of Chiapas moved the seat of state government west to lowland Chiapa de Corzo in 1869 and to Tuxtla Gutiérrez not long after, further undercutting the power of their highland rivals.

The indigenous people of Chiapas were often the pawns and victims of the Liberal-Conservative rivalry, especially during the French Intervention of 1861–1867, when both sides drafted Indians as porters and soldiers and taxed them. The Liberals tried to set natives against the highland Conservatives and the Church by apprising natives of their right to worship freely and their lack of obligation to pay church taxes. Once again, as in 1712, a cult arose among the indigenous people of the highlands, this time centered in the Tzotzil community of Chamula. Alarmed in light of the 1712 rebellion, the elite of San Cristóbal attacked the cult's shrine in 1868 and jailed its leader. This did not deter devotees, however, as the cult spread to neighboring communities. A Liberal schoolteacher warned the Chamulas of an impending confrontation and persuaded them to march peacefully to San Cristóbal in 1869 to negotiate with the authorities there. Unfortunately, it was too late. Ladino hysteria had risen to a fever pitch, and several hundred Indians marched into a massacre.[17]

Meanwhile, the Liberals enacted a series of laws that made it possible for non-Indians to purchase the communal lands held by impoverished native communities. In the highlands, profiteers quickly bought up such land and established private ranches in the former Indian republics, which forced many Indians either to work at the bidding of ranchers who took over their lands or to seek their livelihoods elsewhere. Consequently, large segments of the indigenous population worked on the coffee plantations of the Soconusco or the ranches of the Grijalva River valley, where they invariably labored for a pittance and were trapped into a cycle of working to pay off debts.[18]

Taxes imposed by the state government late in the century were another mechanism through which ranchers induced Indians to enter poorly remunerated labor on the plantations. Head taxes, police levies, school contributions, and other local government charges amounted to about forty days' wages for a rural worker. Indians who could not pay were charged additional fines, leaving them with no alternative but to sell their labor to *enganchadores*—professional agents who advanced debtors' loans and sent them to work off their debts on plantations or on urban construction projects. The Grijalva valley plantations obtained many laborers from such tools of Liberalism, as did the coffee planters of the Soconusco, who would contract native laborers through highland ranch owners.[19]

Liberal use of the law to promote business and commercial agriculture accelerated under dictator Porfirio Díaz, who held the presidency for six terms from 1876 to 1910. Díaz allowed foreign and national entrepreneurs to take advantage of laws designed to free up land, labor, and natural resources. Díaz's policies, which were similar in spirit to the open-market restructuring the Salinas de Gortari government promoted after 1988, did spur development, but often at the expense of villages and communities throughout Mexico whose lands the developers absorbed and whose citizens became impoverished workers.

Chiapas was drawn into Porfirian development during the 1890s, after Guatemala constructed a railway from its western coast to the Atlantic Ocean in order to reduce the cost of transporting its coffee harvest by sea. Concerned that the Soconusco plantation owners would try to secede from Mexico and rejoin Guatemala in order to take advantage of the railway, the Mexican government acted forcefully to integrate the region into the national economy by building a railway along the Pacific coast for the ranchers in northwestern and central Chiapas to ship their goods into the heart of the country. As a result, western and central Chiapas became firmly connected to the rest of Mexico.[20] Eastern Chiapas, however, remained a remote and undeveloped part of the state, a condition that persisted until the Zapatista rebels called attention to the plight of the region in 1994.

MEXICO'S REVOLUTION

When Mexicans speak of their Revolution, they refer not only to the civil war that lasted from 1910 to 1917, but also to the government's implementation, over a period of many decades, of the political and social reforms contained in the 1917 Constitution.[21]

All told, the 1917 Constitution was perhaps the most progressive constitution of its era in its call for fair elections, adequate wages and proper conditions for workers, land for peasants, and other reforms. But Mexico's constitution, like all Latin American constitutions written within the framework of the civil law system, sets forth ideals toward which the government should strive, rather than the iron-clad *guarantees* promised by common law Anglo-Saxon constitutions.[22] What the Mexican constitution promises and what the national and state governments legislate and actually (if ever) deliver are two different things. The present-day Zapatistas, who in August 1994 called for a new constitutional convention, claimed that the 1917 Constitution's promises were not being met and never would be.[23]

The Revolution came to Chiapas in 1914, when followers of the revolutionary hero Venustiano Carranza arrived and imposed a state law abolishing debt servitude. Thousands of indentured native workers were freed from the ranches where they toiled and allowed to return to their homes in the highlands.[24] This radical move changed the status quo for some indigenous workers and poor mestizos, although it did not affect workers on the more remote ranches and plantations in eastern Chiapas.

Freeing the workers, however, angered Chiapas' landholding factions in both the western part of the state and the highlands and inspired them to bury differences and unite to "defend" Chiapas against the revolutionaries. The landowners recruited armed gangs to carry out guerrilla missions against the revolutionaries. Nicknamed the Mapaches (raccoons) for their nighttime military forays and their habit of foraging in peasant cornfields, these gangs waged war against the revolutionary regime for six years, eventually defeating them with the help of impoverished peasants who were pressed into joining the cause. The new government was forced to accommodate the Mapaches and even appointed one of them to be governor of Chiapas, thus leaving power in the hands of landowners.[25]

As a result, the reforms of the Revolution came slowly to Chiapas. Some scholars have argued that, in effect, the Revolution never reached Chiapas at all.[26] While this overstates the case, it is true that reforms were unevenly implemented.

By the late 1920s, some peasants, emboldened by the changes sweeping the country, began to press local elites to comply with new government policies that granted indigenous people and rural workers basic rights. Workers in the Soconusco coffee plantations, for example, participated in Socialist-led labor organizing.[27] In the decade that followed, some of the elites who had sponsored the Mapaches were gradually forced to acknowledge the primacy of the national government as it implemented labor and agrarian reform and established policies that protected Indians.

The situation was quite different on the isolated plantations and ranches of the south and east, where Indians continued to labor in debt peonage for more than a decade after the practice was outlawed and where reformers faced entrenched and recalcitrant ranchers. Such landowners, who had long been allowed to rule the state with a brutal hand, were secure in both their command over the region's poor and their isolation from the capital. They were not inclined to publicize the new laws coming out of Mexico City and knew, too, that no one was likely to interfere when they delayed the implementation of reforms required by the central government.

Students of American history may find a parallel in the experience of some black communities immediately after the Civil War, when African Americans in remote parts of the South remained in slavery, not knowing the Emancipation Proclamation was signed, ostensibly freeing them from their bondage. Former Confederates withheld the news, and black Americans had to begin a second campaign—one of information—before they could claim the liberation that was supposed to be theirs already. The situation was similar in eastern Chiapas, where indigenous peasants had to first educate themselves about the changes in law and then demand that landowners honor them. The politicians proclaimed justice for the poor, but it took many years for the day-to-day experience of most peasants to change for the better. Not until the 1930s did peasants in the furthest reaches of the state inform themselves about their rights and organize into groups to demand compliance from the landlords.

When the newly politicized peasants began to clash with the entrenched elites of eastern Chiapas, who had taken their power for granted for so long, the social order of the countryside changed drastically. In *Balún Canán*, Rosario Castellanos wrote poignantly about these clashes as they were played out on a vast plantation near the border of southeastern Chiapas. She recounts the story of a ladino rancher who responds to government pressure to provide a school for the Tzeltal Indian children on his estate by hiring a barely literate paperboy to be the teacher. The young man, totally unsuited for this task and unable to communicate in Tzeltal, begins drinking heavily and beating the children. The Indians come to demand a new teacher but are rebuffed by the landlord. Eventually, the teacher is killed, the plantation owner leaves for his city home, and the school is abandoned.

Although fictional, this tale portrays the type of interaction that characterized relationships in the outback of Chiapas during the decades following the Revolution. The government did little to ensure that its ostensibly pro-peasant reforms, such as mandatory schooling, were carried out properly. What compliance there was tended to be the result of Indian agitation, not governmental enforcement. And while indigenous people often ended up realizing little in the way of concrete gains from their confrontations with powerful landowners, they did manage to put the ladinos on the defensive and thus began in a gradual way to transform the nature of power on the plantations. The conflict between rancher and indigenous peasant in eastern Chiapas was not simply a story of the past, however, as it was one of the ongoing concerns that the EZLN says galvanized them to rebel.

In western Chiapas, in contrast to the center and east, relations between peasants and landowners gradually improved after the

Revolution. Without a ready supply of laborers, plantation owners began to rent plots of land to their former workers in order to bring in the harvest. This new arrangement, similar to sharecropping, was still exploitative, but preferable to the more coercive previous system. Peasants were able to live in their own homes with their own families and were able to farm their plots of land as they saw fit. Being able to rent small parcels of land may not seem like much of an opportunity, but peasants were enormously creative in turning their farming into small-scale entrepreneurial ventures.

In addition, social interactions between landowners and workers underwent a metamorphosis as the master-servant relationship evolved into more of a patron-client relationship. Although the relationship was unequal, it allowed for more social interaction; it was not uncommon, for example, for peasants to ask landlords to be godparents to their children. This social background is important because it helps explain why peasant-landowner relationships were less conflictual in western Chiapas before the rebellion than in the east. Landlords in the Soconusco area and Grijalva River valley could claim to be more progressive than landlords in other parts of the state.

AGRARIAN REFORM

During the 1930s, under the administration of President Lázaro Cárdenas, the government redistributed thousands of hectares of land in Chiapas. This was by no means a wholesale reorganization, since many large estates remained intact, but it did provide dozens of indigenous communities with their own land.

It is difficult to overstate the power of land reform in winning peasants to the side of the state. Even when land grants were agonizingly slow in coming—and they often were—the federal government was able to hold out the promise of land reform as a way of retaining peasant loyalty. By positioning itself, at least symbolically, as the champion of peasants and the poor, the government was able to inspire tremendous popular support for its programs. Understanding the importance of land reform is thus critical in explaining why Chiapas remained a relatively calm area, except for a few outbursts of political violence, during most of the twentieth century.[28]

How was peace maintained in this region that seemed to have so many factors—poverty, discrimination, injustice—pulling it toward revolution? The answer lies partially in the isolation of Indian hamlets and partially in the national government's shrewd use of various redistributive policies that brought one peasant group after another into the system. While the government did not eliminate the discrimination and injustice that plagued Indians and poor peasants, it did offer them the chance, at least in theory, to farm their own land.

By co-opting one group after another with land redistribution, the government ensured that the peasants' primary loyalty would be to the state and not to their class. The factionalism that developed as each community struggled for its own land helped to contain the potential for organized dissidence because it meant that each village or *municipio* (township) concentrated more on maintaining strong ties with the national government than with other native communities that might well compete for the same land.

It is important to note that the government's emphasis on land reform was not just a bid to win the support of the peasantry. It was also the basis of a strategy for development rooted in agrarian economics that took shape after the American stock market collapsed in 1929. The worldwide depression that ensued sharply curtailed the demand for Mexican exports, resulting in the loss of foreign capital that the government depended upon to fund industrial development. To compensate for this loss, the Cárdenas administration instituted a six-year plan to replace the export-oriented economy with new domestic industrialization predicated on peasant production of cheap food. The government began to expropriate land from stagnant commercial estates to turn over to *ejidos* (lands vested in peasant communities by agrarian reform). On the ejidos, peasant families could join to farm collectively if necessary—arrangements that required minimal capital investment. The huge scale of peasant production kept down prices of foodstuffs, which allowed urban-sector

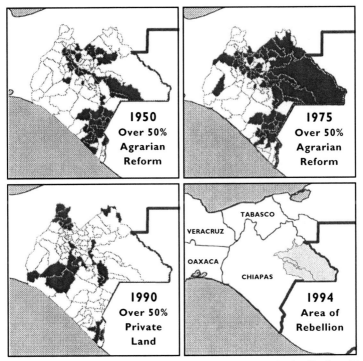

FIGURE 1.3 AGRARIAN REFORM IN CHIAPAS. Most land redistributed by 1950 dates from the 1934–1940 presidency of Lázaro Cárdenas. By 1975, agrarian reform had spread into eastern Chiapas. Large private landholdings remain primarily in western Chiapas where cattle ranching and commercial farming prevail.

wages to be kept low enough for new industry start-up. At the same time, peasants' income from crop sales financed their consumption of manufactured goods, securing a domestic market for the new industries. This approach prefigured the import substitution industrialization strategy of most Latin American countries in subsequent decades and brought Mexico several decades of growth.[29]

As the government began to expropriate land, it also encouraged peasant groups to stake their own claims by occupying and retaking land occupied by private estates and plantations. This tactic not only relieved the government of the burden of having to go on the offensive with landowners, but also ensured that peasants would be more personally invested in the creation of a new economic order. As peasants agitated for land reform, they were brought in to new political organizations, such as the populist Partido Revolucionaro Mexicano (which was later renamed the Partido Revolucionario Institucional or PRI) that had been set up to help orchestrate the peasants' demands, ensuring that they matched the goals of the state.

In Chiapas, Cárdenas' policies firmly established the government as an ally of Indians and peasants against the landowners in the central highlands. Cárdenas rallied indigenous and peasant voters around his candidate for the Chiapas gubernatorial elections in 1936, recruiting voters through a former labor commissioner, Erasto Urbina, who spoke Tzeltal and Tzotzil and had good contacts with Indians throughout the region. Cárdenas then rewarded the indigenous and peasant voters by establishing Urbina as director of a new Department of Indian Protection. Urbina helped his supporters initiate and win claims under agrarian reform, redistributing a substantial amount of land in the highlands and in the Soconusco. Urbina also set up an Indian-run indigenous workers' union with monopoly power to recruit labor from the highlands for coastal coffee plantations. These measures established powerful and long-lasting indigenous and peasant loyalties for the ruling party.[30]

As the 1930s drew to a close and World War II broke out, Mexico once again found itself scrambling to meet U.S. demand for fruits, vegetables, fibers, and textiles. This macroeconomic shift had important consequences for Indians, peasants, and small farmers because the government once again enacted policies that favored the development of large-scale commercial agriculture to meet the sudden demand for exports. The new flow of foreign capital helped the state finance infrastructure, such as irrigation systems, that made large-scale farming viable, especially in the northern part of the country. These changes brought land reform to an abrupt halt and disappointed peasants' expectations of further land redistribution. In some cases, gains made under Lázaro Cárdenas were actually reversed and the types of estates that he had once dismantled prospered again.

Meanwhile, the government continued to develop domestic industry by holding down the relative price of food. As mentioned previously, inexpensive food translated into a subsidy for industrial employers who could thus pay lower wages, but it was a subsidy provided by peasants. Under Cárdenas, many peasants had given up traditional crafts and used manufactured wares when given land to farm. As fiscal policy allowed manufactured items to rise in price more rapidly than food, peasants had to intensify their production simply to make ends meet.[31]

To meet the rising cost of living, many peasants cultivated their land to the limits of its capacity and augmented their income by working part time in the reviving sector of commercial agriculture. Because their own cultivation assured subsistence, many peasants worked for less-than-subsistence wages, which in turn held down wages throughout the economy. As the 1940s drew to a close, many peasants found they were no longer able to focus exclusively on the production of crops. Their numbers swelled, and some peasants began to seek land in eastern Chiapas.

The state's attention to Chiapas' Indians waned during the 1940s, then waxed during the 1950s as the government promoted Indian development projects to curry favor that had been secured with earlier agrarian reform. Endeavors aimed at Indians dated back to the Cárdenas presidency. In 1940, Mexico hosted the first Interamerican Indian Congress, and Indians from all over Mexico were invited to attend. As a result of the congress, Mexico and other Latin American countries established national Indian institutes. Mexico's National Indianist Institute (INI) became the channel through which major funding for rural development was administered, heightening the status of Indians as special clients of the state.

INI officials acknowledged that their goals—rural development through education, improved health, and extension agriculture— were the same as for peasants generally, but that the special characteristics of Indians in regions such as central Chiapas required distinctive efforts to integrate Indian communities into the national agrarian sector. INI sought out Indian leaders to train as *promotores* (local agents) of community development and used them to organize work crews for road construction, to teach curricula designed specially for Indian school children, to run small clinics and promote public sanitation, and to demonstrate new crops and cultivation techniques. In effect, Indian promotores became brokers with a good deal of discretion over who would receive development resources, and through them the state sustained its control over local-level politics.[32]

By making the *municipio* the entity through which development programs were channeled, the government helped to unify those within communities while heightening separation between them. As a consequence, Indian communities remained quite isolated and parochial. Indianist programs, furthermore, reinforced the identity of indigenous people as Indians rather than as part of the class of poor rural workers and peasants. Such identity is part of what has led traditionalists in highland communities like Zinacantán and Chamula, which are closely allied with the PRI, to eschew the Zapatistas. In eastern Chiapas, by contrast, the Zapatistas draw upon the perception of shared interests held by peasants and Indians.

As we shall see in chapters to come, agrarian reform and Indianism were not the only ways in which the government secured support from the exploited rural poor. During the oil boom of the 1970s, Mexico bought popular support by funneling money into development projects and public works. But land reform remained prominent in the public agenda—and in the popular consciousness—as the most cherished legacy of the Mexican Revolution.

When President Salinas de Gortari suspended land reform in 1992, he not only deprived many peasants of their hopes of ever farming their own land but also compromised the peace that held sway in the countryside for most of the twentieth century.

2 ✦ EASTERN CHIAPAS: LAND

Very few frontiers remain for those in search of land. The Selva Lacandona is one of them. Since the 1950s, it has served as a last refuge for impoverished peasants seeking land. The rank and file of Zapatistas are indigenous peasants who embraced the opportunities and the travails of colonizing one of the world's last remaining rain forests. They endured the same adversity that tropical frontiers pose for settlers from other areas—poor soils, unfamiliar and poisonous plants and animals, skin-burrowing insects, and parasitic diseases—and suffered opposition from ranchers who controlled the best land in the region. Since the 1970s, colonists have found it harder and harder to establish homesteads because significant areas of the forest have been set aside as nature reserves. A scramble for land led to conflicts between peasant and rancher, and between peasant and peasant. Conflict in the region was exacerbated first by the government's arbitrary recognition of certain settlements over others and then by agrarian laws that prevented peasants from making further land claims.

It is not surprising that activists, whether Protestant missionaries, Catholic liberation theologians, or political unionizers, found a ready audience in eastern Chiapas, where the government encouraged people to settle, even though there were few roadways, no urban centers, and pitifully few public services.

COLONIZING EASTERN CHIAPAS

In the past five decades, colonization has brought dramatic change to the Selva Lacandona. The two maps in Figure 2.1 underscore this change.

The first map is drawn from information agrarian reform officials had compiled in 1953 and reveals a largely untapped, rugged tropical

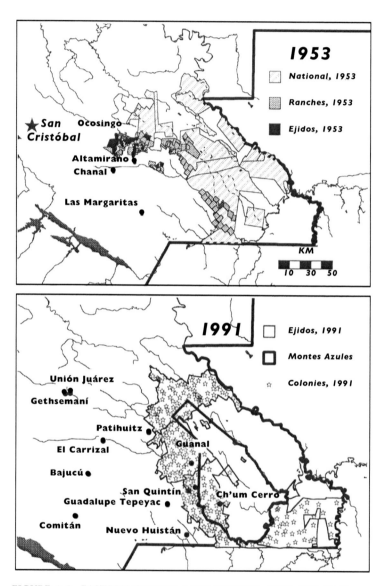

FIGURE 2.1 EASTERN CHIAPAS LAND TENURE, 1953 AND 1991.
Ranches and logging concessions on national lands dominated the eastern Chiapas landscape in 1950. At that time, peasants held ejidal grants only in the Ocosingo valley. By 1991,
the government had granted peasants title to agrarian colonies throughout eastern Chiapas
(illustrated only for the easternmost region), even within the Montes Azules Bioreserve.

forest, sparsely populated by Lacandón Indians.[1] Logging spread from the Usumacinta River up its tributaries beginning in the late nineteenth century until 1949, when the Mexican government declared timber to be a national resource and suspended the logging rights of private corporations. Ranches spread from the outer concentric ring of the old colonial zone into the Ocosingo region and down some of the higher valleys toward the Usumacinta. The only peasant holdings in 1953 were ejidos that the government had set up under 1930s agrarian reform in the higher western valleys close to the township centers of Ocosingo and Altamirano.

Forty years later, the picture had changed drastically. The second map, created in 1991, unveils a mosaic of peasant colonies pressing into the rain forest from the north, west, and south. The Montes Azules and Lacan Tun bioreserves that the government established in the municipio of Ocosingo were most of what remained of the Selva Lacandona.

Peasants in eastern Chiapas hold proportionately more land under agrarian code provisions than almost any other region of the state. But the land they hold is often barely arable, heightening tensions between indigenous and nonindigenous peasants, agrarian reform authorities, and ranchers in the region. Much land in Chiapas is still held privately in large ranches, but such ranches are found mostly in other regions—in the Grijalva River valley, in Cintalapa, and in neighboring townships in the western part of the state (see Figure 1.3 in previous chapter).

Another irony, and one of the major sources of conflict in eastern Chiapas, is that although indigenous peasants dominated its landscape before the rebellion, they did not control local government; instead it continued to be dominated by ranchers and large landowners. In this respect, eastern Chiapas differed markedly from central highland Chiapas, where Indians who benefited from agrarian reform also controlled their own town governments.[2]

This disjunction of power can be traced back to the unfolding of peasant colonization in the northern and western parts of eastern Chiapas, which began in the 1930s when resident workers on ranches began to seek lands on the peripheries of large estates, particularly in Las Margaritas, Ocosingo, and Altamirano. Although the government did establish some ejidos near Ocosingo and Altamirano, many ranchers accommodated "their" workers by selling them marginal lands on the fringes of their properties, thus forestalling expropriation and creating buffers of friendly peasant communities that they could control through patronage.

This tactic also helped ensure a ready supply of labor for the ranchers, who needed workers to herd livestock overland for export through Tabasco; to plant, harvest, and refine sugar; and to cultivate and transport citrus and other crops. Peasants were offered the use of small tracts to farm in exchange for three days' work on the ranch. Such alliances between private landowners and peasants both blurred and complicated lines of potential conflict, eventually igniting feuds not only between ranchers and workers, but also between groups of peasants allied with different landlords. Conflicts sharpened with the passage of time as colonists outstripped their resources and began to press for more land for their maturing families.

Unión Juárez, a peasant settlement located on the fringes of the Sibacá valley in northern Ocosingo, exemplified the type of conflict prevalent in regions dominated by ranchers. Unión Juárez was settled by a small group of families from the town of Tenango and the ranches of Metzá and La Gloria who banded together to purchase two adjacent tracts from separate ranch owners in 1972. By selling the tracts to these aspiring smallholders, the ranch owners forestalled takeover of the tracts by colonists from Sibacá who had petitioned the agrarian reform authorities for enlargement of their holdings. Initially, nine families shared the Unión Juárez holding. By 1987, however, when liberation theologian Brother Pablo Iribarren Pascal visited Unión Juárez on a pastoral mission, the smallholders had come into conflict with neighboring ranchers and colonists by appealing to the agrarian reform authorities for lands for their children, who had matured, and whose young families Unión Juárez could no longer accommodate. One of the parishioners told Iribarren about the opposition claimants encountered from ranchers and other peasants:

We asked for lands, and an engineer came out to identify national lands we could claim, two parcels, one of fifty hectares and the other twenty hectares. But when he came out to survey the parcels, we were set upon by people from the surrounding colonies and ranches, who had been roused by the owner of the Pomalá ranch to thwart our claim. They attacked us with clubs, rifles, and machetes and took the engineer and one of our families prisoner to the settlement at Gethsemaní. People from Batel, Gethsemaní, and Ocotal, all of them Protestant towns, were among those who ganged up on us. In Gethsemaní, they chopped up our clothes, shoes, and hats with machetes. We were sent to Ocosingo, where we were kept in prison for three days while a representative of the Socialist Workers Party (PST) whom we got word to, worked to get us out. The jailing cowed us, we're afraid to pursue the claim with the Reforma Agraria (SRA) and are thinking about getting credits so that we can buy the land and get it without having further problems with neighboring colonists and ranchers.[3]

Colonization came to the region's eastern and southern frontiers when migrants from other parts of the state and from other provinces of Mexico began to arrive and establish settlements in the 1950s. For the most part, these settlers leapfrogged over the ranches of the north and west and began to colonize the tropical forest. Although indigenous colonists predominated in these remote areas far from any township seat, they gained little benefit from the infrastructure and services that the government channeled through town governments.

Many of the newcomers were Tzeltal and Tzotzil Indians from the central highlands of Chiapas; others were Tojolobales and Choles whose ancestors had worked for ranchers in the outer tier of Chiapas' colonial economy. Since the colonial times when conquistadors regrouped decimated native populations in the Chiapas highlands, the highlands have served as a reserve of Indian labor. When Indians began to recover demographically in the nineteenth century, they held so little land for subsistence in the highlands that they had to work on lowland ranches and plantations. Chiapas' populations have grown substantially since 1900, creating further hardships for the

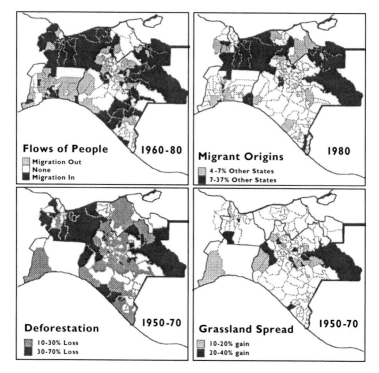

FIGURE 2.2 COLONIZATION AND LANDSCAPE CHANGES IN
EASTERN CHIAPAS. As migrants from the highlands of Chiapas, as well as from
other states, set up colonies in eastern Chiapas, grasslands displaced tropical forests.

already land-poor Indians.[4] Agrarian reform helped abate this pressure temporarily in the 1930s and 1940s, but by the 1950s highland
Indians were once again outgrowing their land and Indian men began
to work in the developed agrarian economies of the central Grijalva
Valley and the Soconusco. After 1950, indigenous people from many
highland communities uprooted their families and ventured into the
forests of eastern Chiapas in search of land to colonize and farm.[5]

Newcomers from other states joined the highland Indians to colonize the Selva Lacandona in the 1970s, responding to then-president
Luis Echeverría's efforts to appease peasant dissidents in other parts
of the country with agrarian reform and colonization. Echeverría
became president two years after the 1968 massacre of student

activists in Mexico's Tlatelolco Square prior to the Olympics, which students had threatened to disrupt. Many held Echeverría, minister of interior in 1968, responsible for the bloodshed. To help polish his image when he became president, Echeverría embraced populist programs and sought the support of peasants, many of whom had been organized by remnants of the student movement in central and northern Mexico. He pressed forward with agrarian reform and opened uncolonized land in Mexico's south to peasants from other areas. Under Echeverría's policies, newcomers came to eastern Chiapas from nearby Tabasco and Campeche, but also from Quintana Roo, Yucatán, Veracruz, Puebla, and Guerrero, Morelos, and Oaxaca, from the federal district, Hidalgo, Jalisco, and Michoacán in central and western Mexico, and even from Sinaloa and Sonora in the northwest.[6]

By 1980, settlers from other states accounted for just over 7 percent of the population of Ocosingo, the highest proportion of any rural municipality in Chiapas. In the early 1980s, officials invited additional out-of-state colonists in to help fill the vacuum of settlement near the border with Guatemala and thus prevent the incursion of Guatemalan refugees, whom the government confined to border camps.

The settlers converged on the tropical forest from the north and west along roadways and trails blazed by government-sanctioned logging, settling on unclaimed national lands or on tracts with prior claims. During the 1950s, for example, peasants from ranches in the Patihuitz Canyon region took over lands that had once belonged to the Bulnes logging firms, claiming them as national lands. Finally, in the 1960s, they received title for them under agrarian reform as expropriations from oversize timbering estates.[7] Timbering firms had allowed many such tracts to fall into arrears in taxes. When families from several different areas banded together to establish the settlement of Ch'um Cerro on other Bulnes lands in the 1960s, they learned from agrarian officials that the Bulnes firm had neglected for twenty-five years to pay taxes for the land on which the colonists happened to settle, and that the settlers could take over in 1970 under a provisional agrarian grant.

Like most tropical rain forests, the Selva Lacandona of eastern Chiapas is a paradise only for those who know how to respect its limitations. Its biomass consists of highly diverse species spread through multiple canopies that protect relatively thin soils from the rapid degradation to which they are prone when exposed to tropical sun. Long-term tropical forest dwellers, such as eastern Chiapas' Lacandón Indians, cultivate by thinning but not destroying the multitiered canopy and by introducing or nurturing useful species in small and multicropped clearings. Skilled cultivators, such as José Camino Viejo, a Lacandón Indian from Mensabak described by the anthropologist-conservationist James D. Nations, raise as many as seventy-nine different crops of food and fiber, more for family use than for sale. In his multicanopied farm plot of three hectares, Camino produced corn, beans, and squash, but also rice, pineapples, sugarcane, bananas, taro, manioc, yams, limes, spices, oranges, cotton, avocados, rubber, cacao, and tobacco.[8]

Newcomers to the region, by contrast, usually introduced intensive cultivation of milpa (the traditional peasant cornfield) appropriate to the higher, cooler climate and richer soils of their original homelands. Having worked in zones of commercial agriculture, they also brought familiarity with cattle and cash crops such as coffee. Producing first for subsistence and then for commercial markets, settlers soon exhausted the land and were forced to press deeper and deeper into the forest. Satellite images of eastern Chiapas starkly reveal this relentless and irreversible march, which has turned wide swaths of the rain forest into grassland suitable only for grazing cattle.

The example of Nuevo Huistán, peopled by Tzotzil speakers from the highland township of Huistán, illustrates how colonists introduced grasslands as they effected the shift from subsistence to commercial farming. Huistecos migrated on foot, with the few possessions they could carry by tumpline, and established Nuevo Huistán in the 1960s on the steep slopes of one of the Las Margaritas canyons.[9] The first to arrive established themselves by working for settlers in nearby, older colonies in exchange for food and a supply of seed that allowed them to begin farming on their own. Once established in subsistence farming, the founding families served as hosts for later-arriving Huistecos; the settlement grew to sixty-three households and won rights to 1,940 hectares authorized by agrarian authorities. Meanwhile, the founders planted coffee for commercial sale as well as cacao, citrus, and other crops. They also seeded a third of their cultivated land in pasture for cattle and other livestock. By 1983, the colony derived seven-eighths of its income from cash crops and cattle, horses, and mules.[10] A 1990 survey of the surrounding zone showed that pasture, much of it induced, made up 60 percent of non-idle acreage, coffee about 10 percent, and subsistence cropping of corn and beans not more than 30 percent.[11]

Over time, Nuevo Huistán emerged as a node linking commerce from the Las Margaritas canyon region outward to a roadway built by the government to control the Guatemalan border. It is important to note that the settlement's increasingly commercial orientation separated settlers (who for the most part had begun production on roughly equal allotments of land) into two groups, one of poorer settlers who relied on subsistence farming and wage work for other compatriots, and a wealthier group involved in marketing cash crops and cattle. When one considers that wealthier colonists attained economies of scale from collective herding and commercial marketing,[12] the distinction between them and private ranchers begins to blur. Such differentiation, which we will discuss further in Chapter Four, created incentives for relative "have-nots" to undertake new colonization of their own, and fed tensions inherent in the multiple and often conflicting claims of colonists seeking legal authorization for new and supplemental land.

AGRARIAN REFORM AND CONFLICT

In 1992, the Mexican government rewrote the agrarian reform section of the Mexican Constitution, bringing an end to the land reform policies that shaped the government's relationship to the peasantry for half a century.[13] In Chiapas, where many land claims have yet to be resolved after languishing in the state bureaucracy for years, the repeal of land reform legislation robbed many peasants not just of the possibility of gaining a piece of land, but, quite simply, of hope.[14] Subcomandante Marcos, in an interview published in *Tiempo*,[15] indicated that the change in Article 27 was the straw that broke the camel's back in persuading Zapatistas to take up arms:

> [The government] really screwed us, now that they destroyed Article 27, for which Zapata and his Revolution fought. Salinas de Gortari arrived on the scene with his lackeys, and his groups, and in a flash they destroyed it. We and our families have been sold down the river, or you could say that they stole our pants and sold them. What can we do? We did everything legal that we could so far as elections and organizations were concerned, and to no avail.

Rage built up in settlements such as El Carrizal, where colonists waited in vain over eleven years for government resolution of their claim to lands. El Carrizal was a community made up of former resident workers from the ranch of San Rafael near Ocosingo. In 1983, these workers learned that the land they had worked for many years as hired hands was going to be sold to other peasants, leaving them without either work or a place to live. They hastily initiated a claim of their own for San Rafael, which for two years went unheeded. In 1985, they went on strike, moved their homes to a site they could defend from expected reprisals, and renewed their claim. Once again it languished, opposed both by ranchers and by other peasant smallholders who coveted the land. Meanwhile, violence broke out. In August of 1988, El Carrizal was burned to the ground by a group of armed men who are said to have acted under the direction of ranchers in cahoots with local police and the army. With support from the Emiliano Zapata Peasant Organization (OCEZ), the El Carrizal peasants marched to San Cristóbal de las Casas, where they camped in protest in the central plaza in front of the San Nicolás church, demanding that agrarian authorities grant their claim. Early in 1989, the government affirmed El Carrizal's legal status pending resolution of the land claim and oversaw rebuilding of the settlement, but violence against El Carrizal continued. By February 1994, when the *New York Times* journalist Anthony DePalma interviewed El Carrizal leaders, they still awaited government resolution of their claim.[16]

The case of El Carrizal poignantly illustrates one of the most troubling aspects of land reform—the fact that the government sometimes took years to recognize claims on which peasants' livelihoods depend. Once a community submitted a petition for land, petitioners often had to wait several years before the government recognized their provisional right to occupy and use the land. The process was arduous. State review boards scrutinized the eligibility of the group to ensure it was actually comprised of at least twenty peasant households. They also scrutinized any documented claims to prior ties to the land in question. Then officials surveyed land within a seven kilometer radius of the community to determine its "affectability"—was it susceptible to expropriation or available for donation to the claimants, or were there competing claims? Finally state-level authorities recommended to federal superiors whether a grant should be awarded. At that point, claimants were sometimes authorized to use land on a provisional basis. But they still had to wait for a federal review of their claim. If their claim was accepted, they awaited a presidential decree and the actual granting of title before the land was legally theirs. Needless to say, the process was often held up by countervailing claims from landowners and, occasionally, other peasant groups.

According to one study,[17] land claims involved some twenty-two different government groups and public agencies and a twenty-seven-step process requiring almost two years of bureaucratic effort, *if the claim was unopposed.* In Chiapas, according to the same study, it took an average of more than seven years for the federal government to approve claims that had already been provisionally accepted by state authorities. It is understandable that being forced to "hurry up and wait" caused tremendous strain between peasants in eastern Chiapas, who generated hundreds of claims in the decades before the rebellion, and agrarian officials. Yet it is worth noting that claims from Las Margaritas and Ocosingo, the heartland of the Zapatista movement, were actually resolved from one to two years faster, on average, than elsewhere in Chiapas.[18]

The strain between peasants and agrarian authorities was not, of course, unique to Chiapas. Conflicts between rural communities and land reform officials had been building since the 1970s, when peasants throughout Mexico's countryside began to lay claim to more valuable lands. Peasants, landowners, and the state generally became more militant in the two decades before the rebellion in disputes over agrarian resources.

When the Mexican government initially brought agrarian reform to the national agenda during the 1930s, peasants were relatively easy to secure as allies without upsetting private agrarian interests. Most of the land that Lázaro Cárdenas' representatives turned over to peasant communities in Chiapas was marginal land that highland ranchers had appropriated from Indian communities in the nineteenth century. When the agrarian communities pushed for augmentation to these holdings in the 1950s, their needs could still be met by granting them small parcels of less valuable lands on the outskirts of plantations.

By the 1960s, it became clear that these parcels were no longer adequate, and peasants began to file claims for more valuable commercial farms and plantations that earlier agrarian reform had spared. Because the law authorized claims only within seven kilometers of peasant settlements of at least twenty households, peasants had to invade coveted lands and settle on them in order to initiate the process.

I know of one such land takeover from my discussions with Zinacanteco Indians who established the Colonia Santa Rosa in the late 1960s. For years, they had weighed the prospects of taking over what were thought to be untitled national lands, but which in fact were claimed by ranchers. But the land was too far from home for them to claim it under the law. They had to establish a settlement there to be able to stake a claim. They organized weeks in advance of a moonless night when, sixty families strong and armed with every available shotgun and machete, they invaded the land. They hastily constructed ramshackle shelters to claim as their "settlement" and set up armed lookouts to defend against rancher reprisals. Then they sent one of their members to notify government authorities of the existence of their settlement and to demand protection while pressing their claim for land as authorized by law.

As such takeovers spread in the late 1960s, landowners called on the government to put a halt to invasions and often fought off settlers with armed force, escalating confrontation in some areas of rural Mexico to the level of guerrilla warfare. In the state of Guerrero, the government used troops to repress peasants. It was in part to defuse such conflict that Luis Echeverría, president from 1970 to 1976, favored the colonization of Mexico's remaining frontiers. To mollify dissident peasant leaders, the Echeverría government also offered many of them jobs in the agrarian reform bureaucracy to help administer colonization efforts.

Ironically, the very mechanisms intended to facilitate colonization often cast the government as the enemy rather than the ally of peasants, especially when they put the agrarian authorities in the contradictory roles of proprietors of national lands as well as arbiters of claims to those lands. This was especially true in the case of legislation that allowed the government to establish relocation centers on national lands to resettle colonists far from their original homelands.[19] These relocation centers sometimes helped facilitate colonization, but in other instances they seemed more to serve state interests than those of peasants.

In 1969 the government initiated a dam project at Angostura that was to flood dozens of peasant communities in the central Grijalva River valley—all of the villages had to be relocated. Relocation inflamed agrarian conflict in Venustiano Carranza, where the government tried to place a new settlement on land that had already been in dispute between ranchers and Venustiano Carranza peasants for more than twenty-five years. After a peasant leader was assassinated in 1975 and several hundred peasants invaded the disputed land in 1976, the government sent in the army to repress the peasants.[20] As a result, Venustiano Carranza became the focal point for independent organizing against the government by the Emiliano Zapata Peasant Organization (OCEZ). Peasant protests actually derailed a government plan to build a fourth dam, the Itzantún dam in the township of Huitiupán, that would have displaced people from their homelands into one of the government relocation centers.[21]

Compounding conflicts over land in eastern Chiapas was the fact that the government began to mark off tracts of land to establish bioreserves, ignoring the fact that the land was already occupied by impoverished peasants who had been encouraged to colonize the region. The government first laid plans in 1968 to set aside small portions of the Selva Lacandona to protect the rain forest. But ten years later, pushed by the international environmental community and by champions of the Lacandón Maya who wanted to protect the Indians from encroachment by colonists, the government set aside another third of a million hectares as the Montes Azules Bioreserve.[22] To relocate 8,000 people already living in twenty-six settlements within the limits of the Montes Azules reserve, the government set up several relocation centers.[23] Then the government set up a logging firm, the Lacandón Forestry Company (COFOLASA), ostensibly to manage the bioreserve's timber on behalf of 400 Lacandón individuals in 66 families deemed to have ancestral claims on the lands of the reserve, completely disregarding claims of 8,000 non-Lacandón Indians and peasants already settled in the area. Theoretically, proceeds from timbering were to be held in trust for the Lacandón families, but critics charge that most of the profit from COFOLASA's timbering operations in Montes Azules ended up in politicians' pockets.

Guanal was one of the colonies whose lands fall within the Montes Azules Bioreserve. Settled in the 1960s by colonists from several areas, Guanal joined with other colonies affected by the bioreserve to prevent authorities from surveying the reserve's boundaries and to resist relocation into the new ejidos. When Brother Pablo

Iribarren visited Guanal in 1988, colonists railed against the agrarian authorities and conservationists who had tried to dislodge Guanal's residents in unsuccessful efforts to relocate them into the government ejidos. Organized with help from Catholic catechists and the peasant organization Unión de Uniones Quiptik ta Lekubtesel (United for Our Improvement Union of Unions), Guanal and the other Montes Azules colonies filed legal briefs against dislodgement, organized protest marches in the state capital, and harassed surveyors and public authorities who tried to persuade them to relocate:

> On one occasion, when Lic. Mario Rivera came as a government delegate to [the colony of] Pichucalco insisting that we sign papers to relocate, he was so insistent that we jailed him. When his bush pilot came to pick him up that afternoon, he found Rivera in jail, so he left. When the pilot flew back the following day, we released Rivera, and he left.
>
> Another time, this same official called us to a meeting at the schoolhouse in Guanal. He got up on a table and harangued us to sign the relocation papers. A storm was brewing, and suddenly the schoolhouse lit up, struck by a bolt of lightening. Everyone was scared, and Lic. Rivera jumped down off the table in fright. After a moment, everyone broke out into applause and began to shout, "Long live Saint Lightning! Another bolt! Another bolt! Viva!" Lic. Rivera left and never returned.[24]

The Agrarian Rehabilitation Plan (PRA) was another mechanism that the government devised to facilitate colonization, but its partisan implementation served only to turn peasants against agrarian authorities. As the governor of Chiapas, General Absalón Castellanos Domínguez set up the PRA in 1984 as a program for the state to buy lands from private owners to turn over to peasants in zones where peasants and ranchers were embattled over agrarian reform. Under the PRA, the state government purchased just over 80,000 hectares of private land in various parts of Chiapas to turn over to 159 peasant settlements. But the beneficiaries were overwhelmingly communities affiliated with the ruling party's National Peasant Confederation (CNC). Communities affiliated with independent organizations not aligned with the ruling party were almost completely excluded from the benefits of the PRA, even though many such peasants had prior claims on ranches bought out with PRA funding.[25]

Rather than allaying conflict, the effect of the PRA was to inflame peasants against the ruling party, agrarian authorities, and the state governor. Peasants' anger was reinforced when it became known that the governor had issued ranchers 2,932 *certificados de inafectabilidad* (exemptions protecting property from expropriation under agrarian reform) for some 1.2 million hectares of commercial farmland and ranchland in the state of Chiapas. One can begin to understand why the Zapatistas later kidnapped Absalón Castellanos and held him prisoner on charges of having betrayed the public trust.

Government intervention into the colonization of one of Mexico's last frontiers thus subtly but irrevocably reversed earlier perceptions of agrarian authorities as allies. The government replaced large landowners as the hated enemy by taking over their role. First, the state came to act as a self-interested proprietor of national lands rather than a facilitator of peasant needs. It set bioreserves off-limits to peasants, exacerbating the pressures on remaining lands. Second, the government, by rewarding peasants loyal to the ruling party, set peasants against peasants, just as hated landlords had once conceded marginal lands to "their" peasants as a bulwark against the claims of other peasants in the earlier phases of agrarian reform. And finally, in 1992, the government changed the law to put an end to the very claims it had encouraged peasants to make as colonists on the final frontier.

3 ✦ EASTERN CHIAPAS: THE BUILDING
OF SOCIAL MOVEMENTS

The Zapatistas have not provided a detailed history of their origins. We know from Subcomandante Marcos' interviews with journalists[1] that the Zapatistas began organizing to go underground in 1983 and that certain other highly politicized peasant groups were also active at this time, but we don't know which, if any, of these groups became the Zapatista National Liberation Army. It seems most likely that the Zapatistas drew strength from various factions of groups who were dissatisfied not only with the government but with other peasant organizations as well. In this chapter, we'll explore the some-times unintentional role the civil and religious movements played in orienting peasants toward political activism, and examine the rise of independent peasant organizations in the eastern part of the state. I hope to illuminate the milieu in which the Zapatista movement began, rather than offer a precise chronology of its development.

Although the Zapatistas did not burst onto the international scene until 1994, their presence in eastern Chiapas had already been an open secret for several years. Even before anyone knew the name of the Zapatista National Liberation Army, people in Ocosingo, Las Margaritas, and Altamirano spoke to journalists about the "armed groups" operating in their midst. In June of 1993, *Proceso*, a progressive Mexican weekly magazine, reported that after five years of denial, the government "acknowledged evidence that there are guerrillas in Chiapas." In August 1993, the Mexico City newspaper *La Jornada* pub-lished interviews with government officials and a Protestant pastor in eastern Chiapas who had heard gunshots in the night, witnessed arms trading, and heard stories about peasants who had been invited to join an "armed uprising" over a period of at least two years. A rep-resentative of a local peasant organization told the paper that "the existence of guerrillas is not a rumor; it has been proven that there are well-armed guerrillas operating near the Guatemalan border and it is known that they have training grounds." In September, a Jesuit priest from the Selva Lacandona told *Proceso* that he had been aware of militant armed groups assembling in the area for eight years.[2]

What led to the formation of this revolutionary underground in eastern Chiapas? Conservatives tend to point their fingers at the Catholic Church, which, in Chiapas, had been heavily influenced by liberation theology and has, in recent years, been at the center of social justice movements throughout the state. The Mexican government initially claimed that the rebellion was instigated by "foreigners," by which they meant Guatemalan or other Central American revolutionaries. Scholars who had studied the region speculated that the Zapatistas were the outgrowth of the independent and mostly left-oriented peasant organizations that formed during the 1970s.[3] Subcomandante Marcos himself hinted that the Zapatistas began ten years before the rebellion, in 1983, when a small group of urban intellectuals arrived in Chiapas with the specific goal of fomenting revolution.[4]

The Zapatistas have been portrayed as a group of indigenous peasants pushed to the breaking point by poverty and exploitation who finally struck out against their oppressors—the government that abandoned them, the army that repressed them, the wealthy ranchers and *caciques* (political bosses) who kept them in subjugation, the ladinos who taunted them. The popular media recounted stories about the hardships of life in eastern Chiapas, including the coffee that was planted and couldn't be sold, the land erosion, the brutality of ranchers, the hunger, the lack of medical care, and the inadequate education. As one reads these chronicles of misery, one can understand why the colonists finally boiled over with anger. The problem with this portrayal, however, is that it makes the rebellion appear to be a spontaneous reaction to injustice when, in fact, a group of organizers had been planning revolution for more than a decade.

The Zapatista uprising was not the first peasant uprising in Chiapas, it was just the first to gain international attention. And while poverty and exploitation may have been the rallying cries of the rebels, the movement also developed in counterpoint to the dozens of other peasant organizations operating in the state. In other words, the Zapatistas were not just fighting what they termed the corrupt government of President Salinas, they were placing themselves in opposition to the tactics used by other peasant groups and fighting to be the voice of the oppressed. The Zapatista consciousness was formed not just by the backbreaking toil of colonizing the Selva Lacandona, but also by dialogue and dissension within and between other organizing groups. By taking over the town hall of San Cristóbal de las Casas on January 1, 1994, the Zapatistas weren't only making a statement to the Mexican government, they were proclaiming their rejection of the peaceful tactics endorsed by other peasant groups.

Before we look at the rise of these alternative peasant groups, however, we have to look further back at the circumstances that combined in eastern Chiapas to make people receptive to grassroots movements. Several things stand out as unique about eastern Chiapas: the region had (and still has) a substantial number of religions that are nontraditional for Mexico—Protestant, Evangelical, Mormon, Seventh-Day Adventist, and others—which means it had a population that already had to challenge the status quo; it had a system of rural networks originally designed to build a sense of religious community among far-flung canyon hamlets but that evolved into a social network grassroots organizers were able to build upon; and, because so many people in eastern Chiapas were refugees from other parts of Mexico, communities tended to be more open, democratic, and diverse than Indian villages in the central highlands, which were often tightly organized around ethnicity, Catholicism, and *costumbre* (traditional indigenous religious practice).

PROTESTANT EVANGELIZATION

The Protestant churches, which made extensive use of lay preachers in eastern Chiapas, inadvertently helped lay the groundwork for the grassroots political organizing that came later. When the Catholic Church responded to the challenge of Protestantism in the region, they used lay catechists of their own, helping to create another "network in the jungle."

Protestant and Evangelical churches also offered more participatory and democratic congregations than many of the colonists were accustomed to. Women and children were welcomed and included in religious services, a sharp contrast to the more patriarchal religious practices found in most of the colonists' hometowns. Because these new forms of worship were so well received, the Catholic Church in eastern Chiapas began to embrace some of the more democratic features of the Protestant churches. The competition between diverse Protestant, Evangelical, and Catholic churches created an environment in which only a *secular* movement, like that of the Zapatistas, could hope to unite peasants across religious lines and attract both women and men, young and old.

The history of Protestantism in Mexico goes back to the mid-nineteenth century, when the Liberal government invited Presbyterian and other Protestant missionaries into the country to provide what the politicians hoped would be a modernizing counterforce to centuries of Catholicism. In the 1930s, during a period of intense anticlericalism, the government forbade the recitation of mass and, to further curtail the influence of the Catholic Church, allowed Protestant Bible translators to establish themselves in various regions, including Chiapas, where it hoped their work would help advance literacy among the peasants.[5]

For many years, the Protestants made few converts. As late as the 1970s, one missionary who had lived in the highland Chiapas hamlet of Nauvenchauk for a decade had yet to convert a single person. Around that time, however, the missionaries began to witness a change of heart, especially among the poor, dispossessed, and politically dissident members of Chiapas villages. But those who did convert met with extreme antagonism on the part of village elders in many communities, most notably San Juan Chamula, where leaders ostracized them, confiscated their land, and in some cases burned their houses and forced them to leave town. Many of these refugees eventually settled in eastern Chiapas or became squatters on the fringes of San Cristóbal.[6]

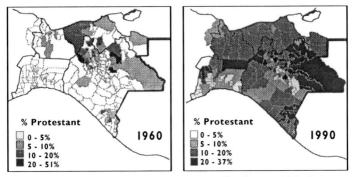

FIGURE 3.1 THE SPREAD OF PROTESTANTISM Already an established presence in eastern Chiapas by 1960, Protestant religions claimed up to 37 percent of the populace by 1990 in many townships.

The animosity between the "traditional" Catholic Indians and Protestants continues today. Because many Protestant converts forswear alcohol and refuse to pay religious taxes or to participate in traditional religious celebrations, they challenge the established village life. Local political leaders often argue that this lack of conformity justifies expelling the Protestants from their villages. Sometimes, nonreligious dissidents are accused of being Protestant as a pretext for ousting them from their homes. Some observers have charged that such expulsions violate Mexico's constitutional guarantees of freedom of religion and the right to property, not to mention internationally recognized human rights.[7] Village traditionalists, however, argue that Mexican civil law has always allowed Indian communities to settle disputes by customary law when felonies are not involved. They claim that expulsions are a time-honored way of dealing with troublesome people. They also say customary law is one way Indian communities preserve their autonomy and argue that forbidding it would be a violation of *their* rights as indigenous peoples. Critics respond that customary law places too much discretion in the hands of village power holders, or caciques, who often use custom and tradition as an excuse for expelling anyone who challenges their authority.[8]

Many Protestants fled to eastern Chiapas, where the Protestant and Evangelical population comprised between 20 and 51 percent in municipios responding to the 1990 population census. About half of these were Seventh-Day Adventists or Presbyterians; Pentecostals, Evangelicals, and Baptists made up another quarter; there were also Jehovah's Witnesses, Mormons, and half a dozen other churches or sects.[9] While some settlers brought religions with them, many others converted to Protestantism after settling in eastern Chiapas, which has a history of evangelicalism, especially along the Guatemalan border.

Why so many different churches? Some of my colleagues who have worked in the area, such as Rosalva Aída Hernández Castillo,[10] suggest that the religions in eastern Chiapas provide homesteaders, who have left their ancestral homes behind, with new ways of forming community. The churches unify people who are trying to establish common ground with neighbors of different origins, ethnic groups, and cultures.

These nontraditional religions may well be more democratic in their practices than their traditional Catholic counterparts in the Chiapas highlands. In the highlands, those who hold religious posts are expected to finance them, and the greater a post's costs, the greater the prestige conferred on those who accept them.[11] In addition to conferring status, completing a term in such a post confers the right to hold forth in public affairs. The costlier the post, the greater the political power. The Protestant, Evangelical, and other nontraditional churches also offer many positions such as elder or deacon that require almost no financial investment. As a result, it is easier for poorer people to become involved, and to attain respected positions. And because religious office is not tied to political power, even those without a church affiliation are able to attain power in civil affairs—something that was once unthinkable in the Chiapas highlands.

The Protestant churches in Chiapas have long attempted to win converts by evangelizing in the native languages of the Maya, a strategy that the Catholic Church had used in the colonial period, but not after Independence, until recently. Markets throughout Chiapas sell cassettes of Protestant and Evangelical hymns sung by indigenous people in their own language and style, spreading the word to the masses. Such grassroots proselytizing not only has helped make the nontraditional churches more accessible but also has helped empower Indians who previously were forced to suffer the indignity of being treated as second-class citizens even in church, where the Catholic priests administered the sacraments only in Spanish. And although Chiapas does not have a high literacy rate compared with the rest of Mexico (69 percent of adults over fifteen years as compared to 87 percent nationally, according to the 1990 census), census statistics show that literacy rates were higher in native-language speaking communities that were Protestant. Even women and girls, whose literacy rates tend to lag far behind those of men, were learning to read.

In 1989, while visiting a town where Protestant exiles from Zinacantán had started a new life, I saw Losha, a five-year-old girl, read a passage aloud from a Tzotzil bible. Later in the day, we accompanied Losha and her family to the settlement's Presbyterian church for the afternoon service, one of several services that the family attends each week. An indigenous pastor delivered the sermon. He also spoke of organizing a visit to Sekemtik, back in Zinacantán, to support the Protestants there. What impressed me most was how the new religion had forged a bond of affinity among the residents of this community, how this church had drawn women and children as well as men into a vibrant congregation, creating a space in which people could challenge the boundaries not just of gender and literacy, but of access, through literacy, to formerly impenetrable domains of law and politics.

Protestantism helped to legitimize literacy, which in the minds of many Indians had negative associations with the repressive laws and policies of the ladino government and, as such, had been viewed historically as a threat to the conventions and costumbre that organize the traditional Maya community. But peasants are learning to read and write about their faith in their indigenous languages as well as Spanish, and literacy is coming to be seen as something that is their own, not as something that signifies the ladino world. As literacy is freed from its repressive political context, Mexican politics become more accessible because peasants no longer fear that it will destroy their traditions.

Women especially seem to have found a place in the Protestant churches of eastern Chiapas. They are *always* present at Sunday and weekday services and hold offices in the church, something they were not able to do in the highlands. The move from the highlands was particularly difficult for women, because whereas many men from impoverished towns were accustomed to doing far-flung wage work, many women had never been beyond neighboring towns and were accustomed to being the ones who held their communities together by performing agricultural work while the men were elsewhere. Migrating to the lowlands, women had to leave behind their networks of day-to-day social relations among kin and neighbors. The churches of their new communities have helped them form new bonds to replace those stretched or broken by resettlement.

As women adapted to their new lives on the frontier, they also began to assume new positions in their communities. Journalists and at least one scholar[12] immediately noted the active participation of women in the Zapatista movement and its armed forces. While no one pretends that the Zapatista movement is a women's liberation movement, it does appear that the Zapatistas at least recognize women as an oppressed group. In a February 1, 1994, interview in *Tiempo*, Subcomandante Marcos described a Tzotzil woman named Susana, who was responsible for visiting dozens of communities to talk with women about their priorities in order to come up with the Zapatista position on women's rights. At a meeting of the movement's leadership that the Zapatistas refer to as the first battle led by the Zapatista women, she read the following list of demands that Marcos claims was unanimously endorsed.

We want not to be obliged to marry with he whom we do not want; we want to have the children we choose to, and whom we can care for. We seek the right to hold *cargos* [religious posts] in the community. We want the right to speak our word and be respected. We want the right to study, and even be truck drivers.[13]

One member of the Comandancia General, the steering committee of the Zapatistas, is a Tzotzil woman named Ramona. In an interview with journalists, Ramona urged all women to join the Zapatista movement:

> Because women also are living in difficult situations, women are the most exploited of all, the most oppressed. Why? Because for so many years, for 500 years, they have not had the right to speak, to participate in assemblies, they have no right to education, nor to speak in public, nor to take cargos in their communities. No. The women are completely oppressed and exploited. We get up at 3:00 AM to cook corn, and we don't get to rest until the evening after everyone else is asleep. And if there isn't enough food, then we give our tortillas to the children, to our husbands. We [women] demand respect, true respect as Indians. We also have rights...and my message to all women who feel exploited, ignored, is take up arms as a Zapatista.[14]

CATHOLIC RESPONSES

While the precise makeup of the Zapatista National Liberation Army and who originally organized the clandestine movement have never been fully disclosed,[15] we have many indications about the roles outside organizations played in its early development.

Most observers trace the beginning of the radical movement in Chiapas to 1974, when the state governor asked Bishop Samuel Ruiz to organize an Indigenous Congress commemorating the birth of Fray Bartolomé de las Casas, the sixteenth-century champion of Indian rights. The purpose of this congress was twofold. On one hand, the Catholic Church, exercising what it called its "preferential option for the poor," wanted to give voice to the sufferings of Indians; the government, on the other hand, wanted to create a more populist image after brutally repressing the student movement of the late 1960s.

Before 1974, the Catholic Church had already begun extensive grassroots evangelizing in eastern Chiapas, in part to ward off the advance of Protestantism. When church planners were asked to help prepare for the congress, they made use of their evangelical networks in the region, which were divided into several districts according to the principal indigenous languages: Chol, Tojolabal, Tzeltal, and Tzotzil. Traveling catechists organized groups of neighboring parishes into evangelical districts and visited them frequently, assembling parishioners each month in a different town, and staying in parishioners' homes. In addition to translating sermons and books of the Bible into indigenous languages, the catechists, many indigenous people themselves, talked about Fray Bartolomé de las Casas and his struggle for Indian rights. They asked indigenous people to think about their current circumstances and difficulties and to delegate members of their communities to come to the congress and talk about their hopes, desires, and priorities for the future.

It is important to note that the Indigenous Congress (and the grassroots evangelizing in indigenous languages that was done by both the Catholic and the Protestant churches) took place at a time when peasants and Indians were held in disregard not just by average citizens but by the intelligentsia as well. Even several strands of Marxist political thought derided ethnicity as "false consciousness," exerting a strong influence over intellectuals who held high positions even in Indianist-oriented government organizations such as PRODESCH, the Socioeconomic Development Program for the Highlands of Chiapas. (PRODESCH was set up in 1970 to coordinate state, federal, and international development efforts in Chiapas.) Because ethnic identity was thought to keep Indians from contributing to development, PRODESCH had abrogated earlier National Indianist Institute efforts to promote bilingual education for Indians. Although PRODESCH worked through indigenous agents, the agency did not hesitate to make decisions for Indians, for example by imposing its own candidates for municipal office on Indian townships.

The Indigenous Congress was unprecedented in the history of Chiapas, for it was the first official meeting of Indians not convened for the government to tell Indians what to do. Indigenous people had been convened before, but usually by Indianist agencies that wanted indigenous people to embrace policies or programs designed by government planners. The Indigenous Congress of 1974, on the other hand, was a grassroots convention for Indians and by Indians and offered a chance for indigenous people to voice their own solutions to the problems that confronted them. Unlike the government-sponsored peasant and indigenous organizations, which are organized from the top down, the congress provided a model of bottom-up organizing upon which independent peasant organizations subsequently drew.

During the Indigenous Congress, the delegates talked about the same bread and butter issues the Zapatistas have: land, food, education, and health. The following passages, the first from the Indigenous Congress and the second, issued twenty years later in the early days of the Zapatista uprising, are almost identical. The demands have remained constant for the past three decades.

FROM THE 1974 INDIGENOUS CONGRESS:[16]

On land: We have problems with ranchers who invade our lands.... We need land, we don't have enough of it, so we have to rent it, or go away to work. The lands we have been given are infertile. We need to be taught our rights under the Agrarian Laws.

On health: Doctors are concentrated in the cities and never attend in the countryside.... The programs of public health are not realistic.... We are sold bad out-of-date medicine that is useless. . . . Merchants are making a business out of selling false medicine, or by selling [government] medicines that are supposed to be free.[17]

On services: We pay taxes, but we don't receive even basic services such as running water.

On food: We all suffer from malnutrition and poverty, because of lack of land.

On education: The education system is very poor and does not serve to improve our communities.

On work: We are paid very unfair salaries and are forced to work from sunrise to sunset.

On commerce: Peasants and Indians work hard but are always exploited. We have to sell our products cheap, but whatever we buy is expensive. For us, merchants and middlemen are like a plague of locusts.

On malnutrition: Our suffering is due to lack of nutrition, poverty, and lack of land.

FROM THE ZAPATISTAS' 34-POINT AGENDA FOR NEGOTIATION IN 1994:[18]

8. Land is for the Indians and peasants who work it, not for the large landlords. We demand that the copious lands in the hands of ranchers, foreign and national landlords, and other nonpeasants be turned over to our communities, which totally lack land. . . .

9. We ask for hospitals in the municipal centers provisioned with enough medicine to attend patients, and for rural clinics staffed with trained and properly paid health agents....

11. We demand the construction of housing...with basic services such as electricity, water, plumbing, telephones..., and such advantages as televisions, stoves, refrigerators, washing machines, etc....

12. We demand an end to illiteracy among the indigenous communities, and for this we need better primary and secondary schools with free textbooks and university-trained teachers who are ready to serve the people, and not just the rich....

18. We demand dignified and fairly paid work for all rural and urban workers....

19. We ask for fair prices for our farm products and markets where we can freely sell and buy without being at the mercy of coyotes [exploitative middlemen]....

21. Let there be an end to hunger and malnutrition, which have caused the deaths of thousands of our rural and urban brothers.

The work of the 1974 Indigenous Congress did not cease with the congress itself—catechists took its lessons back to indigenous communities in the various districts. They screened a film that had been made about the congress and taught courses in native languages on the history of Mexico and Chiapas, political economy, and Mexican commerce. Following the organizing strategy used to prepare for the congress, the catechists continued to meet with indigenous representatives from the various districts, each time in a different place, to build a base for popular participation, including that of women and children.[19]

In the end, however, the catechists' efforts met with the limitations of their association with the Catholic Church in a landscape of religious pluralism. However much the Catholic Church hoped to speak with a universal voice, it could not do so persuasively while attempting to win people away from other religions. Only a truly secular movement appealing broadly to pluralism and democracy could hope to galvanize the indigenous and peasant community across its religious diversity. By 1978, a movement known as Popular Politics (PP) began to do just that, gradually displacing the catechists from their central role in organizing eastern Chiapas.

Although the role of the Church in fomenting revolution remains difficult to assess, it is clear that most later independent organizing in Chiapas drew lessons and inspiration, and in some cases their actual beginnings, from the 1974 congress.

In a September 13, 1993, interview in *Proceso*, Mardonio Morales said, "It [radical peasant organizing] all started shortly after the Indigenous Congress of 1974." The Zapatistas, not quite as bluntly, also pointed to 1974 as the starting point for radical agitation:

Years have passed, since about 1974, when we began trying to get land, dwellings, roads, rural clinics, but without any success. The only response was trickery and false promises.[20]

Morales said some priests did go underground to help bring about revolution, but the Zapatistas were not nearly as forthcoming. In communiques published in *Tiempo* on January 12 and 19, 1994, the Zapatistas denied the influence of outsiders and refuted claims that radical Catholic priests or catechists had inspired them to take up arms:

The EZLN does not have any foreigners in its ranks, and has not received support or advice from revolutionary movements of other countries or other governments. . . . We have never had ties with the Salvadoran FMLN, nor with the URGN of Guatemala, nor with any armed movement of any part of the world. We learned our tactics from Mexican history itself, from Hidalgo, Morelos, Guerrero, Mina, from the resistance to the Yankee invasion of 1846–1847, and from popular resistance to the French intervention, from the heroic deeds of Villa and Zapata and from the long history of indigenous resistance in our country.

We have no links to Catholic religious authorities, nor with those of any other creed. . . . Among the ranks, the majority are Catholic, but there are also other creeds and religions.[21]

And

We are not religious, nor are we against religion. We respect beliefs, but each one of us is in the battle for our poverty. There are catechists among us, also *sabáticos* [Seventh-Day Adventists].[22]

PEASANT ORGANIZATIONS

The 1974 Indigenous Congress had two important consequences for peasant and indigenous organizing in Chiapas. First, by convening indigenous groups from different parts of the state, the congress helped develop an awareness of shared problems across ethnic lines. It established channels for ongoing communication and helped build bridges between groups that would later serve to organize alliances. Second, the congress presented nonindigenous organizers and activists, including teachers and technical advisors, with incontrovertible proof that Indians, even monolingual speakers of different Mayan languages with distinct ethnicities and cultural identities, could organize and share awareness of one another's circumstances.

For years preceding the congress, indigenous and other peasants had been the topic of much debate among Mexico's Left. Many intellectuals[23] denied the political potential of the country's indigenous peoples and claimed that they were not worth organizing because they represented an anachronistic, regressive sector of society that impeded the development of the proletarian class consciousness needed to overthrow capitalism. These scholars, steeped in the tenets of classical Marxism, believed that revolution could only come from a wage-earning working class in a fully developed capitalist society. They rejected the Maoist idea that peasants in a precapitalist society were capable of progressive political action that could lead to the overthrow of the state. They argued that peasant agitation for land reform was not something the Left should support because peasants' inherently inefficient production held back the development of the agrarian sector and, thus, of capitalism. They also believed that Indians were nothing more than pawns of the bourgeois state, easily co-opted as buffers against development of rural proletarians, their ethnicity and culture nothing more than a false consciousness abetted by the Mexican government's Indianist programs. After the Cuban Revolution, the failure of Che Guevarismo—the theory that leaders such as Ernesto "Che" Guevara could appear on the peasant or indigenous scene and ignite latent revolutionary potential—only seemed to further prove the reactionary character of the peasantry.

Other intellectuals on the Left vehemently rejected this characterization of the peasantry. Arturo Warman, author of *We Come to Object: The Peasants of Morelos and the National State*, argued that peasant production, spurred by Lázaro Cárdenas' agrarian reform in the 1930s, had been indispensable to the development of Mexico's urban economy by providing cheap food and thus enabling industry to keep wages low. Alain de Janvry, writing about agrarian reform throughout Latin America in *The Agrarian Question*, pointed out that peasants should be considered semiproletarians because, while they grow food in the countryside, they also sell labor as occasional workers in the city. Other analysts[24] argued that peasants, in their quest for land, were not so different from workers striking for better work conditions in the field or the factory, and that the seeming inefficiency of peasant production was actually a result of middlemen and power holders in the countryside, who robbed them of fair returns by buying corn and beans from them cheaply while selling needed merchandise to them dearly, or by charging usurious interest to peasants who needed loans. If anything, these scholars argued, peasants needed the support of the Left in gaining access to land and assistance in obtaining fair markets and reasonable credits.

Needless to say, the impact of the Indigenous Congress of 1974 was watched closely by intellectuals on both sides of the debate. The success of the congress, and the informal programs—such as the lessons in political economy, commerce, and Mexican history that Indians in the Selva Lacandona requested and received from Catholic catechists in the months following the congress—seemed to underscore both the sophistication and the progressive potential of indigenous peoples. That these courses were taught in the countryside, in Tzeltal, served even further to demonstrate the viability of grassroots education in what had previously been perceived as a backward and conservative sector of society. Activists in other parts of the country busy developing nongovernmental independent popular organizations took note of the congress' accomplishments, and many urban intellectuals were forced to reform their views of the peasantry.

The national government, meanwhile, hoping to capitalize on the effervescence of the congress and co-opt its leaders, convoked its own National Congress of Indian Pueblos in 1975 at Pátzcuaro, Michoacán (the site of the First Interamerican Indian Congress that my grandfather, John Collier, attended in 1940 as U.S. commissioner of Indian affairs). Both developments—the lessons that came out of the church-sponsored Indigenous Congress of 1974 and the government-sponsored congress a year later—drew the indigenous peasants of Chiapas into the national arena. This opened Chiapas to important new currents of organizing and politics, just at the time when federally sponsored colonization was sending peasants from central and northern Mexico to homestead in eastern Chiapas.

During the 1970s, the federal government entered into a rivalry with leftist movements for control of worker and peasant organizations. During the 1970–1976 presidency of Luis Echeverría, the state used populism, agrarian reform, and colonization to draw some peasants into the fold of the ruling party. José López Portillo, in the 1976–1982 presidency that followed, poured money from the oil boom into local programs to win support. At the same time, independent organizers were attempting to win support from peasants frustrated with the government's lack of action on land reform petitions. The repression of the student movement in 1968 had persuaded Mexico's Left to avoid direct political confrontation with the state by pressing for reforms through legal channels. The independent organizations emerging at the time tended to parallel those of the government and competed with them for membership while challenging the government to embrace more radical concerns. Eventually, this competition led to friction not just between government authorities and political organizers, but between independently organized peasants and government-affiliated peasants who ended up challenging each other for the same pieces of land (as I noted in the previous chapter) or the same credits.

The 1970s also marked the beginning of a new way of thinking about peasants and Indians. For decades, Mexican intellectuals had considered the "Indian question" as distinct from the "peasant question." And the government, accordingly, assumed that each group had its own distinct—and not necessarily overlapping—interests. The government and ruling party treated peasants as a social sector (sector social)—comparable to but distinct from labor, industry, or commerce. The social sector was subsidized as such and allocated its own channel of political access within the ruling party through the

National Peasant Confederation (CNC). Peasants, labor, and Indians each had their own, separate PRI-sponsored organization: for peasants, the National Peasant Confederation (CNC); for labor, the Confederation of Mexican Workers (CTM); and for Indians, the National Indianist Institute (INI) and state-level departments of Indian affairs. The CNC and CTM were organizations within the PRI and served both to give members access to and representation within the ruling party leadership and as a channel for the government to reach out to constituents. The INI was responsible for Indianist programs of development. Despite the fact that most Indians were also peasants and the two groups had many areas of shared interest and concern—how to raise better crops, how to improve marginal land, how to gain access to more land, get better prices for crops and obtain credit, for example—no links were made between these organizations. In fact, before the 1970s, even Indians whose communities held land under agrarian reform weren't accepted into the CNC.

But by the 1970s, intellectuals such as André Gunder Frank and Rodolfo Stavenhagen had begun to analyze the Indian *and* peasant questions together as part of Mexico's agrarian class structure.

CHALLENGES TO THE GOVERNMENT

Three distinct independent organizing movements arose in Chiapas in the 1970s and 1980s. One, typified by the Emiliano Zapata Peasant Organization (OCEZ), focused primarily on land reform and was centered initially in the Grijalva River valley town of Venustiano Carranza, where conflict between ranchers and peasants that had brewed for years flared after the government tried to relocate Angostura Dam floodplain settlements there. OCEZ struggled to prevent evictions and relocations of ejidos and to help peasants gain title to contested lands. The second movement, based in northern Chiapas in the area around Simojovel, operated on the premise that peasants were part of a rural proletariat that should be organized into labor unions. The Independent Confederation of Agricultural Workers and Indians (CIOAC) took the lead in this region by organizing resident workers, who were notoriously underpaid and mistreated, to sue ranchers under federal labor laws for back wages and improved working conditions. The third type of organizing focused on making credits available to small producers, and drew strength from the Popular Politics (PP), a Maoist student movement led by a Mexico City economics professor. Although the PP was at the outset primarily a northern Mexican movement, many students involved in the PP eventually came to eastern Chiapas to work among the people who lived in impoverished frontier communities.

Land-focused organizing arrived in Chiapas after the 1975 National Indigenous Congress that the government convoked in Pátzcuaro, Michoacán. Its development illustrates the rivalry between government and independent organizations at the national level that reverberated in peasant organizing in Chiapas. The Pátzcuaro congress brought together indigenous representatives from throughout the country, including Chiapas. After the congress, the government established a National Council of Indian Pueblos (CNPI) to guide development of programs discussed at the congress. At first, the government controlled the council and used it to fund regional programs, such as those of bilingual cultural agents in Oaxaca. But by 1979, when the council's leadership fell into the hands of independent organizers, many of whom were committed to agitating for agrarian reform, the government closed the council down. The independents reorganized the council as the Ayala Plan National Coordinating Committee (CNPA), named after the 1911 Plan de Ayala proclamation setting forth Emiliano Zapata's proposal to expropriate lands, woods, and water that had been usurped from peasants by landlords and politicians.[25]

The CNPA forged a broad alliance of peasant groups from throughout Mexico, including Chiapas, to demand agrarian reform under the banner of Emiliano Zapata. The CNPA also allied itself with another powerful independent union, that of teachers who had split off from the government-controlled national teachers' union.

Together, the two independent organizations led a nationwide mass march on Mexico City on May 12, 1981, to demand the release of political prisoners and the resolution of 315 pending land claims. They organized a second demonstration in June 1982, shortly before their fifth national congress, held in Venustiano Carranza, Chiapas. As a result, Venustiano Carranza became the focal point in Chiapas for long-lasting statewide linkages among the region's CNPA affiliates, who established the OCEZ as a network of independent peasant organizations struggling for agrarian reform in Chiapas, often in alliance with the state's independent teachers movement.[26] Trenchantly opposed to the ruling party's national peasant union, OCEZ spread Zapatista ideology throughout Chiapas during the 1980s.[27]

The second influential current of independent organizing that entered Chiapas from the national arena in the late 1970s focused on labor. The CIOAC was established in 1975 in affiliation with Mexican communists and socialists; its leaders urged the Left to consider peasants as proletarians, pointing out that at the turn of the century, most of Mexico's rural poor had worked as laborers in the developing capitalist agriculture of the period. Should their descendants be considered peasants just because Mexico's agrarian reform had given them some land? After all, many peasants had to hire themselves out as field hands because they still didn't have enough land on which to make a living. And on ranches that had escaped expropriation under agrarian reform, thousands of resident workers lived in poverty. CIOAC argued that all these rural poor should be considered rural proletarians and incorporated into the proletarian workers' movement.[28]

CIOAC arrived on the scene in northern Chiapas in 1977 and began to use federal labor laws as a basis for demanding agrarian reform on behalf of the resident workers on coffee estates in the region of Simojovel. CIOAC organizers argued that ranch owners violated minimum wage and fair labor standards by paying resident workers only token wages and/or giving them marginal plots on which to live and cultivate in exchange for three days' labor per week.

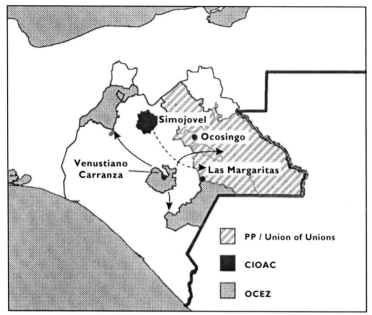

FIGURE 3.2 INDEPENDENT ORGANIZATIONS IN CHIAPAS.
Areas of influence in the 1980s.

CIOAC helped resident workers organize to sue ranch owners in the Simojovel area for back wages—and for the ranches themselves when back wages exceeded the value of a given plantation. In effect, CIOAC opened up a channel for resident workers to claim land *outside* of the conventional application of Mexico's agrarian reform.

This tactic developed at a time when the Mexican government was flush with petrodollars, which the ruling party channeled through state governments to finance development in order to calm dissent. With this goal in mind, Juan Sabines, governor of Chiapas, decided in 1980 to buy out ranches in Simojovel and nearby areas and to offer them for sale to resident workers, financed by CIOAC claims for back pay or by bank loans. For a time, this tactic propelled CIOAC to the forefront of independent peasant organizing in Chiapas. But it also opened CIOAC to criticism, not only from factions within the OCEZ for whom the resort to federal labor laws as a basis for land claims seemed to bypass and thus threaten the agrarian reform laws, but also from independent groups who interpreted the buyout of lands as selling out or compromising with the ruling party.[29]

By far the most powerful current of independent organizing in eastern Chiapas during the 1970s focused on credits and markets and grew out of a political current that began in northern Mexico as the PP and organized by establishing ejido unions as credit and marketing organizations. This movement grew out of a faction of the student movement that decided, after 1968, to live and work with the masses to help them organize in a nonviolent struggle for socialism. A Mexican National Autonomous University economist, Adolfo Orive Berlinguer, had argued in a 1968 pamphlet *Hacia una política popular (Towards a Politics of the People)* that the masses had the capacity to organize at the grassroots, and that the role of theorists and analysts was to help the masses realize their capabilities. An important tenet was to organize from the ground up, with leadership authorized from below—rather than from above. The goal of organizing was to help empower people to become the protagonists of their own destinies without directly challenging the government.

Inspired by Orive and anxious to put his ideas to work, former students turned to the poor in the urban neighborhoods and rural communities of central and northern Mexico, and to the rank and file of teachers' and workers' unions, to build movements that would seek improved living and working conditions for people who had previously been ignored by society. In its rural efforts, the movement met with particular success in collective ejidos among the Yaqui and Mayo Indians of Sinaloa and Sonora[30] and by establishing member-run credit and marketing organizations to circumvent exploitation by merchants, middlemen, and usurers. Adherents of the PP, and of the Proletarian Line (LP), in which the PP joined teachers, metalworkers, and telephone workers organizing in the north, also practiced what they called a "two-faced" politics of "pretexts and objectives." Unlike some more radical groups, which were staunchly against any sort of compromise with the government, the PP advocated interactions with the government that might appear to be compromises but which, in fact, furthered the PP's objectives and could be justified as a means to an end. This tactic was often interpreted by other peasant groups as selling out.

Of all the independent movements, Popular Politics was the most similar in theory and practice to Catholic liberation theology, which explains why PP advocates from the north appeared on the scene both during and in the wake of the 1974 Indigenous Congress in San Cristóbal to offer assistance to catechists organizing and educating peasants and Indians in eastern Chiapas. Orive is said to have offered his personal services to the church, although just what relationship developed between the catechists and the "northerners" isn't clear because some members of the church deny any involvement with Orive or radical politics. Under Mexican law, the church must not step over an imaginary line that separates social service and humanitarian advocacy from politics. Yet in some instances the church may have blurred that line by giving the northerners access to rural assemblies and meetings immediately *after* the catechists had their say.

In an interview with *Proceso* several months before the Zapatista uprising, Mardonio Morales, who served as a Catholic priest in the Selva Lacandona for more than thirty years, recalled what he said was the first meeting between Orive and church activists two decades earlier:

> [Orive said,] "I have come to make you an offer. You take charge of pastoral matters and we will handle political organization. You have the communities in your hands; in this way we can complete our work."
>
> Afterward, he left so that we could discuss it. In general, we thought it would be dishonest to turn the communities over to people who, though apparently very well intentioned, were outsiders. It was a kind of agreement between elites.... We thought that it was not a good idea to ally ourselves with them, that if they wanted to come in and work in the communities, we would not close the doors, but neither would we

turn the communities over to them. Therefore, there was no deal. Mr. Orive was informed and we severed our ties. We never heard from him again.[31]

However, Morales told *Proceso* that some members of the church and some secular missionaries secretly established ties with Orive and the northerners, allowing PP organizers to talk to groups after the catechizers had concluded their meetings in the years following the 1974 congress. At first, Morales is quoted as saying, the northerners seemed to make some concrete improvements in the lives of impoverished eastern Chiapas residents:

> They worked with great sacrifice and devotion, these men and women from Torreón. Thus, they quickly founded the Quiptik ta Lekubtesel, the Union of Unions, then the ARICS, in short, a number of very strong, effective organizations. All indications were that they were on the ascendant.[32]

Within a few years of the 1974 Indigenous Congress, the northerners had displaced the Catholic organizers of the Congress as the dominant intellectual force behind eastern Chiapas' first large coalitions of settlers, formed to obtain credits for peasants. The Quiptik ta Lekubtesel (United for Our Improvement) union galvanized twenty-six communities within the Montes Azules bioreserve and the San Quintín valley of Ocosingo to resist government relocation. In the Selva Lacandona and Las Margaritas, agitation for land and against relocation were used to win a variety of concessions from the government, including credits for small farmers[33] and assistance marketing crops.

One concession won in 1979 was to have INMECAFE, the Mexican Coffee Institute, absorb the considerable cost of transporting coffee produced by member communities in eastern Chiapas to national markets. A second concession, won from Chiapas governor Juan Sabines in September 1980, was to allow the separate independent coalitions to join together in one overarching Union of Unions, which would administer production credits and productivity incentives sponsored by the federal government to revive Mexico's production of basic foods. The Union of Unions quickly expanded to include affiliates in the central highlands of Chiapas and along the Guatemalan border. One year later, from October 12–14, 1981, the Union of Unions mobilized a march and sit-down strike of some 3,000 peasants in Tuxtla Gutiérrez to demand reversal of the eviction orders for the twenty-six communities affected by the Montes Azules bioreserve. Independent teachers', students', and workers' groups accompanied them. In Mexico City, the Independent Workers' Union coordinated a sympathy march in support of the Union of Union's objectives.[34]

By the mid-1980s, the three movements—land-based, labor-based, and credit-based—had spread through the historically undeveloped half of Chiapas from the region around Simojovel to the Selva Lacandona. The movements crossed over one another's original bases of power, sometimes in competition and sometimes in alliance, and established networks of communication across a vast landscape.

The Union of Unions, for example, armed with independent credits and special market access after forming a pact with Chiapas governor Juan Sabines at Bajucú (Las Margaritas) in 1980, quickly became an organizing force in the Simojovel region some one hundred miles to the northwest. There, in the heartland of CIOAC's support, the Union of Unions helped resident workers and Tzotzil colonists band together to take over ranches such as Cucalvitz. Using a combination of violence, threats, and finally bank credits, Tzotzil Indians purchased this ranch, renaming it Kipaltik, or Our Union. They began mixed production of milpa, cattle, and coffee as a collective. When the time came to undertake the first coffee harvests, one of the organizers of the Kipaltik collective, a man who had participated in the Bajucú pact with Governor Sabines in 1980, recruited compatriots (through his network of ties to distant Las Margaritas) to help with the harvest.[35]

The CIOAC and OCEZ began, during the 1980s, to cooperate in militant organizing. Initially they had diverged over the discrepancy between OCEZ's emphasis on using the agrarian code as a basis for militancy and CIOAC's emphasis on federal labor laws. But they began to collaborate in one another's demonstrations and marches, developing networks of mutual support through which protesters could be mobilized to support their organizations' causes. CIOAC and OCEZ also began to expand their activities out of their respective heartlands (northern Chiapas in the area around Simojovel; Venustiano Carranza on the western fringe of the central Grijalva River valley) and into the eastern Chiapas regions once predominantly the domain of the Popular Politics movement and the Union of Unions. By the end of the 1980s, CIOAC and OCEZ had shifted their most militant activity to the Las Margaritas and Ocosingo areas, respectively, making inroads in the heartland of the Union of Unions.

DISILLUSIONMENT AND DISAGREEMENT

What caused those who now support the Zapatistas to lose faith in the alternative peasant groups and in peaceful forms of resistance?

Some of the Zapatistas' most bitter critiques have been directed at leaders of independent movements or organizations who they say have sold out to the ruling party and betrayed their broader constituencies. CIOAC had received some such criticism from the OCEZ during the early 1980s when CIOAC accepted Chiapas governor Juan Sabines' policy of buying out ranches in northern Chiapas and offering them to resident workers. The Union of Unions opened itself to similar criticism by agreeing to tone down militancy in exchange for legal recognition, marketing arrangements with the Mexican Coffee Institute, and support for its independent credit union.

The ARIC Union of Unions split from the Union of Unions (UU) shortly after 1980 to protest the UU's arrangements with the state governor to form its credit union. In 1989, it seemed itself to have compromised with the government when Salinas de Gortari, in the first days of his presidency, recognized the land claims of the twenty-six ARIC communities settled within the Montes Azules Bioreserve and granted ARIC control of a network of subsidized food outlets in the Cañadas region of Las Margaritas, close to the clandestine headquarters of the EZLN. Subcomandante Marcos was outspoken in his disapproval of this arrangement, suggesting that in return for money, ARIC leaders agreed to promote support for the ruling party amongst their followers. In a 1994 statement printed in *Tiempo*, he argued:

> [F]rankly...there are big lies being woven against us with the approval of the army and the evil government. And complicit in those lies are authorities and advisors of the ARIC-Union of Unions, who sold out when the supreme government and their armed forces offered food outlets and money.... Some...of the authorities in the ARIC-Union of Unions and its advisors have sold out and are [government] accomplices. Why? Are they not also poor Indians? The answer, brothers, is that...everyone knows that the majority of the aid that the federal government sent over the past several years to alleviate the hardships of life in our pueblos stayed in their hands. These men fear that their theft will be discovered, as well as their complicity with state and municipal authorities against their brothers of race and blood. Brothers, turn away from those traitors, don't listen to them when they come with their "politics of two faces" to trick others and obtain personal benefits.[36]

In what seemed like a blatant attempt to buy votes for the August 1994 presidential election, the government in May granted almost six million new pesos (approximately 1.8 million U.S. dollars) in credits to ARIC and other Union of Unions subsidiaries,[37] lending credence to Marcos' accusation that the ARIC had compromised its principles for money.

I think that the Zapatista rebellion built upon deep disillusion with both the national state and the independent peasant organizations. In 1974, the Indigenous Congress had inspired the vision that indigenous and nonindigenous peasants could be forged into an alliance with progressive currents from other parts of the country to mobilize for change within the framework of the law. But the 1982 debt crisis, the elimination of government subsidies, Salinas de Gortari's determination to end agrarian reform, and continuing repression, made doing so seem less possible. In a country with little money in a world that demands modernization, peasants have little leverage. When independent peasant organizations won concessions from the government, they paid dearly for them by losing credibility with their wider constituencies. Worse, the leaders of some organizations agreed to compromises that benefited a few peasants at the expense of many others. Each such pact made it seem less likely that the disenfranchised would ever have their day in court. By taking up arms, the EZLN attempted to remove the peasants' struggle from the arena of corrupt Mexican law and politics.

I believe, above all, that the Zapatistas rendered judgment against the fundamental tactic of two decades of independent organizing—that of seeking change through legal channels. Time and again, the national state showed its capacity to exercise the law as a tool for power, selectively and illegitimately, to thwart the revindication of indigenous, peasant, and worker demands.

Every independent movement has experienced repression, either directly from the state's judicial police and military or at the hands of private ranchers' hired gunmen and thugs, who were tolerated and sometimes even abetted by the state. On July 15, 1980, soldiers and ranchers in police uniforms drove over seven hundred resident workers and family members from the ranch they claimed at Wolonchón (Sitalá), left twelve dead and many wounded, and chased survivors into the mountains. Ranchers and their henchmen burned and razed peasant settlements to destroy the nucleus of population legally required as the basis of a land claim. During a six-month period between July and December 1982, independent organizers and the groups they represented in Chiapas experienced five assassinations, violent evictions from two ranches, the destruction of an entire peasant town, and fifty-nine kidnappings. Sometimes peasants acted against other peasants in such incidents, but in the majority (some 80 percent) of cases of repression in Chiapas reported in the press between 1974 and 1987, ranchers (and their gunmen) and public authorities (judicial and security police of the state or federal government or the army) perpetrated the acts of violence against peasants.[38]

If anything, repression escalated in Chiapas after 1982 under the heavy hand of Governor Absalón Castellanos Domínguez, the retired army general later kidnapped by the EZLN from his ranch near Las Margaritas on January 1, 1994. Peasant leaders were assassinated, leaving groups with the memory of their lost heroes, men such as "Bartolomé Martínez Villatoro, Miguel de la Cruz, Alfredo Morales, José Solís, Andulio Gálvez and so many others" who "fell to the bullets of landlords' pistoleros and the state's own police forces."[39] Under the pretext of controlling drug trafficking, judicial police kept up constant repressive vigilance—in one case that I know of personally, a young man "disappeared" in 1989 because they claimed to have found wild poppy growing in his flower gardens. After two weeks during which his family could not even find out where their son was being held, he reappeared, toothless and bruised from the beatings he had received in interrogation. Such ongoing abuses of legally instituted power in Chiapas and elsewhere in Mexico have been documented by Americas Watch and other human rights groups,[40] and underscore the Zapatista contention that

> Constitutional laws have not been complied with by those who govern the country, while, on the contrary, we peasants and Indians are made to pay for the tiniest error, under the full weight of the laws drawn up by those who are the first to violate them.[41]

As for elections, the ruling party did everything it could in 1988 to thwart the Cardenista National Democratic Front (FDN), which united the Left with dissidents who had split off from the PRI. In 1988, for the first time in years, independent groups decided to participate in electoral politics, but to little avail. In Las Margaritas—to take just one of hundreds of examples—Cardenistas charged in June 1988 that PRI municipal authorities had moved polling places out of the settlements known to have FDN sympathizers, had failed to register eight hundred Cardenistas, and had doctored voting lists in PRI-controlled settlements by registering the voters there up to six or seven times. In addition, thousands of Cardenista voter identification cards had been stolen in transit from Ocosingo to Las Margaritas.[42] Official election results strained credulity, reporting overwhelming PRI majorities in the rural regions of eastern Chiapas where the Cardenistas were strongest:

> Why is it that the PRI always wins so many votes in Chiapas, 90 percent of the vote, or more? It's because of fraud.... No one can tell us, "Well, you should have tried elections...." We did everything legal that we could so far as elections and organizations were concerned, and to no avail.[43]

Once again, the government had closed off a channel of legal recourse, justifying an armed rebellion to force Salinas' resignation and to reform the democratic process.

The Zapatistas, moreover, held the national state responsible for corrupting public officials by enabling them to use Indians, peasants, and the working-class poor as rungs on the ladder to power, to be dispensed with or simply forgotten once politicians had attained important positions:

> It has always been easy for the politicians to use us Indians as a step on the ladder for them to climb to power, and once there in power, in their cabinet, they forget about us.[44]
> All of them are to blame, from the highest federal officials to the last of the corrupt "indigenous" leaders, the governor that was not elected by people of Chiapas, the municipal presidents, more concerned with [public] works of adornment and with close ties to the grandees than with governing for their own people, as well as all the other functionaries, who withheld health, education, services, work, justice, food, and above all respect and dignity.[45]

I cannot but wonder whether other leftists of Marcos' generation and background were included in this indictment for having taken up government positions. Arturo Warman, whose *We Come to Object* was a scathing critique of Mexico's use of agrarian policy to exploit the peasants, became director of Mexico's Nationalist Indianist Institute (INI) under Salinas, helped formulate the "reform" of Article 27 of the Constitution and the Agrarian Code, and then served as public attorney for agrarian affairs. Gustavo Gordillo, an activist in Popular Politics in earlier years and, like Warman, a harsh critic of the corruption in the Mexican agrarian policy, also became an advisor to Salinas as subsecretary of agrarian reform and formulated proposals for restructuring the agrarian reform,[46] many of which have been incorporated into the new Agrarian Code.[47] Even Adolfo Orive Berlinguer, the ideologue of Popular Politics, held office in Salinas' National Solidarity Program. There were many others in government positions whom Marcos and his compatriots may have been indicting as sellouts.

THE GROWTH OF THE GUERRILLA MOVEMENT

Although widespread fraud in the 1988 elections may have helped radicalize more segments of society, the Zapatistas had apparently given up on using legal means to change the system long before the elections debacle that brought Salinas de Gortari to power.

According to Major Mario of the EZLN, the clandestine Zapatista army had its inception on November 16, 1983, when six idealists from Mexico's north arrived to join forces with dissident peasants and Indians in a movement that immediately went underground to begin military and political organizing. Mario was a boy at the time, but he remembers one of the six, a charismatic and committed man who was accidentally shot and killed in troop exercises, and whom the Zapatistas commemorate with their left-hand salute to the flag because the man was left-handed.[48] Subcomandante Marcos, who was one of the six, said of that moment,

[I]t was when we arrived that the military question began. There was no military organization before I arrived, we initiated it. We came from a national context similar in process to what is happening now [1994] in the state. Avenues for political action were closing down, and the gap was growing between the two Mexicos that are, in reality three: Mexico of the powerful; Mexico of those who aspire to power; and the Mexico of those who nobody cares about. In Chiapas, these are the Indians. So we decided that something had to be done.[49]

The early 1980s were a time of economic crisis in Mexico. In the last months of the López Portillo presidency in 1982, oil prices collapsed and the stability of the world banking system was threatened because of Mexico's sudden inability to service its huge international debt. The international financial community forced Mexico to make huge cuts in federal expenditures, sharply devalue the peso, slash wages, and remove subsidies for urban and rural poor. The illusions of petrodollar development shattered and with them, no doubt, the expectation that independent organizations could gain economic concessions from the state. On Mexico's southern border, refugees from Guatemala's war fled into Mexico, pursued by the Guatemalan military, and bringing the Mexican military onto the scene to control refugees in what many colonists of the region believed were joint Guatemalan/Mexican military maneuvers to repress the colonists as well. Meanwhile, Zoque Indians and peasants fleeing the northern Chiapas region devastated by ash from the April 1982 eruption of the Chichonal volcano were swelling the flow of colonists into the south. Avenues for political action were indeed closing down, the divide between the powerful and the poor was growing, and frontier Chiapas was becoming a dumping ground for both Guatemalan and Mexican refugees.

Retreating into the jungle, the six northern idealists and their peasant and indigenous compatriots began a process of mutual education. The northerners had to learn how to survive in the rugged backlands. "The Lacandón jungle, for a ladino, is the worst thing that can happen to you, worse than watching 24 Hours [a program of Mexico's Televisa network]," recounts Marcos. "We came here in a process of apprenticeship. The comrades taught me what they know about the mountains, and I taught them what I know.... It was the Indians who taught us how to get around here, to live in the mountains, to hunt, and then we gradually began to study weapons. That's how the EZLN arose, but at first it was sheerly a struggle to survive, to learn how to live in the mountains, make the mountains accept us."[50]

One task for the movement was to develop a political organization that could extend to embrace new constituencies. Following the precepts of Popular Politics, like those of Catholic and independent organizers in eastern Chiapas, political organizing was put entirely into the hands of the movement's indigenous base, in part because of a recognition that the indigenous people of the region would never follow a nonindigenous leadership. In principle, the EZLN organized its leadership upward through the delegation of representation within the ethnic regions that had been established by the 1974 congress. Clearly, the organization did not represent all peoples within various ethnicities, but it did explicitly draw its legitimacy from followers recruited among all ethnicities. It was in the name of this popular base that the EZLN's leadership, the Committee of Clandestine Indigenous Revolution (CCRI), declared war on January 1, 1994, and it was to this base that it submitted the tentative March 2 peace accords, for what proved, on June 12, to be rejection.

Mardonio Morales recalled the period when he told *Proceso* in a September 13, 1993, interview that the "northerner's" movement was taken over by the Emiliano Zapata Peasant Organization (OCEZ) and the National Independent Emiliano Zapata Peasant Alliance (ANCIEZ) and that these organizations then split into two factions, one calling for an armed uprising and one calling for more moderate tactics:

> We do not know at what exact moment the OCEZ and the ANCIEZ, which are extremist organizations, came in and took over the northerner's movement. We learned that the northern advisers were gradually leaving. It seems that the OCEZ and the ANCIEZ are the same thing, with different names and fronts.

They are developing as ejido unions, or production centers, depending on the needs of the region. And on top of this comes all the idealization of the political struggle, which is particularly violent, and the preparation for it. They have a network of economic and organizational advisers. That is how they keep people in line. And behind that mask, they have also organized the whole radio situation, which is how the entire jungle stays in touch.[51]

Marcos and his idealist compatriots were made responsible for military organizing and training, following precepts that Marcos attributed to

Pancho Villa, as far as regular army tactics are concerned, and Emiliano Zapata, with respect to the interchange between guerrilla and peasant. We got the rest out of a manual of the Mexican army that fell into our hands, and a small manual from the Pentagon, and some work by a French general whose name I can't remember.[52]

Gradually, the movement acquired weapons, from several sources, according to Marcos:

[We got weapons from] three sources [sic]. A small portion comes from the "work of ants," of buying arms here and there. Another important source is the Mexican police and army involved in the anti-drug battle. When they arrest drug traffickers, they seize their weapons, but they only turn over only a small portion of the weapons to their superiors, the rest are sold in the black market. That's how we bought AK-47, M16, and other arms. They thought they were selling to other drug traffickers and that they would soon enough arrest them and resell the weapons. The third source was the *guardias blancas* [hired gunmen] of the ranchers, trained by the security forces and the army. They had good weapons and last year began to receive Uzis. Finally, there are the weapons of the peasants themselves, shotguns and rudimentary things. We don't have as many weapons as we would like, nor ammunition.[53]

Over time, the movement began to recruit from among the broader peasantry:

> As far as the peasants are concerned, the EZLN arose as a self-defense group to defend against the ranchers' hired gunmen, who try to take their land and maltreat them, limiting the social and political advancement of the Indians. So they took up arms so as not to be defenseless. Then, later, the comrades saw it wasn't enough to do self-defense of a single ejido or community but rather to establish alliances with others and to begin to make up military and paramilitary contingents on a larger scale, still for the purpose of self-defense.[54]

Before long, youngsters from surrounding regions were coming to the EZLN for training. When young men of the region reached the age of Mexican compulsory military service, many families would urge them to gain training in the mountains rather than with the army—especially after the Salinas government began to pursue what Marcos sarcastically describes as the "brilliant idea" of reforming Article 27 of the Constitution and the Agrarian Code. "That was an important catalyst. The reforms negated any legal possibility of obtaining land, and it was land that was at the basis of peasants' self-defense."[55] Furthermore, by changing the law, the government removed a crucial reason for peasants to try to work within the law.

Salinas de Gortari's reform of Article 27 of the Mexican Constitution and of the Agrarian Code—the very legislation that made land reform a central tenet of the Mexican state—was in fact just one more step in his government's project to restructure the Mexican economy by removing government involvement and support of sectors thought to be "antimodern." Some of the restructuring had been forced on Mexico during the Miguel de la Madrid presidency (1982–1988), as part of an austerity program required by the international banking community for bailing Mexico out from its debt crisis. The austerity program dried up subsidies to peasants for fertilizer and other chemical inputs and eroded price supports for crops. But de la Madrid's restructuring had stemmed from a paucity of economic resources; Salinas de Gortari's reflected a change of will.

Salinas' advisors reached a consensus that Mexico's existing peasantry had to be subjected to major surgery, transformed and absorbed into the modernization of agriculture to increase the productivity of millions of peasant-held hectares used for crops not competitive on world markets, or worked by labor that could be put to more productive use elsewhere. Market subsidies for peasant crops, such as the transport subsidies that the Mexican Coffee Institute had negotiated with the Union of Unions in eastern Chiapas, had to be eliminated. The entire system of agrarian credits needed to be overhauled, advisors concluded, to circumvent corrupt practices wherein bankers and peasants were colluding in fraudulent claims of crop failure to renege on loans. Furthermore, land reform itself should be brought to a standstill to prevent further land from being absorbed into inefficient peasant production. Thus, the advisors advocated the privatization and commercialization of peasant and Indian-held parcels.

Salinas forced these changes through the Mexican Congress in 1992. They were denounced by critics as the death knell for the peasantry, and as potentially devastating to agrarian communities as the Liberal Reform laws of 1856 and 1863 that had robbed Indian communities of their lands and plunged them into penury. The "reform" of Article 27 is certain to have galvanized peasant antagonism to the national state, and may well have contributed to the EZLN decision, in January 1993, that EZLN forces were sufficiently organized and trained, and its alliances with sympathizers and potential supporters developed enough, to launch a revolution. According to Marcos, it was at the end of January 1993 "that the Clandestine Committee decided 'We're going to take up arms,' and they ordered me, 'You take charge of it, we'll give you so much time, and you set the date within those limits.'"[56]

At that moment, evidently, the EZLN was not particularly concerned with NAFTA, the North American Free Trade Agreement passed by the Mexican, Canadian, and United States governments in 1993 and inaugurated on January 1, 1994, the date finally chosen for the EZLN uprising. Although EZLN proclamations first identified

NAFTA as having inspired their revolution, it is apparent that the designation of NAFTA was a pretext. As Marcos explained to reporters who asked why NAFTA's inaugural date had been selected for the uprising,

> It's like the myth of the facemasks. We used facemasks because of the cold. But suddenly the facemasks caught on with the people, and so now we keep them on. We had not planned to rise up on January 1....
> We thought about various dates, taking various factors into account. For example, we needed to show clearly that we weren't drug traffickers. We had to do something related to cities, the pretext couldn't be just about rural conditions so that they couldn't write us off in the jungle, as they did in the incident in the mountains of Corralchén, that garrison of ours they discovered, when they decided we were [a fringe group], marijuana growers, or Guatemalans. We didn't say anything, because we were watching to see what would happen.[57]

In May 1993, the army had raided an EZLN garrison in the remote colony of Corralchén. Although first reports described the raid as having routed out a guerrilla camp, complete with underground bunkers and a scale model of the municipal headtown of Ocosingo, the government subsequently downplayed the reports. At the time, acknowledging the existence of a guerrilla movement in Chiapas would have endangered the chances that the U.S. Congress would accept NAFTA, as it finally did after a battle hard fought and won by U.S. president Bill Clinton in the summer of 1993.

Marcos continued:

> Then there was the problem of the civilian population, and our concern as to what would happen to the guerrilla cause if we attacked the civilian population. For a *guerrillero*, who will die for his cause, nothing is more repugnant than to harm civilians. It's worse than being captured by the army.
> Then there were logistical questions, apart from political ones. For example, when would our food reserves be greatest, given that the war would be long, that we would be surrounded, that they would drive us

into the mountains, so [the uprising] had to begin just after harvest, when we could get money together.

The truth of the matter is that the decision about when to rise up didn't take national politics into account. That's not so important to the comrades, not so much as not being able to stomach things any longer, regardless of national or international conditions.[58]

4 ♦ OIL AND THE CRISIS IN MEXICAN AGRICULTURE

When I think about the impact of energy development on Mexico's southeast, I ponder the situation of two young men whose divergent experiences reflect the contradictions of change that development brought in the 1970s and 1980s and that continue today. One is the gaunt youth from a frontier colony east of Las Margaritas who, shivering, hitched a ride with me in 1991 on his way to Villahermosa, Tabasco, to look for work—any work—in construction near the oil fields. The other is a young man who invested earnings from such work into a combination of farming and a small business selling flowers and vegetables at a market stand in Ocozocuautla, fifty miles away from his home and children in Zinacantán, who was able to purchase a pickup truck to haul wholesale produce to market.

Both young men came from rural areas whose agrarian production was thrown into crisis by energy development in the 1970s, which devalued traditional crops and drew peasants into dependence on jobs far from home to help support their families. Mexico's 1982 debt crisis forced peasants back into farming, which they had to intensify or diversify into crops such as coffee that required purchased chemical inputs and entailed risky credits and markets. Some people, like the young man from Zinacantán who lived close to roads and developed markets, made good by combining farming with nonfarming enterprise. Others, such as those from Las Margaritas frontier areas who invested heavily in coffee production, have been devastated by the collapse of world coffee prices since 1988 and the government's withdrawal of credits and production subsidies. These young men's experiences illustrate the uneven pace of development in rural Mexico and the extent to which participation in the global economy brought new opportunities even as it undermined the agricultural basis of peasant life and created an unprecedented gap between rich and poor in peasant communities.

Their stories also reflect a new reality of peasant life, which is no longer strictly defined by food production. The vast majority of peasant households now participate in some kind of wage work or commercial enterprise in addition to farming. Peasants in today's Mexico double as masons, carpenters, ditch diggers, truck drivers, small store owners, and tailors, and their vocations echo changes in many rural areas of the developing world. The changes stretch the concept of "peasantry" to new limits by encompassing people— including the Zapatista women who want the chance to become truck drivers—who still

> have some ability to produce their own food, or have a close kinship connection to people who have some ability to produce their own food, or interact in a local economy with people who have some ability to produce their own food.... This category includes...petty commodity producers...who produce things for sale or live by trading in local markets...; and semiproletarians...who currently work for wages but who also depend on food production or petty commodity production by themselves or their kinsmen for survival.[1]

That indigenous peasants should participate in a variety of non-farming activities is not in itself new. Colonial Chiapas depended on indigenous labor for more than food production. In the nineteenth century, indigenous peoples were forced from their villages and pressed into service for nominal wages on the coastal coffee plantations and lowland ranches. Indians literally built San Cristóbal at the turn of the century.[2] What has changed—as a consequence of Mexico's energy development—is the dramatic growth of nonagricultural work and the increasing integration of peasant economies into national and international markets.

We must understand these changes if we are to appreciate why some of the Zapatistas wanted to be truck drivers and were demanding work as well as land, consumer goods such as refrigerators and televisions as well as housing, and schooling for real skills as well as basics such as health care.

The world of the Zapatistas, furthermore, is *not just* that of eastern Chiapas. Like others throughout rural Chiapas, the Zapatistas circulate in an economy in which wage work, coffee production, cattle, and commerce mix and move people, stretching the meaning and boundaries of community over a wide landscape.

CRISIS IN AGRICULTURE

Energy development changed the face of Mexico's southeastern region during the 1960s and 1970s. From 1936 onward, when Mexico nationalized the oil fields held by foreign firms, the country developed petroleum for Mexico's internal needs. But after the Organization of Petroleum Exporting Countries (OPEC) shocked the world economy by raising oil prices in 1972, Mexico decided to export petroleum and began to expand coastal and inland oil production. After oil exploration uncovered vast reserves along the Tabasco coast of the Gulf of Mexico, the government found it easy to secure loans from a world banking system glutted by petrodollars. It used the borrowed money to expand oil production and to underwrite ambitious new projects of development. In Chiapas, the government completed two major hydroelectric power projects that had been started in the 1960s on the Grijalva River between the Guatemalan border and the Gulf of Mexico. As energy development shifted into high gear, the southeastern region began to supply Mexico with half its hydroelectric power and much of its oil for export.[3]

During this oil-led boom, Mexican agriculture declined as the country experienced symptoms of what development economists refer to as the oil syndrome, or Dutch disease. This concept refers to how export booms undermine other sectors of a country's economy, a phenomenon that economists nicknamed "Dutch disease" in their analyses of the negative impact of North Sea gas development on

Dutch manufacturing. As oil exports boomed in Holland and other petroleum-producing nations, each country suffered unexpected setbacks in other sectors such as manufacturing, agriculture, or production of other tradeables (exports). Economists explained that the export boom tended to overvalue the exporting country's currency and caused labor and other resources to shift into oil production or sectors producing nontradeables such as construction and infrastructure. In Mexico's case, while industry expanded from 27 percent of the gross domestic product (GDP) in 1965 to 38 percent in 1982, the contribution of agriculture to GDP fell by half, from 14 percent to just 7 percent.[4]

Peasants left the countryside in droves. Many migrated to Mexico City, other cities, or to the United States to look for work. Despite the agrarian redistribution that took place during Luis Echeverría's 1970–1976 presidency, agricultural production shifted away from basic staples such as corn to fruits, vegetables, and meat destined for middle-class consumption and export. Mexico devoted more foreign exchange to purchasing corn from the United States to feed the poorest 40 percent of the population, whose share of the national wealth had not grown since the 1950s. Mexicans quickly came to believe their agriculture was in crisis, even as other sectors of their economy boomed. By 1980, Mexico was importing 25 percent of its corn. Mexican politicians, chastened by American talk of using grain exports as a tool in foreign policy, began to fear that corn imports could jeopardize Mexico's sovereignty.[5]

This food crisis exacerbated Mexican scholars' debates about the place of peasants in Mexican society, and whether they hindered or aided agrarian development. Some argued that peasant production was inefficient and did not contribute to Mexico's growing comparative advantage in producing export commodities such as tomatoes, or beef and animal feed crops. Pro-peasant analysts argued that production of maize was indispensable and that declines in maize production could be reversed by allowing peasants fair access to inputs, credits, and markets, to counterbalance inroads that agribusiness was making in the rural economy.[6] The López Portillo

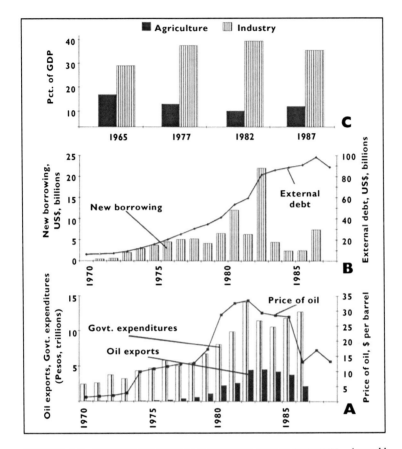

FIGURE 4.1 TRENDS IN MEXICAN ENERGY DEVELOPMENT. As world oil prices rose after the OPEC crisis (A), Mexico began to develop oil fields for exports, which grew during the 1980s. Meanwhile, government expenditures had risen sharply in anticipation of oil revenues. Mexico borrowed heavily to fund expenditures (B), and external debt swelled, generating the debt crisis when world oil prices turned downward in 1982. During the period of energy development up to 1982, Mexican agriculture declined by half (C) from 14 percent to 7 percent of the gross domestic product (GDP), while industry grew. Mexican agriculture recovered slightly after the 1982 debt crisis.

administration of 1976–1982 heeded these arguments. It established mechanisms for credits such as those granted to the Union of Unions in eastern Chiapas in 1980, and launched the Mexican Food System (SAM) to improve the distribution of food to the poor and reinvigorate peasant production through federal subsidies for fertilizer and for other inputs, credits, and price supports. The government also reoriented road-building programs to increase the number of feeder roads linking isolated settlements to national markets.

Mexico's development boom came to an abrupt halt in 1982 when world oil prices declined sharply and Mexico found itself unable to service the huge external debt that the country had taken on during the boom (see Figure 4.1).[7] International bankers did not want to let Mexico default on its debt and insisted on refinancing it, but at the price of steep cuts in Mexico's budget, especially for social programs. The government curtailed subsidies for peasant production, reawakening the debate over policy towards peasants.[8] After 1988, Salinas de Gortari pushed ahead with restructuring the economy through policies leading to NAFTA and to the decision to dismantle the agrarian reform by rewriting Article 27 of the Constitution and the Agrarian Code—one of the actions precipitating the Zapatista rebellion.

ENERGY DEVELOPMENT IN CHIAPAS

I learned about the impact of energy development on hamlets tucked into the mountainsides of central Chiapas in a 1981 economic survey I conducted in Apas, Zinacantán.[9] Fourteen years before, in 1967, virtually every Apas household had almost exclusively farmed milpa. In 1981, I learned that men in household after household had gone off to work on government construction projects near the oil fields or at dams being built for the federal electrical commission. Zinacantecos told me that they could earn far more money in such work than they could by farming corn, and most families farmed only a patch of their land.

Manuel was about fifteen years old when he first went off to a construction job:

> Others from Apas were going off to work far away to earn money. They worked at Concordia. There used to be a place called Old Concordia, but when the dam was built at Angostura, it flooded Old Concordia,

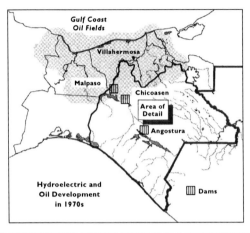

FIGURE 4.2 SITES OF ENERGY DEVELOPMENT.

and so they built a completely new Concordia. And that was the first place I went to look for work, along with others from Apas who were going there, like Antonio, who's now my brother-in-law.

I asked him to take me along, but at the time I didn't speak Spanish and I was afraid of ladinos. "Who knows if you'll get taken on, get given work right away?" Antonio asked me. "Let me go find out." So we went off to work at New Concordia, where the work boss, a contractor, hired me to fill in the ditch for a pipeline for drinking water. I worked for two weeks, but I barely endured it because I didn't understand Spanish and was afraid of the ladinos.

Most Zinacantecos, together with indigenous people from throughout Chiapas who flocked to construction jobs in the 1970s, lacked Spanish language and work skills and had to begin work as unskilled ditch diggers or porters. Many of them picked up Spanish and learned vocational skills on the job. After trying out work at New Concordia, Manuel took up a job assisting a ladino mason, who taught him the trade and helped him improve his Spanish:

"Can you read and write?" he asked me. "Yes, a little bit." "Well, why don't you write down the names of the tools that we use," he suggested. "Write it down, I'll tell you all the names," and he showed me each of the tools and told me what each was called. So I wrote down the name of each tool and what it was used for, and I wrote down the Tzotzil names as well as the Spanish words. And that way, gradually I learned Spanish. So later, when I went to other work, I was no longer scared to go. I had become accustomed to the work and I understood Spanish.

Manuel accompanied this mason from one construction site to another, working near each of the dams that the government built along the Grijalva at Angostura, Chicoasen, and Malpaso. Often working overtime, he earned very good money and used it to marry and to build a tile-roofed house back in Apas, a rarity there at a time when most homes were still made of mud brick and thatch. He paid others to do the building and watch over his milpa while he was away.

Construction work began to differentiate Zinacantecos as some of them acquired enough skills, tools, and capital to become independent masons or carpenters. They could then function as private contractors, hiring other indigenous people to work for them. Juan, another Zinacanteco, told me about how he launched himself as an independent contractor in work near Villahermosa, Tabasco:

> I'd learned how to do almost everything. I'd seen how the work was done, building with stone, with brick, with cement block, tile, mosaic, plastering, and so forth. I had bought some tools, a trowel, hammer, plumb line, level, T-square, chisel, pick, shovel, and wheelbarrow. So I decided to seek a piecework contract. There was a contractor I worked with who saw what I could do, and I asked him if he wouldn't subcontract me work by the meter. And he agreed, turning the blueprints over to me to work from. I didn't really know how to read the blueprint very well, but I could more or less tell where the walls were supposed to go, where cement posts were supposed to be, and I did the job. I had a friend, Mariano, and I hired him to lay bricks for me.
>
> At first I did piecework this way; later I began to contract directly. At the time, a mason's weekly wage was 80,000 pesos, but I found I could take contracts from the engineer paying 4,000 pesos per meter of construction. Mariano and I could complete 80 meters per week. I would get 320,000 pesos for the job and pay Mariano 100,000 per week out of that, more than he could earn as a mason, and twice what he would have earned as a mason's assistant. We worked hard, and I earned a lot of money, and then I quit.

Juan used his earnings to purchase a market stall in Jaltenango where he took up wholesale-retail produce trade as an independent business. Many Zinacantecos started up small market businesses at this time. Others invested in trucks and took up work in transport.[10]

By the height of the boom in 1981, off-farm activities had differentiated the wealthy from the poor and diversified the livelihoods of almost all Zinacantecos. Men of the wealthiest households in Apas were heavily into small businesses. Some were in commerce as

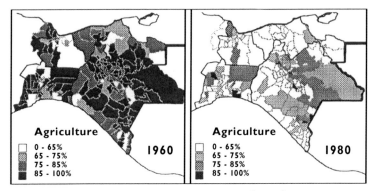

FIGURE 4.3 DECLINES IN AGRICULTURE, 1960–1980. The maps show the percentage of the economically active population (PEA) who were active in agriculture in 1960 and 1980. Agriculture dominated Chiapas in 1960, claiming over 85 percent of the economically active population in most rural townships. By 1980, that figure had declined to less than 75 percent in most areas, reflecting national trends during the 1970s.

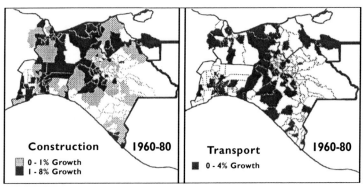

FIGURE 4.4 GROWTH IN CONSTRUCTION AND TRANSPORT, 1960–1980. The maps show the changing percent of PEA who were active in construction and transport between 1960 and 1980. As agriculture declined during the 1970s, construction and transport increased in areas near oil and hydroelectric development.

wholesale-retail traders in produce; others purchased trucks and started transport businesses. Poorer men were almost all engaged in wage work. Among the workers, young and middle-aged men worked predominantly as unskilled hired hands on construction. Older men combined work as hired field hands with small-scale farming on their own. Overall, Zinacantecos had all but abandoned the farming of maize. As will be discussed in the next chapter, these changes also made women, most of whom stayed behind in the hamlet, more dependent on cash incomes than they had been when men and women worked together both in household production and consumption.[11]

Peasants from other municipios also reconfigured their livelihoods in response to opportunities that beckoned from the zones of rapidly expanding Gulf Coast oil production and rapid metropolitan growth in Tabasco and Chiapas.[12] The 1980 census figures show that indigenous people from the rural areas of Chiapas resettled into the Gulf Coast oil zone and into metropolitan centers of Villahermosa, Tuxtla Gutiérrez, San Cristóbal de las Casas, and Tapachula. Colonists also flowed into the frontier areas of eastern Chiapas. Throughout the region, the proportion of the working population active in agriculture declined dramatically as people shifted into nonagricultural employment in commerce, transport, and construction (see Figures 4.3 and 4.4).

It is important to emphasize that these effects of the "oil syndrome" did not affect all areas of agriculture in exactly the same way. While maize farming declined throughout the countryside, some kinds of agrarian production resisted or even advanced against the tide of agrarian decline. Close to the oil fields in Tabasco, where peasants could combine wage work with small-scale farming, lucrative peasant cultivation of cacao flourished. Larger-scale private cacao producers did not fare as well as the peasants, whose smaller scale of production would allow their families to integrate wage work and cultivation. Another factor favoring those peasant cacao producers was a cooperative marketing organization, similar to that developed by the Union of Unions for coffee in eastern Chiapas, that allowed small-scale cacao producers to circumvent middlemen and get better prices for their products.[13]

RESTRUCTURING PEASANT AGRICULTURE

As the 1982 debt crisis unfolded, the government cut employment in the public sector, curtailed development projects, and laid off thousands of construction workers. The Zinacantecos remember their

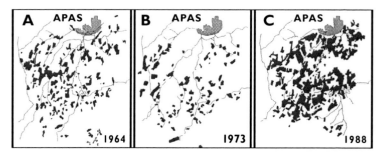

FIGURE 4.5 CHANGING INTENSITY OF APAS FARMLAND USE.
The proportion of farmland in use (shaded parcels) slackened notably from 1964 (A) to 1973 (B) as Zinacantecos shifted to off-farm activities. After 1982, as opportunities for off-farm work decreased, Zinacantecos reinvigorated highland farming by using chemical inputs to farm plots with less fallowing. By 1988 (C), the more intense use of Apas farmland had eliminated most fallow land.

foremen telling them that "the President wants you to go back to farming."[14]

Many Zinacantecos did indeed return to farming, but did not give up off-farm vocations. They were in a fortunate position vis-à-vis other indigenous communities because most Zinacantecos lived near or along the Pan American Highway and had easy access to the off-farm urban work that, although it became scarcer and scarcer, didn't dry up entirely. Many Zinacantecos revived their milpas as part of a "diversified portfolio" of livelihoods.[15] Wealthier wholesale-retail produce vendors and truckers scheduled work for their businesses and maize farming in a rotating fashion, using family labor or hired helpers to meet their overlapping work responsibilities. Poorer Zinacantecos sought seasonal construction jobs during months when maize fields were less demanding of their time, and many of them worked as field hands for other Zinacantecos.

Zinacantecos began to transform their farming by using fertilizer and herbicides to intensify their cultivation in the highlands. By using fertilizers, they could farm plots year after year without fallowing. Doing so effectively increased the number of acres Zinacantecos had at their disposal in their ejidos, reducing the amount of land they needed to rent in the lowlands and saving them the costs of transport to and from lowland fields. The herbicides substantially reduced the work of weeding the milpa, reducing or eliminating the need to hire workers to help, and freeing up family labor to do things in the off-farm economy.

These changes contributed to the gap that had begun to distinguish well-off from poor Zinacantecos during the development boom. Those who had established themselves as independent contractors, truckers, or successful wholesale-retail market vendors had money in their pockets from such off-farm work to pay for the chemical inputs being used in farming. Often they farmed at the expense of poor Zinacantecos who didn't have financial resources to pay for fertilizer and weed sprays, even if they held land to farm. Many poorer Zinacantecos began to rent their ejido plots to their wealthier neighbors who could afford the chemical inputs. One wealthy trader, for example, rented the fields of twenty-five other Zinacantecos who could not afford chemical inputs. He hired the parcels' owners as laborers to farm corn for him, "putting his money to work" at others' expense. Such arrangements are still to be found in ejidos throughout Mexico.

Some Zinacantecos formed cooperative associations—small business collectives—for trucking and flower vending, similar to those established by many Mexican peasant groups for the production and distribution of cash crops such as organic coffee. The associations helped members combine on-and-off farm production, and gained access to credit from banks or the government, which often gave them political support as well. These associations often claimed to be peasant organizations, even though some of their members did not farm land for subsistence. The Zinacanteco truckers, for example, said they unionized in order to obtain routes to transport the produce grown in their communities. In fact, the richest truckers transported flowers that Zinacanteco wholesalers purchased in Mexico City for resale throughout Chiapas.[16]

Indians in other highland communities, Chamula for example, experienced greater adversity when wage work employment slowed after 1982, especially if they had little or no land of their own to farm. Chamulas were and are among the most land-poor of the highland Indians in Chiapas. After 1982, most Chamulas found they could not go back to the work they had once done as hired field hands in the central depression of the Grijalva basin. Landowners, like peasants, had reallocated their production during the energy-led boom. Much of the land once rented to peasants—in effect for sharecropping— had been converted to grasslands for cattle. Furthermore, milpa-farming peasants like the Zinacantecos, for whom Chamulas had also labored, used much less labor because of their access to chemical inputs. Many Chamulas found their families pushed into desperate straits after 1982.[17]

While many indigenous people were set back by unemployment after 1982, a minority did profit from trucking and other commercial enterprises they had taken up during the boom. The development of peasant trucking has been a double-edged sword, on the one hand allowing peasants to retain shipping profits that once flowed out of the countryside into ladino truckers' pockets, and on the other hand enabling peasant truckers to profit at the expense of their rural compatriots. As in the case of Zinacantán, the accumulation of transport capital emerged as a major axis of power and conflict in peasant communities throughout Chiapas. In Tenejapa, trucker organizations acted as a major local political force,[18] just as they did in Zinacantán.

The hardships of unemployed and impoverished Chamulas and other poor peasants were comparable to the circumstances that led Rolando, a major in the EZLN, to join the rebel army around 1986. At the height of the oil boom, Rolando told *San Francisco Chronicle* reporter Robert Collier, he migrated to Tuxtla Gutiérrez, where he lived with Tzeltal relatives and attended school through second grade. Then he took up construction work in Tuxtla. After the 1982 crisis, he could only get construction work at starvation wages. "You go to look for a decent job and they ask you for a resume..., [a]nd of course, I have no resume," he told Collier. He returned to his jungle hometown, but conditions were untenable there as well. He joined one of the independent organizations to press the government for assistance:

> So we went on a march, asking the government for land, and they beat us back with clubs. We kept organizing, but you have to pay to send delegations to San Cristóbal and Tuxtla and Mexico City. It was just going around in circles, and we didn't have any money.

Rolando joined the EZLN out of frustration. "What future do I, or any of us here, have in the new Mexico? I can sell or export my own cheap labor. But I have nothing else."[19]

Not everyone in the Selva Lacandona or other areas of eastern Chiapas suffered because of the boom and bust. Colonization burgeoned at the time, and many settled down, farming milpa and coffee and pasturing livestock. Settlers who arrived first were best off because they were the earliest to secure land. Later arrivals usually had to work for established settlers before gaining land and enough security to farm independently. As Guatemalan refugees flowed into some regions, they took up work at the bottom tier of the wage scale. Gaps between land-rich and land-poor grew when credits became available through the Union of Unions after 1980, in conjunction with federal support for peasant agriculture through the SAM, and as more settlers invested in coffee production.

Nuevo Huistán—the Cañadas region colony in Las Margaritas described in Chapter Two—experienced an increase in tension between rich and poor by 1983. As mentioned before, Nuevo Huistán derived seven-eighths of its income from cash crops and its three hundred head of cattle, horses, and mules.[20] A roadway had established the town as a node of transport and trade, linking more isolated areas of the Cañadas region of Las Margaritas outward to regional and national markets. Commerce distinguished settlers into a wealthier group, involved in bulking and marketing cash crops, and poorer settlers, who relied upon wage work. By 1983, when anthropologist Juan Pohlenz surveyed Nuevo Huistán, this small colony of

316 people had as many truck-owning families as the Zinacanteco hamlet of Apas, which I studied in the central highlands of Chiapas, even though Nuevo Huistán is a smaller community, about one-third the size of Apas.[21]

Austerity hit eastern Chiapas hard after 1982. The region's mixed economy of timber, corn, coffee, and cattle suffered under the eventual removal of fertilizer subsidies. Salinas, after taking office in 1988, dismantled INMECAFE, which had guaranteed markets for the Union of Union's coffee. The world price of coffee fell by 50 percent in 1989, leaving coffee producers in the lurch as their incomes plummeted and their debts spiraled out of control.[22] Since 1998, Vietnamese coffee has come on line in world markets, depressing coffee prices even further. Throughout Chiapas—not just in the east—the hard-won gains of peasants who had taken out loans to finance coffee production evaporated as banks foreclosed on loans and took over land, cattle, or other collateral. The crisis contributed to defection into the Zapatista camp from the Union of Unions and the ARIC-Union of Unions, both of which had promoted peasant coffee production as a way of gaining government credits and assistance in marketing.

Energy development, with its boom in the 1970s and bust after 1982, whiplashed the agrarian economy of southeastern Mexico, leaving both profit and devastation in its wake and sharpening the differentials of wealth and power to which the Zapatista rebellion responded.

5 ✦ THE TOLL OF RESTRUCTURING ON LIVES AND COMMUNITIES

During the oil boom of the 1970s, a new player began to take center stage in the indigenous hamlets of Chiapas. Money. As wage work became more readily available, cash-based transactions between people, even among kin, began to replace exchanges of services and obligations, and purchased foods and commodities began to replace those grown or made at home. This switch brought tremendous change to life in the countryside, transforming the traditional economy, accelerating changes in social and political relationships, and, in some ways, altering the traditional roles of men and women. The new reliance on cash gave distinct advantage to some members of peasant society, particularly young men and those with small businesses, many of whom began to make the kinds of changes in rural production envisioned by government plans of restructuring. But it added new burdens to the lives of others, especially women and those men with less education and property.

In the previous chapter, I looked at the large-scale impact oil and hydroelectric development had on Mexico and Chiapas: how the macroeconomic shifts, the policy revisions, and the undertaking of massive public projects drew peasants from their villages and into a new type of give-and-take with the regional economy that has restructured peasant agriculture. In this chapter, I go back to the village to see how these changes played out *within* communities.

I will examine changes of the sort that were taking place around the world as peasants and workers were drawn increasingly into global markets that displaced subsistence economies and eroded the ability of many to weather downturns in economic cycles.[1]

I will focus on two Maya towns in the central highlands of Chiapas: the hamlet of Apas in the municipio of Zinacantán, as well as hamlets in the neighboring municipio of Chamula, the most populous and one of the poorest of the Indian townships. These neighboring towns refract the shared experience of energy development much like two crystals placed slightly differently in the same light. Although the circumstances described are specific, they typify many of the pressures experienced by peasant communities throughout Chiapas. Both Zinacantán and Chamula have been much studied by anthropologists, but Chamula has come to symbolize the "typical" Indian town in the minds of many ladinos and nonindigenous Mexicans.[2]

Perhaps the most pronounced difference between the two municipios has been their access to land. Although Zinacantecos are by no means land rich, a majority of Zinacanteco families have maintained small plots of land that they can use to supplement their incomes from other sources or use to provide at least a bare minimum of food for their households. The majority of Chamula families, on the other hand, either have no land or are unable to eke out even the most meager subsistence from their tiny plots and so either have hired themselves out as field hands to others, including Zinacantecos, or have left their communities to seek wage work elsewhere. While the safety net that land provides to Zinacantecos is diminishing rapidly, Chamulas have already lost that net and have been living at the very margins of existence. Their financial straits were further exacerbated by the fact many Chamula hamlets were not linked to major roads, which made it expensive and difficult to transport produce or handicrafts to market in San Cristóbal de las Casas or other metropolitan centers.

At the heart of both communities lay the question of the changing nature of maize cultivation. As agriculture changed in rural Mexico, so did the nature of peasant society. It may seem contradictory to place such emphasis on agriculture after pointing out in the previous chapter that most peasants no longer focus exclusively on food production, but the shifting fortunes of Mexican agriculture created real differences in the way people live. And even the wealthiest peasants who made their living primarily in such nonagricultural enterprises as trucking and retailing identified themselves as farmers.

Emotional ties to the land persisted even where the practical ties to the land withered. Peasants considered—and still consider—the land their basis for survival.

After the 1982 economic crisis, when further dam building was put off and construction abated, Zinacantecos returned on a smaller scale to farming maize while continuing, as much as possible, in the pursuits they had begun during the boom years, such as selling food in market stalls or working for wages in San Cristóbal de las Casas. But as I noted in the previous chapter, corn cultivation had been transformed due to the increased use of chemical fertilizers and weed killers, funded by government subsidies and also by peasants' off-farm earnings. In the years between the boom and bust, the land became accustomed to chemical inputs, and fields were not nearly as productive without them. Simple tools and equipment (machete, hoe, billhook, bags) and a reserve of corn sufficient to feed one's household and field workers were no longer enough to enable a Zinacanteco household to farm. Fertilizer and weed sprays had to be purchased. Workers, if they were hired, no longer waited for payment in kind after the harvest; they expected payment in cash at the time of their work. Local truckers had to be paid to haul the harvest home.

The chemically intensive, but not labor intensive, method of farming also undermined the social organization of many peasant hamlets by removing a certain safety net of mutual dependence that kept young and poor people who needed food bound to their older and wealthier neighbors who, when weeding and cultivating had been done by hand, needed people to help them. Prior to the 1980s, Zinacantán had been a place where the disadvantaged could count on others for their basic livelihoods as long as they were willing to help out with corn production. But as maize cultivation was displaced from its once central place in Zinacanteco life, the poor found themselves utterly marginalized; their labor in the fields was no longer required, and they lacked any way of earning the money necessary to buy food.

In Chamula, the fallout of the 1982 debt crisis was even more severe. Anthropologist Diane Rus, who lived in the Chamula hamlet of K'at'ixtik for many years, found that most families were able to extract only a tiny portion (5 percent in 1977) of their food needs from their corn fields before the oil boom. After the bust, that portion diminished even further. Men who had been accustomed to wage work on coffee plantations to make up the shortfall in subsistence suddenly found themselves unable to find jobs. Consequently, many men were forced into the unstable temporary work force and began to leave K'at'ixtik for long periods of time looking for work, leaving women to single-handedly hold their homes and families together.[3]

LAND AND THE CHANGING ECONOMY

Owning and farming one's own land is a relatively recent phenomenon in Zinacantán. Prior to the 1940s, only a handful of wealthy families held tracts of land; other Zinacantecos worked for them. In 1940, almost all married men in Apas received ejidal land, substantially ameliorating differences among them based on property. For the first time, every household in Apas farmed milpa.

At first Zinacantecos concentrated on farming in the highlands using labor-intensive swidden, or slash-and-burn, cultivation. But the ejido could not sustain the Zinacanatecos' population, and the number of landless families increased once again. Zinacantecos then began to rent marginal farmlands in the Grijalva River valley from ranchers who were eager to convert scrub forest to grazing land. As roadways opened up the Grijalva valley during the 1960s, Zinacantecos followed them. They rented little-used marginal ranch land, reaped the higher yields obtainable from fallow lands, and moved on. Farming was still quite labor intensive, and every household member played a role in growing and harvesting the crops. Some Zinacantecos employed workers from Chamula. They farmed for profit as well as subsistence and sold much of their crop directly to the federal corn warehouse system established in the early 1960s. Some began to experiment with hybrid seed and chemical weed sprays.[4]

Not all Zinacantecos were able to reap benefits from the land. The labor-intensive farming methods gave the greatest advantage to older Zinacantecos who were able to maintain an adequate supply of labor either by using their children as workers or by amassing large numbers of followers who would work in their fields in exchange for political favors. During the 1950s and 1960s, a system of costly and time-consuming courtships developed that left young couples financially obligated to continue working in their parents' fields rather than farming independently.

By the 1970s, the population density of the highlands of Chiapas had almost negated the benefits of land reform. As noted in the previous chapter, Zinacantecos and other indigenous peoples found it increasingly difficult to find land to rent in the lowlands, where ranchers had turned over huge sections of property to cattle raising. Some peasants who continued to rent lowland plots lost money if they were unable to wait until after harvest time to sell their crops—the prices prevailing at harvest were the lowest of the year; wealthier Zinacantecos with cash to spare from other enterprises could wait to sell their crops until later in the season. Because the return on the average plot of land was so low, and because the chemical inputs were so expensive, many poorer Zinacantecos—even those with land of their own—no longer had the means to farm unless they borrowed money. By 1981, Zinacantecos had virtually abandoned lowland rental agriculture. The Chamula men from K'at'ixtik who rented lowland plots found their money completely eaten up by the costs of farming—fertilizers, herbicides, labor, and transportation. The situation, according to Rus, was so dismal that "it is commonly remarked that men are more likely to lose money than make it on lowland farming."[5]

One thing that stymies economic planners and development officials is the fact that even though farming is only marginally more profitable in the highlands, today most families attempt to raise milpa on their communal plots if at all possible. The returns are lower to family labor than prevailing wages and rarely high enough to justify hiring field hands. However, this seemingly unprofitable undertaking can sometimes be offset by the other enterprises that invariably make up a family's income. It is also true that the regional economy probably cannot offer every individual full employment and so "working for food" provides a basis for subsistence. Some

Zinacantecos have no land at all and so must either seek food or make money to buy it in other ways. Years ago, there would have been little need to distinguish between "seeking food" and "making money" because most peasants were assured of at least being fed if they worked for other villagers in corn production. But now that those "jobs" are not available, a cash-based economic system has emerged and has led to further hardships for the poorer sector of peasant society

In the years preceding the oil boom, when families were too poor to feed themselves, their members could seek food by working as field hands. Employers were expected to provide food and lodging for their workers, and instead of paying cash, they paid wages in corn at harvest time. After the oil boom, most Zinacanteco employers no longer boarded their field hands but simply paid cash wages, as did most nonindigenous employers. The wages were often not enough to guarantee a minimum subsistence.

Many women, by contrast, still worked for food. Women from households with shortfalls in food—typically women from poor households, or women without husbands or children old enough to help with farming—might take up piecework for other women. They could also make tortillas and hardtack, using the other woman's corn, but supplying their own firewood, and accepting as pay an amount of corn equal to that which they process.

Some Zinacanteco women, predominantly those who were elderly, poor, or widowed, also worked as remunerated field hands, especially in milpas close to home in the highlands. Generally these women were seeking food, rather than seeking money, and received pay in kind with an option of cash. Other women exchanged weaving for money or corn.

In her research in K'at'ixtik, Diane Rus found that as wage work opportunities declined for men, and their family finances became more perilous, women—in addition to performing a multitude of labor-intensive household duties such as grinding corn and making tortillas, hauling water and firewood, and weaving woolen clothes—began to search for additional jobs as well, however ill-paid, to preserve their families' tenuous hold on subsistence. In her survey of village women, she found that more than half produced embroidered shirts, woven bracelets, or some other handicraft for the tourist trade; performed piecework on handicrafts; gathered firewood to sell; made tortillas; or participated in field labor.

Most of these activities, Rus observed, brought in marginal incomes. Women sewing items that took one to two days to complete only earned around 1,500 [old] pesos (about U.S.$0.65) for a finished piece, an inordinately low sum when one considers that the minimum wage in Chiapas at the time was 7,000 pesos per day (about U.S.$3). For many women, however, piecework was the only option, according to Rus, because they lacked the resources to buy the raw materials or felt that trying to sell their wares directly to stores in San Cristóbal de las Casas was too risky because the costs—the high price of transportation, the inability to communicate with Spanish-speaking shop owners, and the possibility that no one will buy anything—outweighed the benefits. Women who worked as field hands or gathered firewood earned an even smaller pittance: 1,000 pesos per day and 1,500–3,000 pesos per week, respectively. Chamula families in such circumstances were barely surviving, says Rus, who likened their living conditions to the days of serfdom on the *fincas* (large ranches and plantations).[6]

GENDER AND GENERATION GAPS

In contrast to the experiences of women, and older and poorer Zinacantecos, who continued to a certain extent to work for food, young men were hastening the change to a cash-based economy. Young men engaged in construction or other nonagricultural jobs expected to feed themselves, as did their Zinacanteco counterparts who ran market stands or did trucking in distant lowland cities and towns. They relished sampling foods other than corn. And, ever attentive to style, they experimented with popular clothing, music, and electronic wares. As they brought new consumer goods home in

the form of noncorn foods, faddish clothes, and even changed construction styles, youthful Zinacantecos were challenging the value
that traditional villagers placed on shared production and consumption of corn.

These conflicts emerged poignantly in marital disputes. In quarrels with their husbands, many women would take their mates to
task for spending their wages on nonessential goods such as soft
drinks and radios rather than on corn and beans for their families. In
disputes that pit young wives against their in-laws, the wives would
seek resolutions by setting up independent households through the
division of corn supplies, even when their husbands earned most of
their income in wage work and commerce. Young men often coun-
tered charges of neglect by pointing out new goods they provided,
such as the different kinds of footwear they bought for their children
(tennis shoes, plastic sandals, boots). And they sometimes tried to
resolve disputes through cash settlements. Family support, for them,
no longer centered on provisioning their homes with corn, but rather
with commodities bought from earnings.

In addition to creating conflicts between husbands and wives, the
focus on wage work contributed to a "generation gap" between young
men and their elders. Previously, there had been a general correlation
of increasing age with wealth. But since 1981, this correlation reversed.
Young construction workers who learned skills and earned the
wherewithal to undertake independent contracting, and young merchants who ventured forth into regional produce marketing,
catapulted ahead of many of their elders. Although wealthy elders
with commercial enterprises of their own, especially truckers, continued to claim leadership within their communities, they increasingly
found themselves confronted with "upstart" youths who contested
their power. In Apas, this conflict was played out dramatically in 1989
by young men who challenged the hegemony of the PRI-affiliated
village elite by persuading a large faction of dissident peasants to join
the rival Party of the Democratic Revolution (PRD). These militant
youth, who flaunted the economic power of earnings from skilled
construction and commerce, were challenging not just the party of

their parents, but the long-standing collusion of village elders with the PRI.

Even though many young men grew up in farming households, and contributed some of their labor to the milpa, their earned income gave them an unprecedented degree of independence. Because they did not draw on household corn supplies while away (selling or working), they justified contributing only a modest portion of their income, if any, to their parents. They felt free to spend their money on clothes—rancher-style boots, pants, hats—or, for that matter, on liquor, and sooner or later on marriage.

The economic independence of youth drastically altered courtship and marriage in Apas. In the heyday of Zinacanteco milpa cultivation in the 1950s and 1960s, long and costly courtships were the rule, and suitors had to borrow from their parents to afford to marry, and to rely on elder kin to negotiate the marriage. Young couples began marriage heavily in debt, which they worked off by contributing their labor to the milpa production of the household in which they lived, usually that of the groom's parents. As the balance of power between parents and children shifted, so did marriage practices. By the 1980s, many couples opted to elope, even though they knew it would anger their parents, rather than participate in the expensive courtship rituals that would leave them penniless.

In the past, marriage brought the parents of the bride and groom into an alliance in which they held considerable power over their children's affairs, and their productive labor after marriage. Young couples had little recourse other than to parents for help in marital quarrels, intervention in disputes with neighbors, and assistance in rituals. Politics, in turn, revolved heavily, and often decisively, around the hold elders had over their married children. Such kin relations continued to be important in the 1980s and 1990s, but their tenor shifted as other bases for power, class for example, grew in importance. The changing economic conditions refigured power relations not only within households but within communities.

In Zinacantán, land ownership shifted over the years to reflect the growing power of youth vis-à-vis their elder kin. When I surveyed farmland in 1967, 56 percent was in the hands of men over 45 years of age, and only 35 percent was held by men aged 25 to 44 years. In 1989, by contrast, elder Zinacantecos controlled only 44 percent of the land, while men aged 25 to 44 held 49 percent. This shift to young men was related to the changing age structure of the population, but it also mirrored young men's increasing economic independence and the concomitant advantages they had in transacting relations with elder kin. Many were unafraid to challenge parents and in-laws in the realm of public politics. And young adults could command the earlier distribution of inheritable assets as the price of supporting their parents in old age, rather than having to demonstrate the right to inheritance through respectful obedience.

THE WIDENING GAP BETWEEN RICH AND POOR

While ejido land itself has not yet become a commodity to be bought and sold in most indigenous communities in Chiapas, the use of land, to a great extent, had—even before the "reform" of Article 27 of the Constitution and the Agrarian Code liberalized the tenure and use of ejido. Firewood once free for women to gather anywhere in the ejido or communal lands is treated today as a private good to be bought and sold. Now that highland farming requires capital expenditures, poor families without assets more readily rent land to wealthier neighbors. The majority of those who rent out their land are single or widowed women "seeking" food in the form of rent in kind and poorer married men who make most of their living from work not requiring capital, as field hands or peons. Those who farm rented land are wealthier young adults, many of whom derive substantial income from skilled wage work and commerce and who thus can afford fertilizer, weed sprays, and even the cost of farm laborers.

Renting farmland is one of the many alternatives, furthermore, in which Zinacantecos with cash can invest their assets flexibly. Rented land need not entail a long-term commitment of renter to landowner. In 1995 Lorenzo de la Torre, a wealthy merchant and truck owner, rented enough Apas farmland to employ as many as twenty-five field hands to work those fields for him; two seasons later he rented no land there having decided instead to farm land he had rented near lowland Villaflores, where he owned and ran his fruit and vegetable business. Such employers are often too deeply involved in activities other than farming to work alongside or directly supervise their workers. They may leave supervision to a dependent, or trust the employees to work on their own. One Zinacanteco, Andrés Hernández, who was working full-time in commerce, simply contracted the work of harvesting his milpa to three Zinacantecos as piecework to be paid a set amount regardless of how they organized the work.

Wealthy Zinacantecos whose small businesses give them cash to spare have come up with a nefarious new way of saving money: prepaying workers at a discount to contract for their future labor. Zinacantecos who are desperate for cash and cannot secure loans resort to selling their labor early, placing themselves at the disposal of their employer to call upon them when their labor is needed throughout the following agricultural cycle. In recent years, as wages have risen to adjust for inflation, the prepayment for future labor early in the agricultural cycle has been at about half the rate that prevails by the close of the cycle. For the employer, prepaying wages at a discount brings the wage down closer to the poor rate of return that milpa farmers receive on their own family labor, making it feasible for the employer to substitute hired labor for family labor. Such employment forces the worker to accept a low wage and strips him of the discretion to work for other employers later in the season except with the consent of the employer to whom he is indebted. The worker may even find himself assigned by his employer to work for someone else—a modern version of debt servitude!

Lending and borrowing have become more prevalent as Zinacantecos need more cash than ever before to farm milpa. Fertilizer and chemical weed sprays must be purchased, if not acquired on credit. Wages for field hands generally are paid in cash close to the time of work rather in kind from the future harvest.

Truckers expect cash payment for transporting farmers to the field or harvest to market. Merchants need funds to purchase their inventory and cover the transport and living costs while on selling trips. Zinacantecos who invest in such capital equipment as trucks or corn mills may resort to banks and government agencies for credits, but they also borrow from compatriots.

Before Salinas restructured the system of government agrarian credits and crop insurance, Zinacantecos who had rights in the ejido of Zinacantán or who owned communal land tracts were eligible for credit from the Banco Rural for the purchase of fertilizer with crop insurance from the National Agriculture and Livestock Insurance Program. After Salinas' reforms, they still obtained credits available through the Solidarity program (discussed in Chapter Six). Farmers received credit in June to pay off after the harvest in February. Zinacantecos used these credits, especially if they lacked cash in June when fertilizers need to be applied, but they felt penalized by having to repay credits in February at harvest time, when crop prices are at their seasonal low. Zinacantecos also borrowed significantly from one another, although at higher interest rates than offered by the Banco Rural, avoiding the paperwork loans require and the unfavorable date of maturity at harvest time.

Through lending, wealthy Zinacantecos have been living in substantial measure from the surplus product of others' work in a manner that used to characterize only nonindigenous usurers. Their advantaged position has let some of them to explore new ways of living and working. A man nicknamed Jaguar, for example, has worked less as a trucker than when he ran both a truck and a van because he earns interest on the money he made when he sold his van. He is reputed to have twenty million pesos out in loans. Unlike elders of yore who gathered followings by making loans to common folk, Jaguar has loaned only to men of substantial means. Jaguar still owns a truck, and he told me that he could easily earn one million pesos per month by running his truck every day. Instead, he runs his truck only on the weekdays that give him the most lucrative business because he earns so much income from interest.

LEADERS WHO NO LONGER NEED FOLLOWERS

In Chamula, political power was for decades monopolized by a small group of indigenous caciques who received their mandate from the ruling party during the 1934–1940 presidency of Lázaro Cárdenas, when they worked as scribes for government Indianist and labor organizers. With direct support from the PRI, their autocratic rule often served the interests of the state rather than the citizens of Chamula, many of whom were unrecognized and unrepresented by the political system.[7] In Zinacantán, PRI-backed authorities traditionally operated with a greater degree of accountability to their constituencies, but they became more oppressive and elitist as a result of the economic changes brought by energy development.

As cash-based transactions became more prevalent and young men challenged the traditional way of doing things, the social stratification of peasant communities underwent tremendous change. Whole new classes of people—wealthy truckers, skilled masons, entrepreneurs—came into being in the 1980s, and their prosperity has heightened the penury of the poorest sectors of peasant society and added a new complexity to productive relations. Those who thus rose to the forefront of their communities in recent years exemplify different values and different styles of leadership than their predecessors.

Since the 1980s, Apas continues to be a place where people care deeply about protecting the integrity of indigenous life and costumbre against the amorality of the ladino world, Mexican law, and the threat of Protestantism and other nontraditional religions. But community members no longer agree on who has the authority to speak for traditional practices. Each political group claims a moral high ground, accusing others of collaborating with ladino politicians and lawyers. Instead of presenting a united front against the outside world, the differing factions have aligned themselves with national parties, and compete for control of state-allocated resources within their hamlets. Community members argue over who "belongs" in ethnic communities, and these arguments are exploited by local politicians to banish their enemies. Apas has become a sharply divided community.

I believe that one of the reasons this happened is that in the post-oil boom society, where maintaining a group of followers was no longer necessary for political or economic ascendancy within peasant hamlets, it became possible for leaders to act with an eye towards individual opportunity rather than community benefit. A primary distinction emerged between people who sold their labor to others and those who undertook commercial ventures for themselves. The wealthy no longer had a need for webs of reciprocal obligations with the poor; the rank and file whose support they once cultivated became expendable. Over the past forty years, I have observed a shift from rank-based politics, in which politicians rose to power through a complex set of community obligations, to class-based politics, in which individuals instead use wealth as a route to power and prestige.

Think of rank-based power in relation to an economic system in which labor was the most important resource and advantage went to those who could organize other people's services. One had first to demonstrate the ability to act effectively on others' behalf and be adept at pooling and channeling others' resources for both the personal and the common good. Rank-based leaders often served their communities by acting as brokers with the outside world or as intermediaries to other groups, for example, by initiating a claim for land on behalf of their municipio. But first, of course, they had to persuade others that they were worthy of being followed. They usually did so by competing with other would-be leaders to demonstrate who was the most willing to sacrifice personal well-being for the common good, often by undertaking ritual posts, which in the highlands of Chiapas were characteristically ranked in terms of cost and prestige.[8] The most effective contenders won respect and support, as well as deference and service, and finally the right to ask for others' resources to promote the common good. Even though they tended to do well by doing good in systems based on labor-intensive production, rank-based leaders usually played down differences in lifestyle from their followers while calling attention to the selfless service they gave in leadership. Rank-based leaders epitomized those the Zapatistas laud today as leaders who obey the will of their constituencies, who subordinate themselves to the needs of their followers. Think of class-based power in relation to a system in which money has become the most important resource and is used to purchase productive inputs, including the work of laborers who can be paid a wage without incurring other cumbersome obligations. In such a system, power holders use political positions to shepherd economic resources in a more exclusive manner, usually to better themselves at the expense of others, even if doing so means excluding others from access to wealth. Class-based leaders often have their power accorded to them from the state through positions from which they can garner benefit from state resources. Class-based leaders may unite with one another against their poor compatriots, the people that a rank-based leader would cultivate as followers.

The political careers of two prominent Apas men illustrate the shift from rank-based toward class-based politics that has taken place in Zinacantán and other communities. In the 1940s, Domingo Gerónimo won the support of Apas residents shortly after the initial distribution of ejido land by insisting on egalitarian division of coffee groves near Ibestik, which other ejidal leaders had wanted to reserve for themselves. He represented Apas in the successful quest for additions to the ejido in the 1950s and pursued an impeccable career of service in Zinacantán's most costly religious posts. By orchestrating his followers and his kin to help fund the costly responsibilities of prestigious cargo positions, he gained the prerogative to speak for others. Community leaders during this period were more than politicians: they were called upon to settle disputes and preserve public civility by fostering feelings of interdependence and connectedness.

Gerónimo's son-in-law, Marcos Bromas, initially rose to power by following the same trajectory. He led the community in a long and ultimately successful effort to establish a lowland colony under the provisions of land reform, served as ejidal officer, and also held a series of prestigious religious positions. He led his followers into the PAN in the late 1970s at a time when Zinacanteco leaders were beginning to make political party affiliations. But by the 1980s, Bromas, a truck driver who wanted to gain a route concession from the state, had begun to put his own interests before those of the community. He reached an agreement with other members of the new trucking elite and, disregarding the wishes of his followers, aligned himself with a powerful faction of the PRI—an action that turned many of his former supporters against him. In conversations about the situation, he admitted to me a certain weariness with the responsibilities of being a leader in the "old style" and expressed a desire for a more "pragmatic" system of politics without so many social obligations:

> I don't want to manage people any more. Let the municipal magistrate do what he's supposed to do and I'll support him. For I have tired of politics, not only party politics, but politicking for agrarian issues, for land.... So that's how it came that there are [political] parties here. It was tied up with the trucks and the fact that we were quarreling with one another before. But today, we truckers are all in agreement.

Local leaders and politicians are currently much less likely to court the support of people they deem unimportant or powerless. They feel they have little stake in maintaining harmony among those who, in the previous era, would have been followers. For example, a young man recently approached a leader for help in resolving a domestic problem. His wife had been complaining that his elderly mother, who lived with them, was eating up too much food without contributing to the household income. Previously, it would have been the job of the leader to help the wife and mother come to some kind of accord, but in this case, the leader simply derided the older woman as a "rat who eats up all the corn of her children" and refused to get involved. He probably thought that since the chances of needing a favor from the woman were slim, she was not worth helping.

The shift from rank-based to class-based society is illustrated by many changes in individual and civic life. In the old days, economic relations were almost always subsumed in social ties. In return for political support, villagers expected jobs to cover their subsistence. Leaders were careful to maintain roughly the same lifestyle as their followers. Today, it is not uncommon for economic relationships to remain purely economic—contracts can be made with strangers, and politicians feel little obligation to support the rank and file. In the past, politicians rose to power by amassing widespread popular support. Today they are most often powerful because Mexico's ruling powers have supported them and given them control of public monies for their communities. As we shall see in the next chapter, such leaders may simply disdain to concern themselves with the poorer members of their communities.

As the gap between rich and poor has widened, a complex set of variables has come into play. The lifestyle of rich and poor differs dramatically: the homes of the wealthy have tile roofs instead of thatch, and their dinners often include meat and chicken, luxuries the poor rarely taste. Studying the demography of Apas over the years, I have found that women and children in wealthy households now enjoy dramatically lower death rates than the poor, who suffer mortality comparable to the highest rates in the underdeveloped world. Peasants have restructured their communities by participating in a new range of activities, but they have also created strains that threaten to pull more and more people into a public arena marked by factionalism, conflict, and inequality and the breakdown of a web of mutual obligation that gave some protection to the poor.

The loss of traditional protections within communities has come at a time when government support, particularly rural subsidies, has been declining. As these protections eroded, the very poorest people in Chiapas' highland villages began to fall out of the bottom strata of their communities into squatter settlements around cities, attempting to eke out a living from street vending or the sale of simple handicrafts.9 The markets and commerce in the cities and larger towns of central and western Chiapas thus provided a safety valve for impoverished people. But in eastern Chiapas, which has no major commercial centers and is largely inaccessible even by road, the impoverished had no place to turn and little to lose by joining the Zapatista rebellion.

The experience in the highlands underscores the risks as well as the opportunities inherent in the economic restructuring that Mexican planners want for the rural economy and that peasants have already begun. Through changes in Article 27 of the Constitution and the Agrarian Code, Salinas and his advisors intended to further liberalize agrarian production. The changes legalized the sharecropping and the rental of ejidal lands that have taken place for years. But they also permitted unprecedented privatization, mortgaging, and the sale of ejidal parcels and even of formerly undivided communal lands. They allowed for outside investors to band together with peasants in joint ventures of commercial production based on the land. There is no question but that the liberalization of land tenure opens up opportunities for peasants to restructure agrarian production even more than they have already since 1982. But the liberalization also exposes poor and disadvantaged individual peasants to the unprecedented risk of losing land altogether to creditors. It thus removes one more protection for the poor.[10]

6 ✦ EXCLUSION: THE NEW POLITICS

It is difficult to imagine what it would be like to live in a place where you could not enter the town hall, use the water system, seek redress for a crime committed against you, obtain a divorce, join in a community celebration, resolve a financial dispute, or participate in a public project unless you were a member of a certain political party. But many towns in Chiapas had become just such places in the years just before the rebellion, and in many cases continue to be so. Throughout Mexico's poorest state, access to public services was based not on need, but on political affiliation.

As support for the ruling party began to crumble, the PRI increasingly turned to coercive tactics to hold on to the peasants' vote, withholding funds and services from those whose loyalty was suspect. Even in the tiniest hamlets of Chiapas, political "litmus tests" came to be used to determine who would benefit from government programs and who would not.

These practices produced sharply fractured villages where hostility has reigned not just between Indian and ladino, but between pro-PRI Indian and anti-PRI Indian, even after the PRI lost the national presidency in 2000 to the PAN's Vicente Fox. Exclusionary politics lent a new, divisive character to the political process in Chiapas' small Mayan towns, and social and economic changes tear at traditional community culture, heightening tensions between young and old, rich and poor, powerful and powerless.

These changes created intense resentments that reinforced emerging class conflict within indigenous communities. Those whom the ruling party favored gained privileged access to resources that should be available to everyone. Those who protested were often locked out of the political process and, in some cases, expelled from their villages. People found numerous ways to express their dissent and reconfigure their communities, often forming their own parallel organizations when denied access to the government's, but they were also subjected to increasing subtle and not-so-subtle repression.

In this chapter,[1] we follow the spread of such exclusionary politics into rural hamlets such as Apas, Zinacantán, continuing our case study of how the transformations that occurred in Chiapas during the past decades of development and modernization have affected everyday life in the countryside. I examine the ways in which local indigenous leaders tacitly or explicitly collaborated with the PRI to stifle opposition, monopolizing government poverty funding for themselves and creating resentments of the same sort as those that galvanized the Zapatista rebels to the east.[2]

"NEW LAW," "NEW POLITICS"

For most of the last half century of the twentieth century, the indigenous peasants of central Chiapas were loyal to the PRI. The ruling party put down strong roots among them in the 1930s when Lázaro Cárdenas instituted agrarian and labor reforms favoring Indians in central Chiapas and the Soconusco coast. Renewed agrarian reform and Indianist development solidified support for the ruling party in the 1950s, 1960s, and especially during the boom of the 1970s when the Mexican government was flush with borrowed petrodollars. The ruling party had reason to take peasants' support for granted.

But the 1982 debt crisis forced the government to cut back on the programs that once bought peasant loyalty, and the government often turned to coercion or bribery to shore up support. Peasants, for their part, showed increasing independence and a greater propensity to join together to speak out against unacceptable policies.

In 1986, for example, the government suddenly raised the guaranteed price it would pay for corn by 32 percent—but only in the northern states, where several gubernatorial races were closely contested. The action backfired on two counts: it was widely interpreted as a blatant attempt to buy support for the PRI candidates, and it infuriated southern farmers, who did not benefit from the price increase.

Peasants in Chiapas responded swiftly, deriding the government's actions and demanding that corn prices be increased across the board. A coalition of corn producers organized public protests, rallying in Tuxtla Gutiérrez and blocking roads when their demands went unheeded. On January 17, 1986, the Chiapas governor Absalón Castellanos Domínguez sent troops to repress a widely publicized blockade of the Pan American Highway near Ixtapa, jailing even bystanders and newspaper reporters who were covering the event. Some of those arrested languished in jail for over two years, a violation of basic human rights and due process.

The incident underscored the state's willingness to use coercive measures to keep its constituency in line, a lesson that was not lost on the indigenous peoples of the highlands. But the protests also demonstrated that the government could no longer take loyalty from the peasants of Chiapas for granted.

After the closely contested 1988 presidential elections, which opposition parties claimed were stolen for Carlos Salinas de Gortari, the PRI stepped up its policing of peasant loyalty. When José Patrocinio González Garrido, a PRI-ista, took office as the new Governor of Chiapas in 1988, he revised the penal code to make it easier for the state government to punish dissent. Referred to as the "new law" in peasant communities, the penal code established González as a hard-liner.[3]

Article 13 of Governor González's new law concerned "unruly crowds" and outlined penalties for those who lead, organize, incite, or support "mob" action. Article 120 criminalized as "rebellion" against the government the actions of anyone who interferes with the function of state institutions or elections. Article 135 penalized those in "mobs" or "riots" deemed to disturb public order or menace public functionaries or authorities on the pretext of exercising a legal right. Article 336 made it illegal to invade property for purposes of appropriation or profit. On its face, this provision seems reasonable—until one takes into account that peasant invasion of lands taken away from them by ranchers was sometimes the only way peasants could reclaim land under the provisions of agrarian reform.

Taken together, these provisions empowered the Chiapas government to quell spontaneous public protest, curb organized opposition, and restrain agrarian activists. According to human rights jurists who criticized Chiapas' penal code,[4] "[t]he provisions, taken together, ...create[d] broad categories of political crimes which embrace[d] every conceivable form of political protest, with the possible exception of the printed word." Put into practice, the penal code "filled [Chiapas'] prisons with political prisoners."

The Chiapas government's implementation of the new law also stripped local non-PRI leaders of their authority. Since colonial times, local authorities in indigenous communities have been allowed to resolve all nonfelony disputes among families and neighbors according to indigenous customary law. Resolving disputes has been one of the responsibilities of each township's elected president, whose administrative functions are similar to those of a mayor. Each township also has judges, and hamlets have magistrates who use customary law to resolve local problems.[5] Beginning in the 1970s, when political factions began to divide hamlets, each faction was allowed its own magistrate, school committee representatives, local tax collectors, and so forth. Thus, in 1988, both the PRI faction in Apas and an opposing faction that called themselves the Campesinos had their own magistrates and local magistrate office. This ensured that people need not rely on someone from a rival political faction to settle their disputes.

This all changed in 1989. The Chiapas government decreed that only one magistrate per hamlet would be allowed and that magistrates had to hold an official appointment from the governor. Because Governor González's appointments for Zinacantán were all in the PRI, only PRI magistrates held legitimate office, leaving people in other factions without their own legal recourse to customary law. When opposition factions complained in Zinacantán Center, PRI town authorities pointedly warned that the new law could be used against anyone who challenged the PRI. The municipal president summoned the magistrates of each hamlet to the town hall and announced his intention to weed out the non-PRI representatives:

There is only one President of the Republic. There is only one state governor. There is only one municipal president. Why should hamlets be the only place where there is more than one chief authority?

In Apas, where twice as many families aligned themselves with the Campesinos as with the PRI, this new policy outraged the Campesinos. Several days after the decision not to authorize faction magistrates, the two factions argued and came to blows. Some of the local PRI authorities were injured and accused the Campesinos of having plotted against them. The municipal president summoned the Campesinos and warned them not to assault PRI representatives again because the new law now allowed those who acted against authorities to be jailed without the possibility of bail.

The municipal secretary then questioned the Campesinos closely as to whether or not they belonged to an opposition party. The Campesinos replied that no, they were simply a division within the PRI. Under the new law, the secretary warned them, opposition to established authorities of the PRI could be punished. He told them that "as a favor" he would write up an official account of the ruckus as merely as a dispute between two "groups," but that in the future the Campesinos could be charged as an illegal opposition group. In effect, Zinacantecos were being told that by opposing local PRI authorities, they were opposing the government itself and could be arrested.

Shortly afterward, several hamlets sent a delegation of Campesino faction members to the state capital to appeal the ruling on magistrates and gain recognition of their own. Although they claimed to be a group within the PRI, Governor González refused to recognize them on this basis. Four months later, Apas' Campesinos gave up any pretense of affiliation with the PRI by joining the Cardenistas— followers of Cuauhtémoc Cárdenas in the Party of the Democratic Revolution (PRD)—in part because a PRD state congressman promised them support in winning recognition of their own magistrate. But once again the governor refused them the magistrate they needed for recourse to customary law.

Shortly thereafter, in the nearby hamlet of Nachih, Cardenistas staged a PRD rally. Violence broke out when PRI local authorities roughed up and jailed several Cardenistas, including Margarito Ruiz Hernández, a PRD deputy to the federal congress who should have enjoyed constitutional immunity from arrest. After protest of the incident, which attracted national publicity because of the flagrant violation of Ruiz Hernández's immunity, the state government pledged to bring the errant PRI-istas to justice. The governor deposed two of the hamlet's PRI authorities, but charges of wrongdoing were eventually dropped for "lack of evidence," indicating that the government would look the other way when PRI militants used violence against the opposition.

CONTROL OF MONEY

In addition to making public protest illegal, the government also used subtle financial controls to ensure that local opposition leaders would never be able to administer public funds. This was another way of disempowering opponents while reserving the opportunity to profit from public funding for PRI loyalists. The government exerted pressure on individuals to toe a party line, withholding permission to operate private enterprise unless the principals involved belong to the PRI. The two anecdotes below illustrate this combination of political and financial discrimination and favoritism.

In 1982, the democratically elected president of Zinacantán, Pedro Vásquez, went to the town hall to assume his position. Instead of a welcoming committee or a celebration, Vásquez, a member of the PAN party, found locked doors, barred windows, and a group of local PRI leaders. They told him that he could not enter the building because it was built with PRI labor and owned by the PRI. Vásquez appealed to the governor, who told local authorities that they had no choice but to allow him into the town hall. After Vásquez took office, however, the state used its power over the municipal budget to persuade Vásquez to leave the PAN and join the PRI. The stakes were substantial because the state government, since 1980, had made a practice of providing block grants to municipal authorities to fund public works, putting control of projects directly in their hands. Zinacanteco factions began to align with national political parties to compete for control of this money.[6]

At around the same time, Marcos Bromas, a prominent Apas citizen (see previous chapter), was also persuaded to leave the PAN and join the PRI. Bromas had been a major leader of the PAN in Zinacantán and had stood for election to the state congress as a PAN candidate. But when Bromas, head of a trucker's union, tried to get a route concession from the state—something he could not operate without—he realized that it would be impossible given his party affiliation. Bromas told me,

> We went to a meeting at PRODESCH [the government's regional development agency] where the lawyers urged us to drop the other party (PAN) and put an end to politics. They tried to convince us that it would be best for the whole of Zinacantán to be of just one party. I said I would agree, for they had told me that otherwise, getting my route authorized would be difficult.

During the 1982–1988 presidency of Miguel de la Madrid, Mexico struggled under a stringent austerity program imposed by the international banking community. The federal government lost the option of trying to cull support by wholesale funding of public projects. In Chiapas, outgoing governor Absalón Castellanos Domínguez emptied state coffers in 1988, leaving the state government without funds even to pay year-end salaries of teachers.

Neither government was in a position to use public money to co-opt support.

When Patrocinio González Garrido became governor, he shrewdly sidestepped the lack of funding by holding out the promise of state money. Without actually earmarking any money for specific projects, he offered Indians a larger role in planning public expenditures. He reorganized the state agencies responsible for Indian affairs under a new State Indigenous Council in 1989, to which he gave authority over state projects for indigenous communities. Officially, the purpose of the council was to "involve Indians in the solution of their own problems, such as the protection of their rights, without paternalism."[7] Each indigenous community sent one of its authorities as a representative to the council.

By establishing the council, Governor González deferred real funding for Indian affairs projects. Because the PRI controlled all but two of the state's 111 town halls, the representatives sent to the council were virtually all of the PRI. That ensured that the council could channel government funding to PRI initiatives when funding eventually became available.

Zinacantecos were never in doubt about the intensely political character of public funding, before or after the establishment of the council. In Apas, politics centered on the use and abuse of public funding. Addressing the Campesino dissidents to persuade them to become Cardenistas at a rally in Apas on April 9, 1989, a lawyer from Tuxtla Gutiérrez representing the PRD spoke in Spanish of the new party's project:

> What is our program? It is a book that perhaps you know. Our program cost one million lives in 1910. Our program is the Constitución Mexicana. It says that every Mexican has a right to land, but that right has not been recognized; we intend to recognize it. It gives people the right to health, but this is not honored; we will honor it. The Constitution grants workers a salary adequate for food, clothing, and housing, which workers don't have. And here in Chiapas, which produces electricity that's even exported to other countries of Central America, here thousands of families lack electricity.
>
> Chiapas has great wealth, but it's the Governors who exploit it, along with PRI officials. Chiapas' wealth doesn't go to all of us, but rather to just a few. And just a handful of millionaires get the wealth; those are the people who join the PRI, because in doing so they know they will be allowed to rob. For the PRI encourages them to be one another's accomplices. Thus when municipal presidents leave office, their successors don't do audits, they know that they will be able to act in their own right for their own benefit. All of them are hiding under the same blanket. But the nation will no longer stand for it.

Claiming that the PRI had stolen the 1988 presidential elections, the PRD lawyer urged the Zinacantecos to form a PRD committee in Apas to prepare for future elections and to channel local requests for immediate public support to state agencies with PRD assistance:

> Without anyone to support you, you are vulnerable to the authorities robbing you without solving any of your problems. But the PRD will help you. If you need potable water, if you need a clinic, school, or kindergarten, you can draw up a request with many signatures and we will help you go to the Presidencia Municipal [town hall] or to Tuxtla.

One of the new Apas Cardenista militants, nicknamed "Master Mason" because of the skills he learned in construction work, took the stand, ostensibly to paraphrase in Tzotzil what the visitor had said. But where the lawyer had voiced the PRD's general appeal to peasants and workers for land, wages, and social justice and had spoken against PRI electoral fraud and graft, Master Mason emphasized government aid and charged that Zinacanteco municipal authorities of the PRI—the trucker elite—corruptly enriched themselves by stealing funds intended for the hamlets:

> The lawyer criticized the way the PRI conducted elections in Zinacantán, and how those who have held office all leave office with trucks and possessions. It's not just the ladinos who are thieves.... The lawyer spoke of the past municipal presidents as thieves. One of them is in jail in Cerro Hueco [the state penitentiary in Tuxtla] for having stolen twenty million pesos. Although that money was supposed to be assistance to the pueblo, the President enriched himself. He didn't give out the aid to each hamlet. This is not just a story, it has come out in the newspaper and on the radio. That's the way the PRI really works. It's not like someone just stealing corn on the cob, or stealing some peaches, it's not just a few thousand pesos, rather it's more like 100 million pesos that they stole.
>
> But now that this new party is here, they can help us scrutinize what happens with each kind of assistance that is supposed to come to our

hamlets. For example, we don't have water, we have to work hard hauling water. If we don't have wells of our own, we have to get water from
people who do. But with this here party, then we can really get *agua
potable* [a water system]. And so with a clinic. We don't have a clinic of
our own. We have to go to San Cristóbal to be treated, and when we do
we aren't really helped. Here again the Cardenista party can help us. It
is not that they are going to give us aid directly, but rather that they will
help us ask the government for aid. What we have to do is tell the party
what it is that we need, and then they will help us ask for it.

Not all of Apas' dissidents were eager to follow Master Mason
and other militants into the PRD. Elders were the most skeptical.
Campesinos were, for the most part, poorer hamlet members among
whom elders had achieved social status by years of civil and religious
service. The militants, by contrast, were young men of new wealth
who, like Master Mason, had learned construction skills in the 1970s
and had gone into contracting or commerce in the 1980s. By inviting
the Campesinos to join the PRD, these young militants were mounting a double challenge, to elders of their own faction and to the PRI
elite in Zinacantán Center and Apas, led by truckers such as Marcos
Bromas. By joining the PRD, which posed as the party of peasants
and workers that would bring benefits such as health clinics and
water systems to all citizens, the young militants deflected attention
away from their own new wealth. After a second PRD rally in late
April, attended by the PRD state deputy Jorge Moscoso Pedrero, the
elders reluctantly followed the militants into the Cardenista party.

As we have seen, the ruling party refused to grant Apas
Cardenistas their own magistrate. The PRI had also sabotaged
Cardenista initiatives for public projects.

Shortly after joining the PRD, Apas Cardenistas submitted an
orchard and water project proposal to CONAFRUT, the agricultural
extension agency that funded orchard projects. They proposed to
plant fruit trees and repair Apas' damaged and long-unused water
system so that it could supply drinking water and water for new
orchards. When Zinacanteco PRI authorities learned of the proposal,

they had their representative to the State Indigenous Council, which monitored CONAFRUT projects, kill the Cardenista proposal. They persuaded the Apas PRI faction to submit a proposal of their own, requesting only trees. When I visited Apas in December 1989, the CONAFRUT seedlings had arrived—the only public project approved for Apas in 1989—and the PRI-istas were planting them. The ruling party had cut off Cardenista access to scarce state funding.

TRADITION VERSUS LITERACY AND LAW

Even as Zinacantecos and other indigenous peasants incorporated changes in agriculture and politics into their traditional villages, they continued to think of themselves as Indians. But new alignments of class and power were jeopardizing disadvantaged peoples' rights to belong to their ethnic communities.

Despite the changes in their lives, Zinacantecos continue to think of themselves as people whose morality, as embodied in costumbre, is superior to that of nonindigenous Mexicans—even though non-Indians hold secular power in the world at large. For Zinacantecos and other indigenous groups, tradition shapes the logic of the familiar ethnic world, whereas literacy and law govern the alien ladino world that exercises power over Indians.

Tzotzil until recently was an unwritten language. Because most Indians are monolingual and illiterate and most ladinos are literate and Spanish-speaking, Zinacantecos link literacy to the power that ladinos have over Indians. As Master Mason put it after translating for the PRD lawyer at the first Cardenista rally:

That's more or less what the ladino lawyer said, as far as I understood it. And you others can add from what you understood. For not all of us know how to read and write. If we did, then we could be thieves like the ladinos living in cities, in San Cristóbal and Tuxtla, rather than working as we do with our machetes. They just want to sit in offices and eat off of that.

Literacy confers the power to "eat" off of those who work with their machetes, especially in the case of those who can use reading to avail themselves of the power of law.

Indians sometimes turn to ladino law, however, to use its repressive power against fellow Indians. When Don Andrés' son Manuel quarreled with his father over land and threatened him, Andrés told him to get out of the house. "Fine," said Manuel, "I'll leave. But I am going to get myself a lawyer in San Cristóbal to get the land for myself." Manuel's threat to go to a lawyer is what Zinacantecos who have anger in their hearts do to make trouble. Rather than seeking settlement by appealing to traditional authorities within the community, those who turn to ladino lawyers can have the lawyers slap their opponents with litigation fees, fines, bribes, and punitive jail terms— the repressive tools of domination.

Lawyers, as far as Indians are concerned, are the ones who connect literacy and law to the power that ladinos hold over Indians. From the time of President Lázaro Cárdenas onward, government agency lawyers have controlled and manipulated indigenous politics. INI and PRODESCH lawyers always worked behind the scenes to guarantee that compliant PRI leaders would hold municipal offices. When Marcos Bromas and other PAN-istas succumbed to pressure to return to the PRI in 1982, PRODESCH lawyers were the ones to press them.

As the rank-based politics of consensus succumbed to the new class-based politics of party, Zinacantecos began to use wealth to compete in politics and even turned to the alien world of law to make trouble for opposing political factions. They often did so in the name of tradition.

Indigenous communities in the Chiapas highlands began splitting into factions affiliated with outside political parties in the late 1970s. They simultaneously adhered to costumbre by competing with one another in ritual performance, each group trying to prove that it was more "Zinacanteco" than the others. Factions collected fiesta taxes separately, forcing every household to chose a side. Opposing factions hired rival bands to play for their members at fiestas and sponsored rival fireworks displays and processions.

Apas Cardenistas lamented what they characterized as the demise of costumbre in the customary law administered by PRI authorities in Zinacantán Center. "It used to be that you could get the President to settle a case with a bottle of liquor," the Cardenistas complained. "But now so much money is involved because of the way the authorities are using the new law." Instead of trying to quiet anger in litigants' hearts in the traditional way, by getting them to drink together to acknowledge settlement, the Cardenistas charged, the president imposed fines in the manner of the ladino judiciary. The PRI officials argued in rebuttal that they tried their best to settle litigation "by costumbre," that opposition litigants like the Cardenistas were the ones who threw tradition to the winds by using outside lawyers and legal maneuvers.

Most town hall litigation no longer involves the proffer of liquor to calm antagonists' hearts, as once it invariably did. What has changed, I believe, is not that offering and accepting liquor has ceased to signify heartfelt casting away of anger, but rather that politicians no longer care to bring fights to resolution. Instead, they often show disdain for people seeking their help—as if others' problems are too petty to be bothered with. Previously, politicians had a stake in settling things amicably; they wanted litigants to depend on them and help bolster their positions in the community. Now, unless the litigant is powerful or wealthy, local politicians are simply not interested, because their power rests in control of capital and public monies, not in retinues of followers.[8]

As a result, those who opposed the PRI before 1994, and even after, lost customary access to reconciliation of debts, marital disputes, quarrels over child support—the very problems that agrarian change and the increasing differentiation of poor and wealthy had sharpened.

When Don Andrés' sister Lorenza begged him to accompany her to Zinacantán Center in 1989 to help her divorce her husband, Andrés' refusal called attention to her isolation, as a Cardenista, from ordinary recourse to traditional justice. Lorenza had to go to Zinacantán Center, the lowest judicial level at which municipal authorities have jurisdiction over divorce. But Lorenza's husband was one of the Cardenistas in Apas. Even though Andrés was a hamlet-level PRI authority, he could not assure her that she would receive a fair hearing in Zinacantán Center. Andrés told me what he had said to his sister, advising her to ask their brother, Mariano, a Cardenista, to help her instead:

"Look, Lorenza, it isn't my affair. If I were a Cardenista, then, sure, I'd go with you to Zinacantán Center, but I'm PRI," I said. "But the Cardenistas don't go to Zinacantán Center. Who knows where they go to settle their problems, perhaps Tuxtla, perhaps elsewhere," I said.

"But I want to give him up for good," said Lorenza [referring to her husband]. "What use is it to me to be living in the same house with him?"

"Do whatever you want. If you want to break up, fine. I'm not going to tell you to leave your husband."

"But Mariano [Lorenza's Cardenista brother] doesn't want to go to Zinacantán Center," she replied.

"Why not?"

"Who knows?"

"Well, I don't want to go either," Andrés said, "for I know that the authorities will ask me if you are from the PRI, and I will have to tell them you and your husband are Cardenistas. Then they're likely to say 'Who knows what municipio the Cardenistas belong to?' And that won't do."

Taunting the Apas Cardenistas repeatedly with the query, "Where is your President, where is your municipio?" the hamlet's PRI minority were insinuating that Cardenistas deserved exile.

The threat to exile fellow Zinacantecos because of their politics is not dissimilar to the exile other highland groups were suffering on religious grounds. Exile was just what "Protestants"—often simply dissidents or disaffected poor—were experiencing at the hands of power holders in many Tzotzil and Tzeltal communities as the strains of agrarian change rippled through the landscape. Chamula, which I have discussed in comparison to Zinacantán as a neighboring township more sharply and adversely differentiated by agrarian changes, had become notorious for the action taken by its PRI-affiliated political leaders against thousands of citizens forced into exile since the early 1970s on the pretext of religious affiliation. During 1989 alone, hundreds of indigenous families were expelled from Amatenango del Valle, Oxchuc, Mitontic, and Chenalhó, ostensibly as Protestants.[9] Zinacantán also exiled Protestant converts, although in far fewer numbers than Chamula. The exiles joined others who took up refuge in squatter settlements that grew up around San Cristóbal as a result of economic and political adversity, rather than simply religious antagonism.

For generations, Zinacantecos have embraced costumbre, as both the Cardenistas and the PRI-istas in Apas still claimed to do. They have defended the integrity of their place in the world as an ethnic community. In a new era of exclusionary politics, would powerful Zinacantecos go so far as to deprive poor compatriots of their ethnic citizenship? Would PRI-istas attempt to cast out the Cardenistas? Before the Zapatista uprising, that seemed like a possibility.

DIVIDED SOLIDARITY

In 1988, six years after the debt crisis forced austerity and restructured the Mexican economy, PRI candidate Carlos Salinas de Gortari claimed the presidency on the basis of elections that many—both Mexicans and non-Mexicans—believed had been stolen from the opposition, a fraud that then-outgoing president Miguel de la Madrid later confirmed in his 2004 memoirs.

Scholars of Mexican politics[10] wondered whether Mexico could continue to liberalize its economy without modernizing its political system. Budget cuts had gutted many of the government programs that helped the ruling party secure popular support, and middle-class standards of living had declined. Some kind of partial democratization or political liberalization seemed advisable to prevent the disgruntled populace from joining with opposition groups to force a political change.

Even world financial planners, who earlier had mandated austerity and the dismantling of third world protected economies (such as Mexico's) to facilitate global flows of capital and goods, began to worry about the social unrest unleashed by economic restructuring. They proposed to strengthen states viewed as too weak and corrupt to provide the legal protections for persons and property necessary for transnational capital flows. The remedies they favored were democratic elections and human rights commissions for defusing social protests triggered by economic restructuring and military abuse. Mexico was a case in point.

Salinas, upon taking office, set a course that seemed to move in the direction of political liberalization. He revised Article 41 of the Constitution and established two federal entities to reform elections: an electoral institute to register voters, prepare elections, and oversee public tabulation of votes; and an electoral tribunal to adjudicate electoral disputes. He also declared amnesty for many who had been jailed for their involvement in social and political battles, and set up a national human rights commission to monitor human rights violations. Salinas took highly publicized and popular actions by arresting strongmen in the powerful oil workers' union (Joaquín Hernández Galicia, nicknamed "La Quina"), in the securities market (Eduardo Legorreta Chauvet), and in the drug trade (Miguel Angel Félix Gallardo) on charges of corruption.[11]

With much fanfare, Salinas also launched a national antipoverty program called Solidarity (PRONASOL, which was administered under the Ministry of Social Development, SEDESOL) to ameliorate the hardships posed by economic restructuring for the nation's poor—the 48 percent of the population who lived below the official poverty line in 1988. Under austerity and in the name of economic restructuring, the government phased out important benefits for Mexico's poor, including price controls and subsidies for basic foods such as tortillas. It also removed subsidies for peasant agriculture and disbanded state-run institutions such as INMECAFE that served peasant producers. Solidarity began to channel funds into five areas: food subsidies for specifically targeted low-income groups; credits for poor farmers engaged in high-risk production; development projects in indigenous communities; social programs to improve access to clinics and schools; and infrastructure such as electricity and water systems for low-income rural and urban homes. As restructuring reduced public funding for social programs through other channels, Solidarity gained prominence by funneling as much as 1.08 percent of Mexico's gross domestic product into these initiatives in 1992.[12]

Solidarity officials, Salinas announced, would collaborate with communities to develop what might be thought of as coparticipative programs based on community initiatives, joint responsibility, and honest administration of resources, without regard to participants' political affiliations. The program epitomized what Salinas hoped his administration would achieve by way of *concertación* or consensus building across the political spectrum. Salinas wanted Solidarity to:

> eliminate all vestiges of paternalism, populism, clientelism, or political conditionality in the improvement of the welfare of the population in poverty.... The activities carried out under the National Solidarity Program represent an investment in physical and social welfare infrastructure that *by their very nature* promote justice and democracy.[13]

Solidarity resources were primarily distributed outside the framework of the ruling party, bypassing traditional power holders in favor of new political actors and institutions. Taken at face value, Solidarity seemed to open up more democratic access to state resources. Coupled with electoral and human rights initiatives, Solidarity looked like the start of a whole new era of government.

Why, then, did Solidarity fail to win popular support in Chiapas, which as one of Mexico's poorest states received more Solidarity funding than any other state in the country?

One reason was that Solidarity funding came too little and too late to ease the hardships that economic restructuring brought to the agrarian sector. One goal of Solidarity in Chiapas was to assist the small producers of coffee who had lost their money and their livelihoods when INMECAFE, the Mexican National Coffee Institute, was disbanded.

During the 1980s, INMECAFE had given peasants credits to purchase fertilizer and other inputs for growing coffee, and had guaranteed a market for their crop. Large commercial plantations grow coffee in the Soconusco region of Chiapas, but so do peasants on ejidos and smallholdings there and in the central and eastern parts of the state, where the Union of Unions won marketing concessions from INMECAFE in 1980. In most regions, INMECAFE tended to favor peasants organized into ejidal unions affiliated with the PRI's national peasant confederation, the National Peasant Confederation (CNC). It also dictated the terms for these unions' production.[14]

After Salinas disbanded INMECAFE as part of his program to get the national government out of state-run enterprises, his Solidarity program targeted small coffee producers in Chiapas to ease the hardships posed by the collapse of world coffee prices in 1989. Solidarity gave credits to individuals organized within local Solidarity committees and provided some support for marketing. But Solidarity could support only the most impoverished of coffee producers. For most peasants, the program's assistance was inadequate, according to one expert appraisal:

> Has [Solidarity] been successful in combating extreme poverty in the coffee sector? In the 1989–1990 season, a small producer with two hectares in coffee, producing a crop of 500 pounds, earned the equivalent of 369 days of work at the minimum wage. In 1991 and 1992, that same producer earned the equivalent of 195 days of work at the minimum wage. Thus, the answer must be "no." Small coffee producers are poorer today than when Solidarity began. Clearly [Solidarity] is not to blame for this situation, though it did not prevent it either. It is true that, given the withdrawal of INMECAFE, without [Solidarity] things would be worse. But the situation is, nevertheless, far from good.[15]

A more telling criticism of Solidarity was that its implementation in Chiapas did not honor the program's promise to hand out funding without regard to the political affiliation of its recipients. Solidarity channeled substantial support to indigenous peasants in Chiapas through the National Indian Institute (INI), which set up regional councils of indigenous representatives to formulate strategic projects.[16] At first it appeared as though INI-sponsored initiatives would actually reach out to indigenous and peasant groups regardless of their political affiliation. But in 1992, Chiapas governor Patrocinio González Garrido arrested and jailed three top INI officials in Chiapas on what many believed to be trumped-up charges of corruption. Critics maintained that the governor was angry that INI was dispensing Solidarity funds to PRI opposition in independent peasant groups in eastern Chiapas.[17] After the governor put his own people in charge of INI, the agency's Solidarity program once again became an instrument for ruling party clientelism.[18] In Zinacantán, for example, Cardenistas lost Solidarity's support for a community project after new directors took charge at INI in 1992.

INI's administration of Solidarity also fell short of the program's commitment to aid grassroots initiatives without paternalism. Indigenous representatives complained about this failing during an August 1993 meeting convoked by INI in San Cristóbal de las Casas.

A video of the meeting made by one of the indigenous representatives called attention to subtle paternalism inherent in the very organization of the meeting. With one exception, the high-ranking officials who led the meeting were nonindigenous men. The women of INI's nonindigenous staff were given responsibility for running the workshops. The organizers relegated indigenous staff and indigenous representatives to the audience in plenary sessions, and to roles in workshops that to my eye treated them like schoolchildren, seating them around tables to write their ideas with colored pens on paper posters to put up on the blackboard under the supervision of the INI staff members. My own impression was that such paternalism is so deeply embedded in Mexico's treatment of Indians that those who exercise it are not always conscious of the resentment paternalism engenders—resentment that the Zapatistas voiced through Juan, one of the delegates to the February 1994 peace negotiations:

> We fight to gain respect for our dignity.... What offends us most is the inability to express our sentiments, our demands. Let it be clear that we fight for our dignity as Indians and so that we will not be stigmatized.... For years we have not been respected.... We say this in order that we stop being sold like animals in a zoo, so that we get treated as persons and humans.[19]

An indigenous representative at the August 1993 INI meeting angrily voiced his criticisms of INI's Solidarity programs in one of the workshops, urging compatriots to reject INI's paternalistic and heavy-handed management:

> We can't let them tell us what to do and what not to do, comrades. Those bastards treat us as though to say, "You, Indians, sit down and keep quiet...." We've heard from one another how we're told to run things at our own initiative but then not allowed to do so. They want us to do things only the INI way.
>
> The fact is that our enemies control the different institutions, such as INI, right now. They've decided to support Indians, or, you might say, to put up with the scourge of the Indians, but what kind of relation to the state can we really enter into?

Like Zinacantecos in Apas, and Zapatistas who accused public officials of merely using Indians as a stepping stone to positions of advantage and power, he complained that bureaucrats were using literacy and legalism to take advantage of Indians:

> For two days we've shown that we know how to work, how to get things done. Sure, we have setbacks, we have delays, but we're also making progress. I think that shows that we Indians are real *chingones* [studs/fuckers], that we know how to survive even on our few grains of corn. Why, then, won't they let us keep on making progress?
>
> It's because we have trouble doing the paperwork. Now they want us to fill out all these forms. If we don't do all the paperwork, they won't give us the money. The money's there. But if you don't know how to fill out the paperwork, then you have to give all the money back....
>
> The truth is that the staff secretaries don't want to do the work. The truth is that not all of the INI employees are hard workers, many of them want to be there behind a desk, just like other functionaries.
>
> You gentlemen [he said, addressing the INI officials], help us. We need your support and your advice. But we don't want your impositions. We don't want you to tell us our projects are no good, but rather to help us strengthen our projects. You have to realize that the projects

we propose are not our personal projects, not something dreamed up by just anyone, but rather by our public assemblies....

We [Indians] have been working on these projects for just three years, comrades. Think about it. For seventy years, they say, they've been trying to help Indians. But they haven't been able to make any progress, they haven't found the right shot, the right pill, to cure the Indians' poverty. And here we are, wanting to progress, willing to work, and now they change the accounting system on us, after seventy years of perpetrating abuses and robbing money from the poor.

At which point, the conference organizers interrupted to shut this man up.

Perhaps the most important shortcoming of Solidarity administration in Chiapas was that the majority of its support was administered directly through municipal governments, virtually assuring that its benefits would flow to supporters of the ruling party, and not to opponents. The ostensible purpose of administering Solidarity funds through municipalities was to encourage locally planned initiatives. But in Chiapas, where the ruling party had deposed virtually every opposition candidate who won a town hall presidency, block grants to municipalities perpetuated and sharpened the subtle and not so subtle politics of exclusion that we have seen at work in Zinacantán. In Zinacantán, PRI authorities used Solidarity funding to build a grandiose new municipal hall, one of several public building projects that primarily benefited the truckers paid to transport the construction materials. Not surprisingly, in the wake of the Zapatista rebellion, other Zinacantecos began to hold the PRI authorities accountable for purported misappropriation of the public works funding.

In the central highlands of Chiapas, the politics of exclusion seemed to have worked for the PRI up to the moment of the Zapatista uprising. Then, as Mexicans contemplated the seeming debacle of Salinas de Gortari's triumphalist modernizing, and as peasant and indigenous groups throughout Mexico began to acknowledge the legitimacy of Zapatista grievances, it appeared that the PRI had gravely jeopardized its ability to hold on to power, in Chiapas or elsewhere, without radically reconsidering the nation's goals.

Shortly after the Zapatista's January 1, 1994, uprising, opposition groups in dozens of municipalities in Chiapas seized town halls to protest the purportedly corrupt practices of PRI authorities imposed on many municipalities by the ruling party. Those protests within communities were understandable when one considers that the politics of exclusion spread throughout the Mexican countryside under the tenure of state governors such as Patrocinio González Garrido.

Analysts on the left of the political spectrum[20] argue that the Mexican bourgeois state, by stirring up factionalism among the peasantry, has been able to make class contradictions in Mexican society—between those who own the means of production and those whom production exploits—seem to disappear. Conflicts that have roots in fundamental inequalities separating peasants from large landowners, they say, have been written off as "Indian problems." I think there is merit to the claim that the government has deliberately fostered factionalism in the peasantry in order to divide and rule in the Mexican countryside. But I also believe it is important not to overlook how such tactics resonate with and sharpen the class divisions fostered within rural society by energy development and agrarian change in Zinacantán and throughout Mexico's southeast.

In this light, the Zapatista rebellion becomes understandable as a response to the growing differentials between rich and poor, and between favored and excluded groups within the rural society of Chiapas. We can better understand why the Zapatistas felt betrayed by peasant groups within the Union of Unions or the ARIC, which accepted ruling party patronage and commercial support and, consequently, were criticized for selling out their compatriots. We can also understand why the Zapatistas call for leaders to govern "by obeying" those whom they govern; why they vow that they will themselves govern uncorruptly, "for everyone and not for ourselves"; and why the Zapatistas have refused government funding or support until such time as a peace based on political reforms has come into being. But above all, we know that the conflict in Chiapas arose directly from a quarter of a century of Mexican development and modernization, and that solutions must take this into account.

7 ✦ TRANSITIONS

The weeks before the August 21, 1994 Mexican presidential elections were a time of great anxiety within Mexico about the country's immediate future, given the prospect that the ruling party might not credibly win the vote:

> The problem is that not even once in this country's recent history—not since 1911—has power been transferred by means of elections. Never. There is no tradition of that here whatsoever. None. None. None at all!

That, said Jorge G. Castañeda, a prominent Mexican political scientist, was why he and some forty members of the so-called San Angel group, named after the district in Mexico City where many politicians, intellectuals, and social leaders live, had been discussing privately how to ward off a political crisis that could accompany the 1994 presidential elections.[1]

Modern Mexicans could not look to a precedent for a model for a peaceful transfer of power from the PRI in the event of a loss. There had been no transfer of power since the Revolution of 1910–1920, and opposing parties had never held office—and would not until six years later, after the 2000 elections. In what had become institutionalized as the *dedazo*, PRI leaders transferred power by "fingering" their candidate for the next elections at the end of each six-year presidential term.

While the 1994 elections were relatively free of violence, many Mexicans were looking back to the Revolution of 1910–1920 itself for ways of imagining how a change of government might someday take place. The last change in the system of Mexican government had come after the 1911 elections in which Madero forced six-term president and virtual dictator Porfirio Díaz out of office. Chaos and the

Revolution ensued. During the Revolution, contending forces convoked two constitutional conventions. The first, at Aguascalientes in 1914, was so dominated by Villistas, Zapatistas, and socialists that it proved unacceptable to middle-class "Constitutionalists" and was followed by three years of anarchy and civil war. The second, held in Querétaro in 1917, drafted the constitution that has been Mexico's charter since the Revolution. Did Mexico's current circumstances warrant a new constitutional convention?

According to the Zapatistas, they did. Rejecting the peace accords in June 1994, the Zapatistas' *Segunda Declaración de la Selva Lacandona* stated that "the Carta Magna [Constitution] that governs us is no longer the will of the Mexican people.... [We need] new national law, a new Constitution, one that guarantees implementation of the popular will."[2] The statement called for a convention of delegates designated by "civilians" from ejidos, colonies, schools, and factories to meet in EZLN territory at an opportune time and place.

Other Mexicans made similar proposals. Amado Avendaño Figueroa, owner of San Cristóbal de las Casas' independent newspaper, *Tiempo*, served as the PRD candidate for governor of the state of Chiapas. In his platform he promised to form a transitional state government while convoking a convention drawn from "civil society" to write a new Constitución Política de Chiapas—in this case under the provisions of the existing 1917 Constitution that empowers citizens to change their form of government.[3]

Neither proposal clarified just who belongs or does not belong to "civil society," but this imprecision did not deter a large group of independent peasant organizations and citizens from meeting in Tuxtla Gutiérrez at the self-proclaimed Chiapas State Democratic Convention on July 2–3, 1994, to endorse both proposals. On July 9, the Zapatistas and the leaders of the state convention issued a convocation for an August 6–9 National Democratic Convention, this time claiming a basis in the existing constitution. Several thousand people responded to the EZLN invitation. The convention was held before the elections, at the beginning of August in a place in the Selva Lacandona called Aguascalientes—in memory of the Revolution's first constitutional convention in 1914, signaling the intention to draft a more radical constitution than that on which Mexican government currently is based. Although many were supporters of PRD candidate Cuauhtémoc Cárdenas, the assembly refused to endorse any candidate and pledged to take to the streets in the event of a PRI "victory."[4]

Meanwhile, in San Cristóbal de las Casas, the ladino property and business owners most threatened by Zapatista demands and land takeovers organized themselves as "authentic Coletos" (nicknamed after the original colonial settlers of the city). Their reaction against supposed Zapatista sympathizers—individuals and groups (including the Catholic Church) who supported the peace negotiations—crescendoed into death threats. Fear of an indigenous uprising was widespread among the ladino poor, fed by memories and lore of the eighteenth- and nineteenth-century uprisings.

It had become clear in the weeks leading up to the presidential elections that many indigenous and peasant groups had gained both the courage and the political consciousness to demand vindication and redress for their grievances. Such groups said they had been awakened by the Zapatista uprising, and some of them embraced the organizational structure adopted by the Zapatistas (communal decision making, bottom-up management). In Zinacantán, a broad-based citizens' group formed a Consejo Municipal (municipal council) to govern the township with responsibility to what Zinacantecos were calling "the base" ("the masses"), after charging that the incumbent municipal president, Domingo Vázquez Jiménez, and his associates had misappropriated public works money and solidarity funds. Rumors spread that Vázquez held a private account in Oaxaca with deposits over U.S.$270,000. The state legislature declined to depose Vázquez; Zinacantecos proceeded to take matters into their own hands by beating Vázquez and jailing him along with others accused of corruption.[5]

What did Chiapas—and Mexico—have to look forward to as the 1994 elections approached in the wake of the Zapatista rebellion?

At the time, Mexicans faced the very real possibility of further armed confrontation. Either the Zapatistas or the government could have broken the truce that had held since January 12, 1994, and hostilities could have resumed at any point. Some people thought that the military might renew its advance against the Zapatistas unilaterally, by way of a coup. The ensuing conflict would have extended well beyond Chiapas.

In the event, the elections took place as scheduled on August 21, uninterrupted by the conflict or coup that many feared. Mexicans preferred not to risk changing course at such a critical moment and rewarded the PRI with yet another presidency, that of Ernesto Zedillo Ponce de León. Mexico was to face a six-year period in which the PRI would cling to power, using counterinsurgency to contain the Zapatistas in a stalemate that led to little constructive change in Chiapas.

The Zapatistas, for their part, had to reconsider how to sustain the momentum of their movement after the PRI presidential victory. When they convoked a second gathering of Mexican civil society at their Aguascalientes center in the autumn of 1994, fewer people attended, and most were demoralized by the election. There seemed little prospect that civil society would heed the Zapatista call to rewrite the Mexican Constitution. By the end of 1994, the Zapatistas shifted emphasis, placing indigenous rights at the center of their agenda, reformulating their quest for social rights (land, health, housing, schooling, work, equitable markets, etc.) as fulfillment of indigenous rights long neglected in Mexican law and policy. This is the topic of Chapter Eight.

Yet as the Zapatistas began negotiations over indigenous rights with the Zedillo government in 1995, they found that the government would not allow them to bring agrarian reform or social rights to the negotiating table. I think it was at that point, finally, that the Zapatistas decided to take the cause of social and economic equity to the world public by deepening their involvement with Mexican and international civil society in efforts to consider alternatives to neoliberal economic globalization—the topic of Chapter Nine.

LESSONS FROM THE PAST

Before turning to what has happened in Chiapas and in Mexico since the Zapatistas initiated their rebellion in 1994, I want to underscore some of the lessons that I believe the background to the rebellion compels us to keep in mind.

First, Mexico suffered a prolonged crisis in agriculture that substantially antedated NAFTA, the North American Free Trade Agreement that the Zapatistas chose to protest by rebelling at its moment of inauguration. This is important to remember because, since the Zapatista rebellion, NAFTA has come to be seen as one of the principal causes of the problems in the Mexican countryside. But even if Mexico were to turn back the clock and somehow annul NAFTA, many of the problems that rural cultivators face would remain.

Let me explain. Mexico's agrarian problems stem at least in part from the development Mexico pursued more than a half century ago by having peasant production indirectly subsidize national industry by providing cheap foods to help industrial employers hold down workers' wages (see Chapter One, page 32). Rural small producers were placed in a position of always having to contribute more than their fair share to the country's growth. That meant pressing agrarian resources to the limit, and ultimately beyond, to the point of forcing smallholders to send family members into the Mexican urban informal economy or into the United States to work. In this sense, the older model of peasant agriculture was inherently unsustainable.

At least, however, Mexico had a national policy of sovereignty over food. When Mexico entered the global economy of oil in the 1970s and undertook development that sharpened the crisis in agriculture and the flow of rural producers into other sectors of the economy (as we have documented happened in Chiapas), the government had to face up to growing corn imports. It did so by attempting to restore the country's basic food security, subsidizing rural producers to intensify corn production through the use of chemical inputs. The technical inputs staved off the declines in corn harvests but at tremendous social costs in the countryside, with growing disparities of wealth and impoverishment—another model that was inherently unsustainable.

Mexico, of course, was forced by global financial managers to undergo economic restructuring after 1982, and many of the supports for rural small producers withered away. Ultimately, the country's leaders abandoned even the vision of Mexican sovereignty over food. They embraced NAFTA, which required phasing out all Mexican support for basic grains, notably corn, while opening the country's markets to imports under the neoliberal model of global free trade.

NAFTA sounded a death knell for peasant production, the Zapatistas have claimed. A decade later, activists are arguing for reversal or modification of free trade agreements for agricultural products to restore policies of sovereignty over food (see Chapter Nine). But return to sovereignty over food would still require Mexican policy makers to grapple with the underlying structural changes—such as growing dependence on fertilizer and other inputs for agriculture, yet declining government support for the inputs— that sharpened the agrarian crisis and reshaped peasant agricultural production before NAFTA. At the very least, the Mexican countryside would have to consider how to make rural production more sustainable. To their credit, the Zapatistas are undertaking production projects with substantial attention to economic and technical approaches to sustainability.

A second, related lesson of the background to the Zapatista rebellion is that the time has passed for considering the "peasant question" simply in terms of price guarantees for corn or redistribution of land for labor-intensive household-based production. While peasants do continue to produce for subsistence and survival, their livelihoods also range off the farm, not just in wage work, but in a wide array of activities that combine surprisingly modern and flexible enterprise with collective or cooperative endeavor.

Zinacantecos, for example, use cooperative trading arrangements in their wholesale and retail marketing of flowers. Rather than competing individually in the flower trade, groups of Zinacantecos band together to market flowers. Robert Alvarez and I (1994) found that Zinacanteco flower merchants who supply the markets of Tuxtla Gutiérrez work in groups of up to six or eight associates selling flowers at a given market stall. Members work together to bulk and ship goods they obtain from local producers, even though each purchases his produce separately. Every day, a different member of the group travels to Tuxtla Gutiérrez to sell. Members rotate the use of the market stall among their group, sharing the risk of fixed expenses as well as the opportunities for profit, leaving each member enough time for farming milpa or for other activities.

Most Chiapanecans do not realize that Zinacantecos travel as far as Mexico City to obtain flowers for southern markets, and that while Zinacantecos are investing in plastic greenhouses to produce flowers in the Chiapas highlands, they are also procuring as many as half of the flowers sold in central Chiapas from wholesale markets in central Mexico. One of my godsons belongs to one of six groups of Zinacantecos who pay a trucker to make a weekly round trip to Mexico City to purchase flowers. Each group sends one of its members, on a rotating basis, to buy flowers for his associates. For such trips to be profitable, the eight-ton truck must return from Mexico City fully loaded, hauling far more produce than any given group can afford alone. In effect, a large number of vendors are sharing the costs, risks, and profits available to those involved in national commercial circuits by banding together. Doing so allows them to capture some of the profit that would otherwise go to shippers and to realize economies of scale unavailable to individual vendors. Like many Zinacantecos, these flower vendors use at least part of their off-farm proceeds to pay for inputs to intensify their farming.[6]

It is encouraging to me that peasant organizations in Chiapas have been experimenting for some time with alternatives to chemical-intensive agrarian technologies of the "Green Revolution." Many small producers have embraced the use of chemical fertilizers and labor-reducing herbicides that were heavily promoted by government agencies and by advisors to many of the independent peasant organizations. But others have been encouraged by niche markets to draw upon centuries of experience with nonchemical multiple cropping to intensify organic production. For example, ISMAM, an organization of indigenous peoples from the Sierra Madre of Motozintla, Chiapas, took up the production of organic coffee for markets in Canada, the United States, the Netherlands, Germany, and Switzerland some twenty years ago. (The Zapatistas have since taken up organic production of coffee for such niche markets.) In Pantelhó, before the rebellion, Indians formed a cooperative with the assistance of a French agronomist to produce and market organic honey.[7] Environmentally sustainable production (which, as we shall see, the Zapatistas have also begun) needs to be encouraged, and peasants should undertake more multicropping to protect themselves against fickle markets that expose producers to devastation when world prices of a given cash crop collapse.

Economists and planners need to recognize in such examples how diverse and flexible peasants' enterprises can be. In an epoch of global change that rewards those who tailor production to niches of economic opportunity, peasants are demonstrating they can do just that. Those who plan agrarian development need to recognize the potential of such peasant enterprise. They need to plan beyond agricultural extension in rural communities to develop the infrastructures for transport, marketing, and commerce that help indigenous people diversify their livelihoods and invigorate the agrarian economy.

A 1994 study of NAFTA's impact on peasant corn producers argued that just such infrastructural support was needed to facilitate either the modernization of corn production to reach higher yields or the diversification into nontraditional fruits, vegetables, or field crops. Yet economic restructuring has removed the essential government services of credit, technical assistance, insurance, marketing, and agricultural advising precisely at the time when peasants still need such services to diversify and modernize their production.[8]

I believe that Mexican economists also need to reconsider the relationship Mexico's agrarian economy has to the world economy. A decent living in the countryside and the value of subsistence foods need to be factored into the equations that set the terms in which the country balances agrarian needs against those of urban-industrial producers and consumers. In addition, appropriate valuation of the peso could do much to help small producers of coffee and corn recuperate from market setbacks. Following the devaluation of Mexican currency after the debt crisis, Mexico controlled its rate of exchange to reign in inflation. But some Mexican and North American economists argued that the peso was overvalued by as much as 5 to 20 percent in 1994,[9] and it may still be overvalued in 2004, despite depreciation over the decade. An artificially strong peso reduces the cost of imports encouraged by NAFTA, but it also creates a disadvantage for Mexican producers whose crops are destined for foreign markets or which compete with imported foods. Those who claim that peasant corn is not competitive with imported corn have ignored the impact of Mexico's often overvalued currency on domestic prices as a competitive disadvantage along with the subsidies that farmers in the United States receive from the U.S. government for exporting grains.

The Zapatistas have emphasized agrarian reform as key to survival in the countryside, together with demands for work, land, housing, nutrition, health, education, independence, freedom,

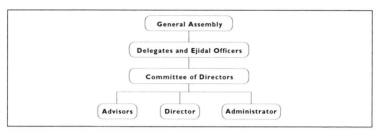

FIGURE 7.1 ORGANIZATIONAL CHART, UNIÓN DE EJIDOS
"PROFESOR OTILIO MONTAÑO."

democracy, and justice. Other independent organizations in the region have emphasized marketing and credits as adjuncts to enhance indigenous production on the farm. It is important to recognize that a variety of off-farm commercial enterprises can also play a role in agrarian development, and that small producers of indigenous rural Chiapas have demonstrated their capacity to develop such enterprise to capture the profits that customarily have gone to others.

The third lesson I believe we should carry from the background to the Chiapas uprising is that the Zapatistas built their movement from a long trajectory of social activism and experiment. Ten years after the rebellion, observers tend to forget that many Zapatista initiatives drew upon earlier inspiration and accomplishment.

Planners have as much to learn from indigenous cooperative associations of the 1980s as they do from the post-1994 Zapatistas about accountability, namely that government agencies and public institutions must be accountable to the constituencies they serve, rather than vice versa.

In this regard, I am struck by the organization of the Unión de Ejidos "Profesor Otilio Montaño," an ejidal union founded in the 1980s near Motozintla in the Pacific coastal range of Chiapas. Made up of sixteen member ejidos and six additional settlements, this union was dedicated to the organic production of coffee, apples, beans, corn, honey, and mushrooms for niche markets in Mexico and abroad. Its administrative organization placed the union's general assembly on top and its administrators and officers on the bottom, symbolically inverting the hierarchies of power that are familiar to us for most corporations and governmental entities.

It is notable that the Zapatistas describe themselves as similarly organized with popular assemblies governing the "Clandestine Committee of Indigenous Revolution," to which Subcomandante Marcos is in turn subordinate. Whether or not the Zapatistas or ejidal unions fully achieve the ideal that Marcos has described in terms of leaders who serve and who obey the will of the many, such commitment to accountability beckons powerfully to people who have experienced decades of disenfranchisement in which politicians, bureaucrats, and power holders treat the populace as beholden to them rather than vice versa.

A broader accountability is also called for on behalf of those who have been disadvantaged by the growing differentiation in the Mexican countryside. It is alarming to me that new alignments of wealth and power in indigenous communities allow leaders to turn their backs on their poorest and weakest compatriots, among whom women and children have most to lose. But I am equally alarmed by the willingness of planners, in Mexico and in the United States, to shuck off responsibility for the impoverished for the sake of economic restructuring, especially when restructuring has actually swelled the ranks of the homeless, the unemployed, and those women and men who must work at multiple minimum-wage jobs with no benefits just to survive. In Mexico as in the United States, federal and state governments have sacrificed social safety nets in the name of austerity and free market minimal governance. Mexico is now paying the costs of such callous neglect.

More generally, "modernizers" need to reconsider whether our societies can afford the impoverishment of the masses that accompanies economic restructuring. Corporations pursue cheap labor and hefty profits on a global scale that escapes responsibility for conditions in any given nation. But concentrations of new wealth do not readily trickle down to the masses. In the final analysis, can modern economies and modern states afford societies in which so many people are losing their economic power as purchasers and consumers? For over a decade, the indigenous people of Chiapas and the Zapatistas have been forcing North Americans—of Canada, the United States, and Mexico—and citizens of the world to ponder this question.

8 ✦ THE NEW INDIGENOUS MOVEMENT

At the time of the Zapatista rebellion, Mexico was synonymous with "economic modernization." Indeed, the North American press heralded the election of Harvard-educated Salinas de Gortari, portraying him as an enlightened technocrat who would lead Mexico into a new economic era. Like leaders of other countries faced with the burden of massive debt restructuring, Salinas de Gortari and the Mexican government embraced the course imposed by the International Monetary Fund and most favored by foreign debt holders: continued structural adjustment and neoliberal reform. Breaking the social pact with peasants, workers, and Mexican business that the government had forged after the Revolution, especially in the 1930s, the ruling party began eliminating social programs, privatizing state industries, removing price controls, and courting international investment. The government dropped price guarantees for agricultural products and phased out credits for rural producers. These measures were applauded by many, but exacted a deep toll on Mexico's poor, especially the rural poor who had been the traditional backbone of support for the government.

Against this backdrop, Subcomandante Marcos and the Zapatistas burst onto the scene. With their unusual blend of Internet sophistication and rural guerrilla tactics, they drew international attention to the plight of those at the losing end of Mexico's economic globalization, particularly the indigenous groups who were losing both their livelihood and, increasingly forced into migration, their hopes for self-determination. At least for a time, the Zapatistas successfully directed attention to the high costs of modernization, and they forced a change in the public discourse over Mexico's future.

The movement served as a wake-up call to other Mexicans to question the established authority of the ruling party that had governed for so long, yet was no longer committed to the welfare of most of its citizens. During 1994, the Zapatista rebellion seemed to stop the steamroller of Salinas de Gortari's modernizing project in its tracks. The hegemony of the ruling party, sustained by generally accepted voter fraud in elections, began to erode. Even though the PRI's Zedillo won the 1994 elections as Salinas' successor, opposition parties have since made important gains in state and federal elections, notably the capture of the Mexican presidency by the PAN's Vicente Fox in 2000. Electoral reform, which began under Salinas, advanced even further. Mexican civil society has flourished, boosted by the call of the Zapatistas to carry the revitalization of Mexico's democratic life and social organizations from Chiapas to the rest of the nation. The Zapatistas brought new attention to gender rights. The independent labor movement, to which the Zapatistas had ties before the rebellion, has advanced, symbolized by the first independent May Day march in Mexico City in 1995. Peasant and indigenous Mexico, which in the wake of the 1992 "reform" of the agrarian law appeared to be on the verge of extinction, or at least starvation and emigration, has been reinvigorated. There is no question but that Mexico has changed.[1]

Those of my readers who view the Zapatista movement from afar will be surprised at how sobering the Zapatistas' situation appears to me on the basis of ongoing work in Chiapas since the rebellion. Although the movement has brought a new public focus to the topic of indigenous rights, the situation in Chiapas is at an impasse.

There have been no real negotiations between the government and the Zapatistas since 1996, not even after Fox took office, vowing to work with the Zapatistas to resolve their demands. Assertions to the contrary on both sides, I do not believe either party really wants to negotiate. During the Zedillo presidency, the PRI regained ground steadily in Chiapas and seemed determined to treat the Zapatistas as a regional issue in a peripheral area not important to Mexico's modernization—all the evidence presented in previous chapters notwithstanding. The Zapatistas, for their part, hemmed in by the Mexican military, had little reason to trust Zedillo, who would not honor agreements that his own representatives negotiated with them. The Zapatistas hoped instead that international scrutiny would see them through until the political climate changed in their favor. As we shall see, Fox's historic wresting of the presidency from the PRI has not led to a peace in Chiapas that builds on the Zapatistas many provocative and worthwhile proposals.

Yet to appraise the rebellion's future, we must look deeper than the daunting realities in Chiapas, attending (as in past chapters) to the structural factors underlying surface appearances. Mexican and global society are exploring new terrain. The very processes of globalization that brought the Zapatistas into rebellion have led Mexicans to conceptualize the world in new ways. Because modernization brought unexpected hardship to many, Mexicans have come to question economic restructuring, and especially the government's embracing of "neoliberal" reforms, which look to the marketplace to solve all of society's problems and meet all its needs. Neoliberalism has changed society, both for the better by contributing to dramatic growth of civil institutions independent of the government, and for the worse by leading the government to militarization and repression to hold onto power. Assessing whether the Zapatistas' current prospects look like a glass half empty or a glass half full requires recognition of these changes.

THE NEW ZAPATISMO

In the ten years that have passed since the Chiapas rebellion broke out, Zapatismo has come to stand for the new indigenous rights movement in Mexico. Yet when I began research in Mexico forty-four years ago, Emiliano Zapata, although a popular hero in central Mexico,[2] was hardly known among indigenous people in Chiapas. They did remember Venustiano Carranza and Pancho Villa, whose forces were active in Chiapas at the time of the Mexican Revolution. But they thought of agrarian reform (which was won in 1917 by Mexico's original Zapatistas but was not implemented in Chiapas until after 1934) as a government program to benefit them as campesinos. Each year on April 10, the anniversary of Zapata's assassination, the national state would memorialize Zapata as a symbol of Mexico's institutionalized revolutionary commitment, not to Indians per se, but to peasants. These days, no one thinks of Zapata without thinking of Chiapas and Mexico's new indigenous movement. How did this remarkable conceptual change come about?

When activists such as Marcos' predecessors turned to the countryside (as well as to urban barrios) after the government crushed the student movement in 1968, they began to protagonize Zapatismo in areas where Zapata had never acted—in Chiapas and other parts of the country—as a way of holding the national state accountable for fulfilling the agrarian reform inscribed in the law but never completed. In Chiapas, Zapatismo grew after the Indigenous Congress of 1974, as indigenous communities allied themselves with indigenous and peasant counterparts in national organizations such as CNPA and OCEZ. Yet even the activists most involved with indigenous populations referred to themselves as *campesinistas* (activists on behalf of peasants). But after Salinas' 1992 abrogation of agrarian reform and the 1994 Zapatista rebellion, the ruling party lost virtually any credible claim to Emiliano Zapata as one of its heroes.[3] Zapatismo now symbolizes the demands for fundamental reform of the Mexican state, especially on behalf of indigenous people.

This important symbolic shift is one of many that the Zapatista rebellion has helped consolidate. Before neoliberalism, indigenous groups represented themselves as peasants because most national programs directed to the countryside were for peasants, not for Indians. Mexico's Indian programs, notably those of the National Indianist Institute (INI), were designed more to assimilate indigenous people into the peasantry rather than to help them as Indians. But with economic restructuring, land became more important to economic planners as a market commodity and peasants became more important as a mobile and increasingly transnational labor force. The government thus decided it no longer needed to fund the programs that supported peasants. As resources for rural support dried up, indigenous people found little basis for continuing to represent themselves as peasants. They began to protagonize themselves as distinct and worthy in their own right.[4]

The end of the cold war also contributed to a conceptual shift in the new indigenous movement because it seemed to invalidate the analysis of Mexican society in terms of Marxist or socialist concepts of class struggle. Much activism on behalf of peasants against the national state had been based on such analysis. Support for *indigenous* activism, by contrast, reflects the analysis of society in terms of identity and plurality, a new kind of analysis that responds to the world-wide emergence of demands by minority groups for representation and rights.[5]

"Rights" activism became important in Mexico in the 1980s when the universal human rights movement began to protest the repression that the Mexican government had applied to its own urban and rural dissidents after 1968, which occurred even as the country became a haven for those suffering human rights violations under authoritarian regimes such as Pinochet's Chile.[6] Private citizens set up the Mexican Academy for Human Rights in 1984. They argued that Mexico, as a signatory to the UN Charter, had a legal and moral obligation to conform to the Universal Declaration of Human Rights, and they called on the international community to put pressure on Mexico to do so. Human rights advocacy began to gain ground in Mexico after Amnesty International called attention to repression in rural Mexico[7] that resulted in hundreds of unwarranted jailings, including that of Chiapas journalist Jorge E. Hernández Aguilar, who had written many articles on agrarian injustice and whom Amnesty International identified as a "prisoner of conscience."

In the decade that followed, human rights organizations spread all over Mexico (by 1990 at least thirteen were active in Chiapas), pressing Mexico for both electoral and judicial reform. Prisoners began hunger strikes to demand review of their cases, and a distinct concern for indigenous prisoners emerged, for example in Chiapas in 1987, when the Committee for the Defense of Indigenous Liberty (CDLI) pointed out that most of the victims of rural repression in Chiapas were indigenous and that indigenous people make up the majority of the prison population in Chiapas (as is true of African Americans among the prison populations of the United States). The CDLI was particularly strong in northern Chiapas, contributing to new activism on behalf of indigenous rights.[8]

While this activism for indigenous collective rights was new, it built on earlier indigenous rights concerns. As early as the 1950s, INI had pressed for fair treatment of indigenous people before the law. INI developed bilingual education for schools it controlled in the highlands of Chiapas in the 1960s and 1970s. The Mexican government sponsored native language programs led by Mixtecs and Zapotecs in Oaxaca in the 1970s and 1980s. These and other efforts prefigured later demands for linguistic rights, which Maya nationalists in neighboring Guatemala began to demand in the late 1980s. Prominent Mexicans such as Guillermo Bonfil had called in the 1980s for a pluricultural Mexico to accord indigenous people greater political participation and recognition.[9] But in the 1990s, for the first time, indigenous collective rights were being treated as distinct from citizenship rights or general human rights and thus deserving of separate legal recognition—another symbolic and conceptual shift.[10]

In 1990, Mexico ratified additions to the International Labor Organization (ILO) charter, including Conventions 107 and 169, which accord specific collective rights to cultural and ethnic minorities and require nation states to protect their indigenous communities. Convention 169 had provided a strong legal basis for indigenous groups in Guatemala to demand protection of cultural rights after the Guatemalan war died down in the late 1980s. In Mexico it helped activists pressure the government to revise Article 4 of the Mexican Constitution in 1992 to recognize Indians for the first time as part of a pluricultural nation and to accord them rights. As the year of the Columbian Quincentennial, 1992 also brought hemisphere-wide indigenous activism to bear on Mexicans organizing for indigenous rights. Indigenous groups from around the nation formed the Mexican Committee for "500 Years of Indigenous, Black, and Popular

Resistance" and contributed to marches on behalf of indigenous rights, including the Xi Nich (Ants) march from northern Chiapas to Mexico City.[11]

The movements from peasant to indigenous concerns, from class to identity, and from individual human rights to indigenous collective rights have all been apparent within the Zapatista movement itself. As discussed in earlier chapters, the Zapatista movement grew out of peasant organizing. When the Zapatistas first called for revolution on January 1, 1994, they used the rhetoric of socialism to appeal for support from other parts of the country, urban as well as rural, that have less indigenous representation and activism than Chiapas. On behalf of Mexico's indigenous and nonindigenous poor, they demanded land, work, housing, nutrition, health, education, liberty, democracy, peace, and justice. These points provided the basis for negotiation with government representative Camacho Solís before the assassination of PRI presidential candidate Colosio in March 1994 (see Introduction). Later, after rejecting the Camacho accords, the Zapatistas convoked their first Aguascalientes convention to promote a national movement for constitutional reform. But when the second Aguascalientes convention from November 2–4, 1994[12] drew a disappointing turnout, the Zapatistas began to heed the calls of indigenous groups elsewhere in Chiapas and Mexico. These included the Chiapas State Indigenous Peasant Council (CEOIC) in Chiapas and the Indigenous Peoples Independent Front (FIPI), who, together with nonindigenous scholars and writers working as advisors, called for more explicitly *indigenous* demands, notably collective rights of "autonomy." In December 1994 the Zapatistas announced that they were setting up thirty-seven autonomous municipios in the regions of Chiapas under their control.[13]

"Autonomy" hardly existed as a concept in rural Chiapas before 1994. Mexican law accords certain kinds of autonomy to universities, to labor unions, to the *municipio libre* (Mexican municipality), and to the recently formed National Human Rights Commission (CNDH). In some parts of the Americas, indigenous communities have legally recognized tribal governments and enjoy some autonomy within state law (as in the United States), and others form part of autonomous regions (for example, the Miskito Indians of Nicaragua), but not in Mexico. It is true that indigenous communities in Mexico enjoy a certain degree of de facto autonomy in the practices of customary law inherited from the colonial era. The government has also found it convenient to allow them to run some of their internal affairs under traditional authorities. In the 1980s, some indigenous communities held up their right to *usos y costumbres* (usual and customary practices, but also supposedly "traditional" and culturally distinctive practices). But the idea of legally recognized collective rights of "autonomy" was little known until the indigenous rights movement gained momentum in the 1990s.[14]

Now, "autonomy" has become the central demand of the Zapatista movement. Autonomy was the central basis of the San Andrés Accords on Indigenous Rights and Culture negotiated with the government on February 16, 1996, but subsequently rejected by President Ernesto Zedillo. Autonomy continued to be what the Zapatistas turned to the world to hold the Mexican government accountable for through Zapatista-organized referenda. In conjunction with their supporters in Mexico and other parts of the world, the Zapatistas convoked a *consulta* (referendum) for autonomy on March 21, 1999, which won support from more than three million balloters in Mexico and other parts of the world for demands that the Mexican government honor the accords.[15]

There are many provisions of the San Andrés accords, but the fundamental agreement was for a new, constitutionally based "social pact" recognizing indigenous pueblos as having collective rights within a framework of autonomy. The agreement provided a framework for consideration of other issues in future negotiations: legislation to recognize indigenous economic, political, and social rights as *collective* rights. It called for judicial reform to recognize indigenous norms as different and at the same time legitimate. Indigenous culture was to be promoted, together with education and training that respects and uses indigenous traditional knowledge. The accords recognized the need for new laws, both state and federal, to implement the agreements. Under the accords, indigenous people were to be key actors in forging the new relation to the state, defining themselves as groups, organizing themselves within a framework of state and national government, and managing many aspects of their own internal governance and administration.[16]

When Fox became president in 2000, he vowed to seek constitutional changes that would honor the San Andrés accords. The Zapatistas organized an impressive March for Indigenous Dignity to Mexico City in February and March 2001: 1,100 from within the Zapatista Army accompanied by many more hundreds of sympathetic Mexicans and foreigners—to promote constitutional changes to recognize indigenous rights and culture. Comandante Esther's impassioned appeal to the Congress of the Union for the reforms galvanized the media in Mexico and abroad. But on April 25, 2001, the congress, instead, enacted a constitutional "Indigenous Law" that set aside almost all of the San Andrés provisions for indigenous rights and culture and that adds up to little more than antidiscrimination clauses. Commentators quipped that the constitutional change was "reforma light." The Zapatistas angrily accused Fox of betrayal.

Autonomy, as defined in the San Andrés accords, is a lofty agenda for Mexico's new indigenous movement. But what are the chances that the government will ever grant it? And what are the prospects for the movement? I believe that the answers to these questions may lie in the profound structural changes that Mexico continues to undergo as a consequence of neoliberalism. The changes give rise both to pessimism and optimism for the movement's future.

THE DOUBLE-EDGED SWORD OF NEOLIBERALISM

Mexico simply is not the same place that it was before 1982. One profound change has been that neoliberal restructuring created the space for Mexican society, which had a long tradition of activism, to blossom independently of the government and the ruling party. The austerity forced on Mexico after the 1982 debt crisis, and the financial planners' subsequent embracing of neoliberalism, removed the government's capacity and will to sustain programs that for half a century held Mexico together in a social pact. Independent organizations, churches, human rights activists, and political opposition parties stepped into the breach, for example after Mexico City's 1985 earthquake, when the government proved to be incapable of responding to the crisis.

Networked with counterparts throughout the world, these alternative groups and associations mobilized international leverage over Mexico's internal affairs to pressure the government for reform and democracy. In the emerging global order, citizens of the world were more likely after 1994 to "buy Marcos" than to "buy Mexican"—both figuratively and literally, such as by pressuring their own governments to accept or reject trade agreements with Mexico—if Mexico was seen as violating the rights of citizens and minorities. Because the government wanted the international community to accept Mexico as a new player in the modern order, leverage such as that mobilized by opposition groups had efficacy. This was a development that advanced the cause of indigenous autonomy and rights.

But as the growth of independent opposition penetrated Mexico's social and cultural landscape, the result was often division and conflict that undermined the solidarity of traditional communities that had enjoyed considerable de facto autonomy in the past. In Chapter Six I described the spread in Chiapas in the 1980s of what I characterize as "parallel/independent" organization (for the lack of a better term). Take political party affiliation, for example. In communities where there were loyalties in opposition, such as to the PRI and to the PRD in Apas (Zinacantán), almost every aspect of public life began to revolve around mutual opposition. Where the community once conducted its fiestas and agricultural ritual as one group, it began to conduct them as two (or even three or more), each functioning in opposition to the other(s). There would be two rock bands at the fiesta, two school committees, two sets of curers for agricultural rituals, two agencies for settling local conflicts, and so on. While such oppositional factionalism often grew out of efforts of the disenfranchised to challenge local power holders (as seen in the earlier discussion of the politics of exclusion), it frequently took on a life of its own. The affiliation of a given group to a political party or cause was often less important than the opposition itself. Ironically, during 1995, most of Apas' earlier PRD-istas became PRI-istas, and most of the PRI-istas became PRD-istas, for reasons connected to wider politics[17] yet underscoring that structural opposition, in itself, came to play a key and often polarizing role in local affairs. At least one writer has characterized the result as a "breakdown of community"[18] that undermined the solidarities on which autonomy may be based.

We have also seen that organized structural opposition could take the form of intolerance and exclusion, as happened in the case of expulsions on the pretext of religion that have plagued the highlands of Chiapas in recent years. It is evident in the polarization of Chiapas society that followed upon the Zapatista rebellion, in outbreaks of paramilitary violence, and in polemical discussion of public life. *La Jornada*, the national newspaper that best represents the progressive and independent Left in Mexico and that features most coverage of the new indigenous movement, rarely has had anything good to say about the PRI, whatever the party may propose or do. Other papers and the media, sympathetic to the PRI, if they cannot discredit the opposition, simply have ignored what is going on in Chiapas as though it were irrelevant. There was almost no television coverage of the March 21, 1999, referendum on the San Andrés accords, even though 5,000 masked Zapatistas (equal numbers of men and women) had dispersed all over the country to administer it! Much of what one reads or hears about Chiapas is thus thoroughly partisan and needs to be interpreted in light of the propaganda war going on. Such dogmatic partisanship is an impediment to negotiating a peaceful settlement in Chiapas, much less a solution that can fulfill indigenous aspirations.

At the same time, as organized structural opposition extended across multiple levels of public life, it helped build up alliances on which new solidarities and new types of shared community could be based. As communities or factions within them affiliated with one or another Protestant or evangelical church, or with Bishop Samuel Ruiz's Catholic catechists, indigenous groups of a given religion began to support one another to fight expulsions and to secure religious rights. When the national government set up its National Human Rights Commission (CNDH) in 1990, the Diocese of San Cristóbal lost no time in setting up its own Fray Bartolomé de Las Casas Human Rights Center to make sure that the rights of progressive communities would not be ignored. The EZLN won recruits facing military service by offering itself as an alternative to the Mexican army, and it has continued to build its movement as a quest for an alternative to the current Mexican political system. In 1994, after the PRD contested state-level elections claimed by the PRI, PRD gubernatorial candidate Amado Avendaño set up an independent state shadow government—which the ruling party tolerated yet ignored—that afforded indigenous organizations opportunities for banding together. Since the 1994 uprising, the Zapatistas have organized international conferences to formulate alternatives to the neoliberalism embraced by many of the world's governments. In fact, the Zapatistas themselves negotiated with the government as a parallel, independent national movement with international overtones and support that helped empower the quest for autonomy and rights.

While the oppositional patterns have their drawbacks, on balance I believe they enhance the prospect for respect of pluralism. The oppositional tendency has become so entrenched in life in Chiapas that I consider it to be one of the structural givens that will shape the future possibilities of the Zapatistas and the new indigenous movement. One can be certain that the discourses and the practices of the government and the ruling party will never again be taken for granted as the only path for Mexican life. The very fact of structural opposition at almost every juncture means that Mexicans have to formulate and to consider alternatives in public policy, and this cannot but help contribute to democracy.

MILITARIZATION AND CONTAINMENT

Militarization was another outcome of Mexico's neoliberal turn. Although Mexico had always used the carrot and stick to win political support, the drying up of state economic resources weakened the government's capacity for retaining loyalties other than by policing them. That left the regional elite, but also dissident rural poor, free to act on their own, with growing impunity, especially after the economic crash of December 1994 devastated Mexican living standards. Hooliganism, organized crime, insecurity, and violence have been on the rise in Mexico City and elsewhere, while private security guards police the growing gap between rich and poor at storefronts and gated communities. Drug trafficking has been growing and is reported to net Mexico as much foreign revenue as oil. When the Popular Revolutionary Army (EPR) sprang up in August 1996 in rural Oaxaca and Guerrero as a new guerrilla movement, it spread rapidly into Puebla, Tabasco, Guanajuato, and the Federal District, seemingly making rural areas ungovernable except through military intervention. Militarization was significant in Chiapas in the wake of the 1994 rebellion, but it actually began in the late 1980s. (I vividly remember the arrival in 1989 of a contingent of troops in Zinacantán to persuade the municipal authorities there to acquire arms to defend against rogues and dissidents.) Today, the military is deployed in much greater numbers even than at the end of 1994, not only in Chiapas but in other parts of the country as well, and has assumed an unprecedented role in public life, for example heading up police forces in major Mexican cities.[19]

Troops moved into Chiapas during 1994 to contain the Zapatista movement and undercut its strategic options. Even as the government declared a truce and negotiated with the Zapatistas, the army built roads to surround and penetrate the Zapatista heartland in eastern Chiapas, and it set up barracks throughout the region. The Zapatistas lost no time in flouting the army, in December 1994, by showing up in the Sierra de Motozintla and Simojovel outside the heartland, sparking a crisis in foreign investors' confidence in Mexico, and a collapse in the peso requiring a bailout of some $25 billion from President Clinton. Zedillo lost no time in sending troops on February 9, 1995, to capture the Zapatista leadership, while "unmasking" Marcos as Rafael Santiago Guillén Vicente, a former philosophy student of Mexico's national university (UNAM). Guillén and other Mexicans of the National Liberation Forces (FLN) were described as having had ties to the Farabundo Martí National Liberation Front (FMLN) in El Salvador before establishing themselves in Chiapas. Zapatista sympathizers immediately used the Internet to denounce the armed advance. Although international outcry at the apparent breakdown of the truce with the Zapatistas halted the army's advance, the militarization intensified and spread—and now extends through the highlands of Chiapas where the Zapatistas have sought sympathizers and recruits. Under Zedillo there were at least 30,000 federal troops deployed in Chiapas—some say more than double that number. Fox reduced that number, yet the military presence is still substantial. Although the Zapatistas have mobility in the rugged backlands of Chiapas, there is no question that the army has the upper hand militarily.

Stamping out the Zapatista movement was another matter, in part because Mexicans and the international community would not accept a genocidal war in Chiapas of the kind the Guatemalan army undertook. Legally, the government could not advance militarily on the Zapatistas under the terms of the law for dialogue passed by the federal Congress in 1995 after the failed effort by the army to arrest the Zapatista leadership. Instead, the government took advantage of ungovernability of the region[20] to mount a low-intensity war of attrition. Regional elites and power holders were not, for the most part, curbed by the army. Up until 1999, a vigilante group in northern Chiapas self-styled as advocating Paz y Justicia (Peace and Justice) was free to organize a dirty war against Zapatistas and their sympathizers. The sympathizers, in turn, have brought forth ample evidence that Peace and Justice was covertly armed by state security forces.[21]

The low-intensity warfare extended to the media. When the Diocese of San Cristóbal's Fray Bartolomé Human Rights Center published *Ni Paz Ni Justicia (Neither Peace Nor Justice)* to expose Peace and Justice's impunity to carry out killings and repression,[22] the latter group published *Ni Derechos Ni Humanos (Neither Rights Nor Human)* attacking the Fray Bartolomé center as partisan in overlooking Zapatista and PRD human rights violations. But for the most part, Zapatistas and their sympathizers have held the upper hand in the media warfare, using the press, the Internet, and Marcos' famous ironic wit to put the government on the moral defensive. The Zapatistas have been so effective in the use of the media to prevent the government from annihilating them militarily that their rebellion has been characterized as the *"first informational guerrilla movement."*[23]

The dirty war took advantage of long-festering conflict and factionalism that antedated the Zapatista rebellion, a facet of the oppositional processes discussed in the previous section. It was easy for groups of whatever political persuasion to arm themselves, and such groups readily lent themselves to manipulation. In the highland Chiapas municipio of Chenalhó, long-standing factionalism and conflict dating back well into the 1980s coalesced into pro-Zapatista and anti-Zapatista fronts vying for territory, loyalties, and the power to govern local affairs.[24] On December 22, 1997, the smoldering conflict flared into a massacre in the Catholic chapel at Acteal of forty-five Tzotzil Indians, mostly women and children. The massacre was carried out by a paramilitary group from nearby Los Chorros that was affiliated with the ruling party and had been armed and egged on by state security police.[25] Although the government responded primarily by stepping up militarization of the Chiapas highlands, the Acteal massacre drew major national and international protest, which ultimately led to arrests of eighty-four people held responsible. The tragedy of Acteal was thus something of a turning point, in that it revealed the limits of militarization, which could besiege communities aligned with the Zapatistas but not eliminate them without inviting even greater international attention to the cause of indigenous rights and autonomy. After Acteal, increasing numbers of foreigners began to flock to "peace camps" set up by the Fray Bartolomé Human Rights Center between the military and the Zapatista communities for volunteers willing to witness and report on rights abuses.

The Zedillo government nonetheless tried to rein in the churches, civil associations, and independent groups in Chiapas so as to close down their contacts with international counterparts. Several foreign

Catholic priests working for the San Cristóbal Diocese were deported. The diocese was represented as so partial to the Zapatistas in its role in the National Mediation Commission (CONAI) that Bishop Samuel Ruiz decided to disband the CONAI. Leaders of nongovernment organizations (NGOs) received anonymous threats and in some instances were alleged to have provided war materiel to the Zapatistas. Beginning in August 1994, journalists were being restricted in their access to the Zapatistas in eastern Chiapas. After the Acteal massacre, the immigration authorities stepped up vigilance of foreigners visiting Chiapas in curiosity about the Zapatistas, and the government attempted to dissuade foreign human rights observers by limiting the visas of foreigners entering Chiapas to only fifteen days. The government expelled scores of foreigners who attended what was to be the inauguration of the Zapatista autonomous municipality of Taniperla. But the effort was counterproductive, because among those expelled were many prominent Italian jurists and legislators who later helped mobilize European pressure against Mexican rights violations. President Fox subsequently backed off from such tactics.[26]

The Chiapas state government contributed to federal efforts to undermine the Zapatistas by mounting a vigorous program of "law and order," as called for by regional elites in the anarchic months of 1994 and 1995 when no one seemed to be able to control the self-arming of local groups, land invasions, and the spread of pirate transport fleets apparently supplied by stolen vehicles. The state government used the judicial police to remove squatters from lands they had invaded around San Cristóbal de Las Casas. In collaboration with the army, the state authorities raided hamlets in Zinacantán and Tenejapa where car thieves were hiding vehicles, and they arrested and jailed the indigenous and nonindigenous leaders of the pirate taxi movement. Municipal checkpoints were set up at town entrances to check the papers of suspicious vehicles and to search for arms. In his much publicized campaign for "Peace and Reconciliation" in Chiapas, interim PRI governor Lic. Roberto Armando Albores Guillén proposed, and the state government legislated, a new law offering amnesty to those who would give up their arms—a measure much criticized by progressives who claimed it granted immunity to those who participated in paramilitary operations against Zapatista sympathizers while affording no protection to Zapatistas. With much fanfare, Albores declared illegal the autonomous municipalities that the Zapatistas had set up for governing their territory and sent in military and state police forces to disband four of the thirty-seven autonomous centers and arrest their leaders. These law-and-order measures won praise from conservatives but also created concern on the part of many non-Zapatistas that the state government had become too reactionary.[27]

As if militarization, restrictions on foreigners, and "law-and-order" measures were not enough, the government also attempted to buy indigenous loyalties by offering benefits of various kinds. Programs such as food aid and health care supplied at military outposts or aid in school construction thus served as tools of counterinsurgency. Such enticements had some effect on populations that were close to army encampments or bases, but they also hardened the Zapatistas' resolve to reject all material aid from the government as fundamentally corrupt.

The government's most notable effort to regain indigenous loyalties was negotiation over land claims. In January 1994, Zapatistas and their followers invaded 65,000 hectares of private land in the Chiapas eastern lowlands. Further invasions followed the Zapatista example in almost every part of the state, especially in the western highlands and northern areas, where independent peasant groups organized under CIOAC, OCEZ, and the Union of Unions had been most active (see Chapter Three), and where indigenous peasants took over almost all remaining ladino private holdings. Overall, some 6 percent of the state's private holdings had been invaded by 1998, giving indigenous peasants unprecedented control of the countryside and the Zapatistas one of the strongest claims on their grassroots base, at least initially. The government used the army and state judicial police to evict invaders in some areas, but the invasions were too widespread to deal with by force.

Instead the government negotiated with peasants over invaded property and other land claims. Although the government had "ended" agrarian distribution with Salinas' 1992 "reform" of the agrarian code, it proposed that some invasions could be dealt with as "unfinished business" within the old framework. Others could be handled as conflicts over ownership to be negotiated through the new federal Agrarian Attorney General's Office. A third approach was to set up trusts (*fideicomisos*) to fund thirty-year interest-free loans for peasants to buy private property, either from owners whose lands they had invaded or from any landowners willing to sell.[28] Just weeks after the government negotiated the San Andrés Accords on Indigenous Rights and Culture with the Zapatistas, the government signed a March 19, 1996, Agrarian Accord with sixty-two official peasant organizations and eighty-five additional independent peasant groups from Chiapas, including those affiliated with ARIC, CIOAC, CNC, FIPI, and OCEZ-CNPA—but notably *not* with the Zapatistas, who were holding out for repeal of the government's 1992 "reform" of the agrarian code. By 2000, these groups had won legal title to 242,000 hectares in agrarian colonies and 244,000 hectares of purchased land. It should be noted, however, that the government did not provide support for the infrastructure that would be needed to make these lands productive. By 2002, some 40 percent of the lands granted through the Agrarian Accords had been abandoned. Nonetheless, the Agrarian Accords, which never would have come about if Zapatista-led land invasions had not presented the government with a virtual fait accompli, considerably eroded the Zapatista base.[29]

The war of attrition bore fruit for the government. The euphoria that spread through indigenous Chiapas during 1994 has sobered.[30] The Zapatistas were forced to hunker down in the countryside while the government wooed away their sympathizers with offers of goods and services funded by special programs for Chiapas. Even in their heartland, the Zapatistas faced peasant and indigenous opposition, and these were the groups that for the most part had won land concessions under the Agrarian Accords. The Zapatistas do not permit their followers to accept any government aid, and they have ordered them to abstain from elections. As a result the PRI regained the upper hand in regions where the PRD or other opposition groups could have won local elections in 1995 and 1997 if the Zapatistas had voted. In many areas, rank-and-file Zapatistas reaped few rewards and much hardship from loyalty to their movement. Some renounced their Zapatismo and rejoined the PRI.[31]

Yet the war of attrition has also sharpened the resolve of Zapatista communities to survive under siege—learning to do without unessential consumption, to develop production that does not rely on government aid or costly inputs, and to share the collective burdens and responsibilities of their cause. Zapatista communities contribute war taxes to the EZLN, and they mobilize to help one another face off external threats. Such commitments underscore the autonomy through which the Zapatistas are seeking alternatives to neoliberalism's erosion of Mexican society.

LEGAL CONCESSIONS AND CO-OPTATION

The Mexican government has always been adept at appropriating the initiatives of adversaries and thus undercutting or mollifying its challengers. Decades ago, the government appropriated Zapata as a symbol of revolutionary commitment even though Mexico's post-Revolutionary leaders were responsible for Zapata's assassination. After repressing the 1968 student movement as interior minister, Luis Echeverría embraced populism and Marxism as president and made overtures to many who had supported the movement. When independent organizations developed artisan production in Chiapas in the 1980s, the state government established its own program, restricting funding and marketing of crafts to groups that joined its efforts.

The arena of indigenous rights is one in which state attempts at co-optation have had mixed results, bringing at least some positive change for indigenous people. When Mexico signed the ILO Convention 169 in 1989, which requires nation-states to recognize and protect their indigenous peoples, it opened itself to pressure from indigenous rights advocates in the international community. One result was the revision in 1992 of Article 4 of the Mexican Constitution to recognize Mexico's Indians legally for the first time. The revision of Article 4, the efficacy of which really depended on additional federal and state legislation, evoked pressure for further legal reform. In Oaxaca, which has a substantial indigenous population and activism, the state government undertook a series of legislative changes, beginning in 1993, to reform the legal code to recognize indigenous rights.[32] While the Oaxaca legislation may be seen as a state effort to co-opt indigenous initiatives, it did grant substantial legal recognition of indigenous rights.

I view such ostensibly conciliatory initiatives in Chiapas somewhat more skeptically. During the Zedillo presidency, for example, Interim Governor Albores announced his own program to partially "implement" the San Andrés accords. While his government was forcibly disbanding the Zapatistas' autonomous municipalities, Albores sent the state congress a proposal for remunicipalization in the current municipios of Altamirano, Las Margaritas, Ocosingo, Chilón, Sabanilla, Salto de Agua, and Tila, all territories which supported the Albores Guillen proposal in the 1998 elections from which the Zapatistas abstained. Albores touted his remunicipalization plan as compliance with the San Andrés accords even though the procedures for remunicipalization pointedly ignored the provisions in the San Andrés accords for indigenous (and Zapatista) initiative and self-determination in designing new municipalities.

Albores also claimed to be granting the recognition of indigenous rights and law by implementing President Zedillo's call, in his September 3, 1996, state of the union message, for legal changes to establish a new relationship between the Mexican state and indigenous communities. Zedillo pointedly made no mention of the San Andrés accords, so angering the Zapatistas that two days later they pulled out of further negotiation with the government.[33] While Zedillo had appropriated the rhetoric of a new social pact with indigenous Mexico, he indicated that federal and state governments would generously design the initiatives—that is, the reforms would emanate from the state, top-down, rather than from the rights of indigenous peoples, from below.

As the Zapatistas deployed nationally to conduct their March 21, 1999, referendum in favor of the San Andrés accords, Albores announced his own proposal for a State of Chiapas Law of Indigenous Rights and Culture. Critics lambasted the Albores proposal as ignoring indigenous collective (as opposed to individual) rights, and for failing to recognize the rights of indigenous pueblos to define themselves, to organize themselves politically, and to govern themselves internally. The initiative, indeed, left it entirely to the state to decide who is indigenous and what rights should be recognized and respected, seemingly rigidifying the existing structures of traditional power holders that the Zapatista rebellion undertook to replace.

These legal initiatives, despite their limitations, have afforded some favorable change in the indigenous experience of the administration of justice. In Chiapas, the Albores government set up a branch of the state public defenders office that employs legally trained indigenous public defenders to help represent indigenous defendants. A state law passed establishing seven Indigenous Courts of Peace and Reconciliation that, for the first time in state history, legally acknowledged the legitimacy of indigenous customary law as a basis for arriving at the resolution of conflict. The law constituting the Indigenous Courts of Peace and Reconciliation established the principle that disputes involving indigenous parties should be heard by indigenous authorities before flowing into the state judicial system, and that reconciliation attained by the indigenous courts would stand before Mexican positive law as legally binding. Reconciliation continues to be an important basis for managing indigenous conflict and has functioned well in some communities. And indigenous courts have retained considerable autonomy, largely because they conduct business in indigenous languages that make their proceedings unintelligible to would-be government observers.[34]

What is interesting to note is that even though the state and federal legal initiatives subverted the very principles of indigenous collective rights and self-determination, they nonetheless were put forward "in the spirit of the San Andrés accords." This suggests to me that the Zapatistas and their sympathizers, while failing to win legal enactment of the San Andrés accords, have nonetheless begun to reshape the agenda for Mexico's future.

I gain perspective on what is happening in Chiapas from developments in neighboring Guatemala, where a vibrant movement of Mayan nationalists, centered around indigenous language and education, is also pressing for legal recognition of indigenous collective rights and culture in the wake of Guatemala's genocidal civil war.[35] Like the Zapatistas in Chiapas, the Maya in Guatemala have moved away from popular and class-based demands and toward those based on identity and rights. Like the Zapatistas, they seek autonomy. Like Mexico's indigenous rights activists, the Guatemalan Maya build upon broad international support and accountability. The pan-Maya activism in Guatemala has drawn fire from skeptics and even charges of essentialism and ethnic fundamentalism. Yet the controversy over Guatemala's Maya movement underscores a fundamentally new reality, that no group in Guatemala can pretend to ignore the Maya as in the past.

The Guatemalan Maya may be said to have advanced in Guatemala what the Zapatistas seek for their country, "Nunca más un México sin nosotros" (Never again a Mexico without us). And to a substantial extent Mexicans have shifted academic, cultural, educational, and research programs toward the Zapatista agenda. In Chiapas, agencies promoting indigenous concerns range from small NGOs such as Maya Women's Power (FOMMA), devoted to assisting Maya women coping with displacement in urban migration, and House of the Writers (Sna Jtz'ibahom, A.C.) a Maya writers' group, to larger, internationally funded NGOs. For example, Chiapas is now the base for the Forum for Sustainable Development (FORO), which promotes sustainable development and ecotourism for the indigenous countryside; for the state-supported Center for Chiapas Indigenous Languages, Art, and Literature (CELALI); and for government programs such as the Ministry for Assistance to Indigenous Pueblos (SEAPI), just to name a few. While such endeavors fall short of the legally protected collective rights and autonomy that the new indigenous movement seeks, they are a step in the right direction.

As the world has changed, so has Mexico. Where the international labor movement has failed to find ways of confronting the daunting transnational mobility of capital and industry, the new indigenous movement has at least succeeded in building transnational networks to stave off and in some cases reverse the forces that threaten indigenous peoples. The new indigenous movement's demand for collective rights and autonomy has been acknowledged by the world. It may yet bear fruit.

CHIAPAS AT AN IMPASSE

As should be clear from the above, the situation in Chiapas is at an impasse. In a way, the stalemate reflects one of the dilemmas of the nation-state in the emerging neoliberal order, namely that state sovereignty is being challenged simultaneously, and in new ways, from below and from above, from within and internationally. The old rules of the game of Mexican statecraft no longer hold. The government does not want to grant indigenous people the special status they demand in a new social pact it cannot afford. In the post–cold war era, Mexico can no longer count on the legitimacy it once held internationally as having offered, with its commitments to both social welfare and private development, a compromise between socialism and capitalism.

Caught in the impasse, the Zapatistas have assumed a stance of intransigent resistance—to the government and political party system that the Zapatistas believe has betrayed the Mexican people, and to the neoliberal policies that the government has pursued. Rebuffed on many fronts, most recently by failure to win constitutional reforms on behalf of indigenous rights and culture, the Zapatistas have assumed a stance of refusal that verges on the dogmatic. As we have noted, the Zapatistas do not permit their followers to accept any government aid, and they have ordered them to abstain from

182 THE NEW INDIGENOUS MOVEMENT

elections. Zapatista communities do not even accept the services of
the Mexican postal system and are busily attempting to set up clinics
and schools totally independent of those of the government.

The Zapatistas also steadfastly oppose the government's plans to
expand free trade. For example, Mexico's President Fox proposed that
Mexico form a free-trade zone to the south with Central American
states and Panama. The so-called Plan Puebla-Panamá (PPP) would
foster transnational industrial development in Mexico's south, taking
advantage of Central American resources and labor. One idea is to set
up a maquiladora industrial corridor along the rail lines connecting
the Isthmus of Tehuantepec to the south along the Pacific coast, and
to the east through Tabasco and northern Chiapas. Another element
is to promote investment in ecotourism, which can "grow" the tourist
sector of the regional economy in development that preserves the
environment. More generally, the plan would develop infrastructure
to expand free trade into the region. While many indigenous people
of Chiapas would welcome the jobs that would accompany
maquiladora and infrastructural projects, most groups fear that the
benefits of the PPP would be concentrated among elites. The
Zapatistas, in concert with many Mexican progressives, have
mounted a bitter campaign against the Plan Puebla-Panama, which
the Zapatistas have declared shall not be allowed in the territories
under their control.[36] So far, the Plan Puebla-Panama has not progressed, not just because of Zapatista opposition, but also because
Mexico's economy has been dragged down by the post-2001 recession
in the United States and lacks the resources to develop the plan.

9 ✦ CONNECTING THE LOCAL TO THE NATIONAL AND THE GLOBAL

If the grimness of the Zapatistas' situation as I have described it in Chiapas seems surprising, this is in part because the Zapatistas have had some of their greatest successes outside of Chiapas.

National and international supporters have helped the Zapatistas weather counterinsurgency and avoid annihilation by the Mexican military. For their part, the Zapatistas have helped bring together activists in a vocal and increasingly effective movement against neoliberal corporate globalization. While undertaking autonomy projects of their own, the Zapatistas have been networking with other disempowered groups to contribute to a plural movement that can both challenge neoliberalism and be independent of it. They are advocating alternative forms of globalization that advance social and political integration and not just economic integration, and urging people to link their efforts in ways that reflect "local" needs.

NETWORKING FOR SURVIVAL

The Zapatistas have been portrayed as the first "postmodern" revolutionaries because of their novel use of the media and Internet.[1] The Zapatistas have used web pages set up by affiliates on the Internet to sustain contacts with national and international sympathizers. A network of organizations that work to support indigenous rights in Chiapas, such as the International Service for Peace (SIPAZ) and the Center for Economic and Political Research on Community Action (CIEPAC), have mobilized e-mail and letter writing to protest at any hint of military action against the Zapatistas.[2] The Zapatistas have convoked international conventions in Chiapas, drawing hundreds of foreign participants that the government did not dare to interfere with because of the negative publicity that it would have drawn. In addition, the Zapatistas have civilian affiliates in the National Convention for Democracy, established at the second Aguascalientes convention in eastern Chiapas in November 1994, which later failed and was replaced by the Zapatista National Liberation Front (FZLN), a political arm of the Zapatista movement that acts with government acquiescence. These organizations reached out to sympathetic groups all over the country, throughout the Americas, and in Europe. Much internationalist support for the Zapatistas is coordinated through the civilian network Enlace Civil (Civic Network, described below) that was set up to help the Zapatistas interface with supporters.

In the United States, the Zapatistas have Chicano backing and assistance from the Chiapas Support Committee in California. An attempt was even made to set up a Zapatista consulate in Chicago. In Spain, Catalans set up a Zapatista consulate in Barcelona. In France, Mme Danielle Mitterand counts herself as one of the most ardent of thousands of Zapatista supporters in Europe. And each year, hundreds of European sympathizers vacation in Chiapas, some to savor the scene, others to witness the conflict firsthand and in many instances to aid the besieged Zapatistas.

International support has been crucial for the Zapatistas' survival. Hundreds of internationalists have participated in the "peace camps" set up by the Fray Bartolomé Human Rights Center and by Enlace Civil as buffers between Zapatista communities and the army in eastern Chiapas where the very presence of observers dampens the likelihood of repression. San Francisco–based NGO Global Exchange has been conducting "reality tours" in Chiapas to educate foreigners thirsty for information about the Zapatistas. Economic resources have flowed from abroad in support of the Zapatista movement. For example, after the massacre at Acteal, the largesse of many well-wishers and sympathizers has developed and transformed the town. Internationally, human rights activists use boycotts and similar tactics, such as the threat of the European Union not to sign trade agreements with Mexico, to pressure the government into observing human rights.

ANTINOMIES OF SOLIDARITY

An irony of international solidarity is that outside support for the Zapatista movement, while crucial to the movement's survival, has to some degree sharpened divisions within indigenous Chiapas while hardening the Zapatista's resolve to break off relationships with the state and federal governments.

The Zapatistas have never enjoyed full support from indigenous Chiapas. Although the rebellion sparked a wave of pride and sympathy within indigenous communities in Chiapas and throughout Mexico, the movement continues to confront the competing religious and independently organized social movements that were at work in the development of the 1994 uprising (see Chapter Three). Divisions persist even in the eastern Chiapas heartland of the rebellion, where some groups still affiliate with the PRI and with other official parties (which the Zapatistas boycott), and where many communities have divided loyalties, even among kin. Indigenous leaders of the Chiapas State Indigenous Peasant Council (CEOIC) and the Indigenous Peoples Independent Front (FIPI) have differed from the Zapatista Committee of Clandestine Indigenous Revolution (CCRI) over issues such as whether to press for regional autonomy in the negotiation of the 1996 San Andrés accords, which the Zapatistas negotiated on their own with representatives of the Zedillo government.[3] Who speaks for the indigenous movement? The Zapatistas? The Catholic Church? Other indigenous organizations? At times all have spoken for the movement, and not in the same voice.

Government concessions have also divided the indigenous movement by creating points of engagement with the indigenous movement while evoking Zapatista rejections. Even though the San Andrés accords were never enacted, both state and federal governments have undertaken to "implement" facets of the accords, as noted in the previous chapter. Indigenous groups willing to meet with the government have won concessions. Thus, for example, after the Mexican Congress and some state governments legislated linguistic rights for indigenous people in legal proceedings, a cadre of indigenous lawyers and translators stepped forward to help implement these rights. Concessions have divided the Zapatistas from their indigenous compatriots and hardened Zapatista rejection of government initiatives—even though the government would not have made them had it not been for the Zapatista rebellion. In 2001, Vicente Fox established a program of Intercultural and Bilingual Education, borrowing the concept from the San Andrés accords and providing the program with some resources. The Zapatistas, who have an autonomous education of their own, refused these resources, as they have shunned all government assistance since the 2001 congressional debacle over the San Andrés accords. But the federal initiative has attracted indigenous educators who once deemed themselves "Zapatistas."

Internationalists who support the Zapatistas are not always aware of the differing currents within the indigenous movement. To their credit, a good number bring political sophistication with them from their own experiences. Yet many outsiders are not aware of the history of the rebellion that this book describes, nor of how international solidarity with the Zapatistas inadvertently sharpens divisions within the indigenous movement or isolates Zapatistas from others in their grassroots communities. Some support only the Zapatistas in respect of the rebels' own decisions to separate themselves from other groups. Most internationalist support for indigenous education in Chiapas, for example, has flowed to Zapatista autonomous schools, but *not* to the official schools that are often in the same communities, forcing many indigenous educators in those schools to turn to the government's Intercultural and Bilingual Education program for resources, even as the Zapatista educators are enabled to do without government support.

Human rights workers from abroad contribute immeasurably to restraining counterinsurgency in Chiapas. But they have not always been aware of how, in the polarized landscape of indigenous Chiapas, "human rights" are often invoked as a political tool against one's enemies. I remember speaking with an educator from a university in the United States who visited Chiapas to train human rights workers in how to manage cases so as to increase the likelihood that they could *not* be settled within the framework of Mexican law. Thus litigants, having exhausted Mexican legal remedies, could appeal to the Inter-American Court of Human Rights in Costa Rica, where human rights suits are more likely to win. This educator had little interest in or understanding of the divisions within indigenous Chiapas from which much litigation arises, or of the tradition of indigenous customary law that seeks to reconcile litigants rather than to adjudge "right" or "wrong" or allow one party to "win."

Such ironies notwithstanding, internationalists and the Zapatistas have worked together not only to keep the Zapatista movement alive in the face of considerable adversity, but also to link the Zapatista cause to broader regional, national, and global concerns.

NEOLIBERALISM AND ANTI-NEOLIBERALISM

The Zapatista leadership[4] argues that free market globalization falsely promises to benefit all through trickle-down economic growth, while actually enriching transnational corporations and financiers at the expense of people and communities around the globe. The Zapatistas call for a different kind of global planning that enhances rather than diminishes social equity in diverse local and regional landscapes by networking people and communities in grassroots initiatives for their own futures. Appealing for "a world in which many worlds fit" (*un mundo donde quepan muchos mundos*), the Zapatistas stand for a globalization that is radically democratic and yet diverse, in which different people work together to find solutions that accommodate the differing world views and needs of their local, regional, and national circumstances.

One of the Zapatistas' most notable successes has been to appeal to others who are being marginalized by globalization, forming alliances with them to protest neoliberalism. The Zapatistas began by convoking an international anti-neoliberal convention in their own territory in 1996—the first of a series of International

Meetings for Humanity and against Neoliberalism (Encuentros Intercontinentales por la Humanidad y Contra el Neoliberalismo). They then joined or supported others to protest neoliberal planning, globally and publicly, at the very places where world financial planners met to promote the free trade agenda—Seattle, Prague, Quebec, Genoa, Evian, and Cancún. Meanwhile, the Zapatistas have urged their allies to implement anti-neoliberal planning in their own countries, and to provide resources and advice for projects that the Zapatistas undertake, autonomously, in southeastern Mexico. The Zapatistas are thus enacting—globally *and* locally—their own contribution to "a world in which many worlds fit."

Just what is the "neoliberalism" to which the Zapatistas and their allies are opposed? Those who speak of "neoliberalism" are generally critics of economic restructuring within countries that began when Ronald Reagan and Margaret Thatcher brought structural adjustment—antilabor policies and reduction in taxes and in government programs—to the United States and the United Kingdom. They also criticize the opening of national economies to unrestricted trade, foreign investment, and economic globalization, often on terms that are unfavorable to countries saddled by debt or reliance on aid.[5] Critics decry the surrendering of economic sovereignty that has allowed corporations to avoid accountability to governments and step out of the framework of national economies. One result is that national governments have lost revenues that could otherwise be used for the public good. It has become increasingly common for corporations to establish off-shore headquarters, where they are sheltered from taxes.[6]

I have used "neoliberalism" sparingly in describing the background to the Zapatista rebellion, preferring to examine concretely what happened in Mexico when petrodollar loans undermined Mexican food security; when international financial institutions forced Mexico to undergo economic restructuring after the 1982 debt crisis; and when the country's leaders embraced policies such as the 1992 agrarian "reform," which permitted privatization of the country's ejidos. In 1994, NAFTA speeded the removal of Mexico's protective trade barriers, including those preventing dumping of subsidized U.S. corn on the Mexican market, and opened the country further to foreign investment. NAFTA thus made the economy more susceptible to international financial booms and busts and capital flight. All of these experiences in Mexico were part of a worldwide movement on the part of financial planners and firms to "liberalize" the economy. As economic globalization unfolded in the two decades before the Zapatista rebellion, critics had analyzed its negative consequences from various perspectives, in anticapitalist critiques from the old and new Left, in human geographers' recognition of changes in industrial organization, in critiques of GATT (the General Agreement on Tariffs and Trade) as it evolved into the World Trade Organization (WTO), and in analyses by organizations such as Global Exchange and Food First of the economic and social injustices accompanying these changes.[7]

As globalization has progressed, the erosion of nations' sovereignty has had high costs with different consequences for people in different places in the global order. In the United States, we have seen cutbacks in welfare; the loss of public funding for health, education, and social services; and the outsourcing of manufacturing and service jobs to lower-wage countries. Europeans have faced the privatization of public services and threats to their benefits and pensions. Developing countries have had to rescind protections to their national industries and agriculture. Labor unions have found their ability to bargain collectively under national law jeopardized. Environmentalists worry about corporations' moving production to parts of the world that lack environmental laws or enforcement. Peasants and small farmers face ruin as markets for their products are flooded by lower-cost, often subsidized imports. Around the world, people without labor safeguards, often women and children, have worked for manufacturers at rock-bottom wages, only to see their jobs moved away when corporations found even cheaper labor elsewhere.

The very diverse character of economic globalization's impact on the world poses a paradox for Zapatistas. Neoliberalism thrives on the existence of multiple (semi)autonomous jurisdictions, so that it can shop around for the lowest labor and transaction costs. Regionalism and local autonomy are policies pursued by neoliberalizing states. There is at the very least a double-edgedness to the Zapatista response in that it risks building the very variation and lack of state-level safeguards that economic globalization thrives upon.

The Zapatista rebellion deserves credit for catalyzing "anti-neoliberalism"—the sense that economic globalization was at the root of the plural and sometimes very different perceptions of marginalization that people had been experiencing. The 1994 rebellion came as official socialism was collapsing and Marxist insurgencies, such as occurred in Guatemala, seemed only to provoke genocidal repression. The Zapatistas offered a less violent rebellion coupled to a new and different hope, one that sought to unify people rather than divide them. The original Zapatista demands for land, housing, education, and health care were not only ones that resonated with people around the world whose lifestyles were threatened or deteriorating due to economic restructuring, but also echoed the past promises of capitalist as well as socialist states. Unlike earlier communist insurgencies, the Zapatistas were not trying to overthrow a government. They were merely asking the Mexican government to live up to its promises. When the Mexican government proved incapable of responding to the legitimate demands expressed by the Zapatistas—demands which were, after all, enshrined in Articles 22 through 27 of the 1948 United Nations Universal Declaration of Human Rights—it gradually became evident that the global system, rather than individual states, was responsible for governments' inability to meet the legitimate demands of citizens.

LAUNCHING THE GLOBAL
ANTI-NEOLIBERAL CAUSE

From around the globe, hundreds of foreign and Mexican sympathizers responded to the Zapatista call to the First Intercontinental Meeting for Humanity and against Neoliberalism in July 1996.

Among them were people with roots in the old Left and New Left movements, labor organizing, Liberation Church and Christian base communities, and in Central American solidarity organizing of the 1970s and 1980s, but also younger people enthusiastic about the Zapatista opening.[8] Making their way past Mexican Army checkpoints, they converged on Oventic, where the Zapatistas had built another of their Aguascalientes convention centers to greet them. Then they split up into working groups, at four other Aguascalientes centers, to analyze neoliberalism and to draft recommendations for resisting it in five thematic areas—politics, economy, media and communications, civil society, and identity. While some in attendance found the discussions unorganized, contentious, ideological, and more like a political rally than a substantive consideration of issues and solutions, many felt energized by the experience. When they reconvened a few days later, they pooled recommendations and planned how to mobilize around them both in their own ways in their home countries and in international alliances. The proceedings of this convention, published by the Zapatistas in a remarkable crimson-bound volume, the *Crónicas Intergalácticas EZLN*, have become a handbook of the international anti-neoliberal movement.

The July 1996 convention identified the various repercussions of globalization experienced by different groups; allowed people to listen to and learn from their differences; and identified a shared strategy for resisting neoliberalism at its highest levels of planning while mobilizing a broad range of politically and socially responsible alternatives.

Encouraged by this first anti-neoliberal congress, and by a similar meeting that the Zapatistas convoked in Spain in 1997, anti-neoliberal alliances began to coordinate public protests against the financial planners of globalization. The protests brought together many different groups—Zapatistas from Chiapas and Mexico, but also internationalists identifying with the Zapatista cause, such as in Italy's Basta Ya! movement; labor organizations fearful of losing workers' rights; advocates for indigenous peoples and human rights; and groups marginalized by unemployment, gender discrimination, and migration. In November 1999 protesters mobilized to derail the Seattle ministerial meeting of the World Trade Organization (WTO) summit meeting in Seattle. Fending off riot police, they blockaded entrances to WTO meeting places to prevent delegates from attending. In the streets, some used carnivalesque theater to critique the WTO. While most protesters used tactics of peaceful civil disobedience, a minority of direct-action anarchists trashed downtown banks and offices linked to financial and corporate globalization. Newspapers and television broadcast images of protestors in the streets and WTO officials attempting to meet behind closed doors to draw up financial plans that would affect millions of people who had no representation in the planning. The WTO summit ended in failure when delegates from the global South refused to consent to a new round of trade agreements.

After Seattle, anti-neoliberal protestors moved on to the meetings of the International Monetary Fund and World Bank in Prague in September 2000. They went to Quebec's April 2001 Summit of the Americas, where secret plans for a hemispheric free-trade zone were being proposed behind heavily fortified barriers protected by Canadian Mounties. This use of police helped the protestors call attention to the antidemocratic character of international financial governance. The movement gained considerable public sympathy in Europe from police atrocities committed against protestors at the July 2001 Genoa meeting of leaders of major industrial nations (G-8). The movement has grown in influence and helped provoke divisions within the World Trade Organization that led to the collapse of efforts to negotiate tariff reductions at Cancún in September 2003.

Anti-neoliberalism is today as fervent a cause as was advocacy for civil and social rights for my generation during the 1960s. Indymedia (www.indymedia.org) is a clearinghouse for activists who travel from one international financial meeting to another to protest globalization. *The Zapatistas: A Rough Guide*—"anti-copyright @ 2000" (spoofing the copyrighted Rough Guide travel books)—was published by Chiapaslink to educate United Kingdom activists about Chiapas and anti-neoliberalism. Chiapas activists are involved with

Global Exchange (in San Francisco), with the Colleciu de Solidaritat amb la Rebellió Zapatista (Barcelona), with the Comitato Chiapas Torino (Turin, Italy), and with many similar organizations around the world.[9]

"The Movement," as some call it, has grown far beyond the initial identification of many of its members with Zapatismo. There are many networks within it. One is ATTAC (Action for a Tobin Tax to Assist the Citizen), which works internationally to advocate taxes on currency speculation, outlawing of tax havens, cancellation of third world debt, and reform of the World Trade Organization.[10] People's Global Action is another global network coordinating direct action and civil disobedience in grassroots activism against inequitable economic globalization and on behalf of social causes. The World Social Forum began in protest of the World Economic Forum meeting in Davos, Switzerland, in 2001. It has been meeting annually at Porto Alegre, Brazil, and in Mumbai, India, as a world-wide consortium of groups and organizations seeking "peace and global social justice," including environmental justice, human rights, and race and gender equity. The Movement, which is as diverse as it is broad, ranges from militant to peaceful in tactics, including street theater, performance art, training to counteract police repression, and research and publication to rebut the claims and arguments of neoliberal think tanks.

The Movement is not without weaknesses, however. Linking people and causes primarily through web sites, it manifests the Internet's variable quality of information. Its antihierarchical values and plural organization make mobilization difficult to focus, and spark dilemmas over who is in charge and what tactics to use. The Movement's broad opposition to global capitalism and capitalism's influence on culture and human relations does not always clarify what mobilization is *for*. Marcos has characterized it as a movement of one big no [to capitalism] and many small yeses. Articulating the yeses is the challenge.[11]

NETWORKING FOR AUTONOMY IN CHIAPAS

For their part, the Zapatistas have been implementing projects of autonomy in the areas they control in Chiapas. We should remember that indigenous communities of Chiapas held a great deal of de facto autonomy for living according to their own custom before the Zapatistas demanded "autonomy" under the law. There is an ideal behind their "autonomy": the prerogative for people everywhere to govern themselves locally and regionally, to control the resources essential for their livelihoods, and to enjoy culturally plural social rights—the "world of many worlds" that the Zapatistas idealize and that they would like to construct for their offspring to protect them from the effects of economic globalization. At the same time, grim realities threaten their projects: surviving military containment and counterinsurgency, especially in the early years; and their own refusal of any involvement with Mexican government, either by co-optation or concession. Furthermore, as a member of the Zapatista Junta of Good Government in Oventic put it to me recently, it will be years before their movement can bring revolutionary change to Mexico as a whole. First the Zapatistas must develop projects[12] that will generate resources to sustain their struggle.

There has been an interesting evolution on the part of Zapatista initiatives for autonomy as the EZLN has gradually realized that it cannot hold the Mexican state accountable for its problematic political system and its unfulfilled social pact. Autonomy was not on the Zapatistas' agenda when they initially held out for reformed politics and a renewed commitment of state resources to social programs. They soon were made to realize that Mexico was too compromised by structural adjustment and economic "modernization"—the race to develop in the image of the global North—to devote resources to indigenous Chiapas. (Under the Agrarian Accords of 1996, for example, the government helped indigenous groups gain legal title to land, but it did not provide them with the resources needed to make the land productive.) With each failed effort to negotiate with the government, for example over indigenous rights, the Zapatistas grew more aware that they would have to act independently of the government. The result has been increasing urgency for Zapatista autonomy projects of greater scope, undertaken without any hope or expectation of government support in collaboration with nongovernment sympathizers through the horizontal, nonhierarchical networks that have become the hallmark of Zapatista anti-neoliberalism. At the same time, with many indigenous people of Chiapas accepting government concessions, Zapatista autonomy, which eschews such engagement, has become more isolated and appears more dogmatic.

Zapatista autonomy projects began at the end of 1995, with the establishment of the first autonomous Zapatista municipalities in areas of strongest Zapatista control.[13] At the outset, the Zapatistas set up autonomous municipalities primarily to afford their followers local governance that they could not expect to experience justly within the framework of Chiapas' official municipal jurisdictions. When the Zapatistas began negotiations with the government that led to the 1996 San Andrés accords for indigenous rights and culture, they continued to emphasize autonomous municipal organization, which they expected would be recognized upon ratification of the accords. In doing so, the Zapatistas set aside proposals for jurisdictions for regional autonomous governance that others within the broader indigenous movement advocated. After the San Andrés accords failed to gain meaningful enactment in the Mexican congressional legislation of the April 25, 2001, "Indigenous Law," the Zapatista autonomous municipalities lost hope for recognition of juridical standing within the framework of the Mexican Constitution. It was not until 2003 that the Zapatistas decided to establish—on their own authority—autonomous jurisdictions for *regional* governance in all the areas of their influence in Chiapas—the "Juntas of Good Government," pointedly named in contrast to "bad" official governance. The Juntas of Good Government are supposed to mediate affairs within and between autonomous municipalities and to promote productive projects in collaboration with national and international civil society. But in attempting to extend authority over regions that sometimes include more indigenous non-Zapatistas than Zapatistas, the Juntas of Good Government have sometimes found themselves in conflict with indigenous communities and their elected authorities.[14]

This evolution has also been apparent in Zapatista autonomous education. With the collaboration of sympathetic educators, the Zapatistas have been developing a program of autonomous elementary education with culturally appropriate curriculum in native languages taught by indigenous educators. Although the Zapatistas refuse government resources, they initially worked with government-funded educators in research institutions and in the officially tolerated independent teachers' unions to design programs that would have received federal funding *if* the San Andrés accords had been implemented. This possibility has now been dashed, making networking with sympathetic Mexicans and foreigners for material and intellectual support to build and supply schools and provide them with volunteer teachers far more essential. But aid channeled to Zapatista schools, and not to schools attended by non-Zapatista children, has led to invidious comparison. Ironically, the heavy involvement of volunteer educators, who do not speak indigenous languages, has brought about ever greater use of Spanish (rather than in Mayan) language in Zapatista education, for example at Oventic, where the Zapatista secondary school curriculum is being taught primarily in Spanish rather than bilingually.

In other respects, the implementation of autonomy and resistance has been as varied as the local and regional realities of the Zapatista struggle. While the Zapatistas have set up their own "autonomous" jurisdictions, administering local governance and justice under *usos y costumbres*—traditional/customary practices of indigenous communities—these jurisdictions vary from region to region, shaped by the complex background discussed in this book as well as by militarization and counterinsurgency, especially since 1994, and the growing tensions between Zapatistas and non-Zapatistas.

AGROECOLOGY AND RESISTANCE

In areas with substantial Zapatista followings, it has been possible for autonomy to build on the collaboration of adjacent Zapatista communities in local and regional governance. In the Chol area near Palenque, the Municipio de Trabajo (Municipality of Work) has been implementing agroecology as its project of autonomy and resistance, first on its own, later in collaboration with two neighboring Zapatista communities, and more recently in extension to all thirteen of the autonomous municipalities that make up the Zapatista Northern Region under the authority of the Junta of Good Government located in the village of Roberto Barrios.[15] Agroecology is the approach to sustainable and preferably organic agriculture promoted by progressive agronomists in the Americas after farm organizations from the Americas and Europe issued their 1992 "Managua Declaration."

Like many communities settled in the lowlands by milpa farmers of an earlier generation, the Municipio de Trabajo's corn yields have declined since the government removed its support for the fertilizers and herbicides needed to avoid fallowing. NAFTA went into effect, the government phased out price supports for corn, and heavily subsidized United States corn began to swamp the markets. Local farmers found that their corn harvests sold for less than what they cost to produce. Their livelihoods were also disrupted by militarization in the wake of the rebellion. After NAFTA, families were producing only about one-third of the corn they needed to subsist. The Zapatistas realized they had to do something to reinvigorate the milpa agriculture if they wanted to resist the forces of neoliberalism pushing youth out of the countryside into migration or dishonest pursuits.[16] Their hoped-for solution was agroecology.

Following the Zapatista principle of egalitarian self-governance, the community appointed a group of its young adults, mostly men, to serve as *promotores de agro ecología*—agroecology advocates/agents— and another group, mostly young women, as *promotores de salud* (health workers), as well as a group of *promotores de educación* (primary educators), charging all three groups to implement their initiatives without aid from the national state.[17] The agroecology promotores were also asked to find farming techniques that use no inputs from the marketplace, chemical or otherwise. The goal was to develop sustainable production adequate for people's subsistence and without any reliance on neoliberal markets—thus combining autonomy with resistance.

The agroecology promotores turned to the Civic Network (Enlace Civil) for technical advice. Enlace Civil, A.C. was formed in 1996 at the request of the Zapatista anti-neoliberal convention as an organization to link Zapatista communities to experts in national and international civil society who could advise Zapatista projects of health, education, production, and commercialization—outside the framework of neoliberal or government institutions.[18] Enlace Civil found two agronomists with training from the Universidad Autónoma Chapingo who recommended that the Municipio de Trabajo farmers introduce *Mucuna* (the velvet bean, also known in tropical Mexico and Central America as *frijol Nescafé* because of its common use as a coffee substitute) into their cornfields. The *Mucuna* vine fixes and adds nitrogen and other nutrients to the soil. Under tropical conditions it forms a dense mass of vine that can be left in place after the corn is harvested. Later, the vines are cut down, but not to the ground, and are left in place as erosion-preventing mulch through which corn grows in the next season's milpa.[19] *Mucuna* and mulching improved Municipio de Trabajo milpa yields and allowed farmers to intensify cultivation without fallowing, without having to depend on fertilizers and herbicides or off-farm income to purchase them, and perhaps without the sharp class divisions resulting from such input dependency in Apas (Chapter Four).

If Municipio de Trabajo milpa farming appears to have become much more self-sufficient and sustainable, it also drew strength from networking, initially with advisors from Enlace Civil, and subsequently with other local projects and other Zapatista communities. The agroecology promotores of the Municipio de Trabajo began to hold grassroots end-of-season meetings to describe their results to others in their own and neighboring Zapatista communities. Some adjacent communities decided to join in the experiment, appointing agroecology promotores of their own. Health workers argued that proper nutrition depended on the innovations in farming and that they, too, should be trained in agroecology. The communities' promotores for education, who were developing curriculum for autonomous education, proposed that primary school children study milpa yields as a way to learn arithmetic. The autonomy projects in health, education, and agroecology thus began to work together synergistically.

The Municipio de Trabajo invited outsiders from Enlace Civil to attend their end-of-year meetings, for which they prepared posters analyzing the results of their various autonomous experiments. In the spirit of the Zapatista principle that leaders should obey their followers, the promotores asked the technical experts to listen and learn from the communities' experiences, and to offer advice only at the very end of each annual meeting. Ultimately, representatives from the Municipio de Trabajo traveled to Oventic in the highlands of Chiapas, one of the places where Zapatistas periodically gather to share experiences in projects for autonomy and resistance.

By 2004, the Municipio de Trabajo promotores had extended both the scope and geographic reach of their project. They were making use of land donated to them for a demonstration center where they were training a new generation of promotores from many more of the region's Zapatista communities. They planned to involve all thirteen of the northern region's Zapatista municipalities. They were developing techniques to raise sheep, chickens, and pigs using organic feeds grown locally. They were also experimenting with organic horticulture of vegetables. Twenty-six enthusiastic and very dedicated young promotores, including three women, were devoting three days per month to training in an ongoing seminar, which the first generation of promotores taught. The project was coordinated with initiatives in health and nutrition for the entire Zapatista northern region through its Junta of Good Government.

Although the Municipio de Trabajo experiment marks an apparent success, use of the *Mucuna* bean should not be thought of as a magic cure for all tropical agriculture. *Mucuna* does not grow in the tropical highlands and may not work as well in other lowland areas where the soils are less volcanic than in the Chol area. Nonetheless, other agroecological approaches can make cultivation more sustainable elsewhere, and there are certainly lessons to learn from the synergy among the Municipio de Trabajo's experiments in agroecology, education, and health and with the initiatives of neighboring Zapatista communities. Regional coordination through the Junta of Good Government is also notable.

THE MUT VITZ ORGANIC COFFEE COOPERATIVE

Although Zapatista authority has become established in many parts of Chiapas, in many regions, especially the central highlands, the Zapatistas are forced to compete with political parties, the national government, and even the Catholic Church for indigenous loyalties. "Autonomous" Zapatista jurisdictions often consist of territorially disconnected hamlets, family clusters, and even individual households of Zapatistas dispersed among groups of different persuasion— requiring different implementations of autonomy and resistance. Such is the landscape in which the Zapatistas have launched a very differently organized autonomous project, Mut Vitz (Bird Mountain), a cooperative that produces organic coffee and honey for export to niche markets in France, Germany, Italy, Switzerland, Spain, and the United States through international solidarity groups.[20]

Mut Vitz formed in 1997 as a Zapatista group in the western part of the highlands of Chiapas. The Mut Vitz group split from another coffee-producing organization that would not agree to the Zapatista dictum of accepting no government aid. Initially, there were 500 producers in Mut Vitz, spread over the official municipalities of Bochil, El Bosque, Jitotol, and Simojovel, as well as San Andrés Larraínzar and San Pedro Chenalhó, just to the east. This was the region where CIOAC and the Union of Unions mobilized resident workers to take over coffee fincas in the late 1970s and 1980s, and where earlier production cooperatives such as Kipaltik (see page 77) had formed before the rebellion. In 2004 there were 705 producers, some of them isolated families or clusters of families, others in settlements, all self-affiliated to the Zapatista autonomous municipalities of 16 de Febrero, San Juan de la Libertad, San Andrés Sacamch'en de los Pobres, as well as in the municipalities of Chalchihuitán and Magdalenas. If this sounds complex, it is because the Mut Vitz region is one of multiple competing and overlapping official and Zapatista jurisdictions, divided by competing politics and religion and troubled by paramilitary counterinsurgency. The members of Mut Vitz thus have no single community to organize their cultural and social life other than their cooperative and the overarching Zapatista Junta of Good Government of Oventic.

The cooperative has fifty promotores who train members in agro-ecological improvements to organic coffee cultivation. In an informative video, *The Strength of the Indigenous People of Mut Vitz* (Chiapas Media Project 2000a), José, one of these promotores, demonstrates these approaches. These include planting and nurturing coffee seedlings in nurseries and preparation of terraces where the coffee will be transplanted using wooden slats to shore up the soil and prevent erosion. Additionally, the co-op members use composting to enrich the soil, to which they apply ash to control pests. They transport seedlings in banana leaves to protect them en route to planting. During the growing season, they use mulching to control weeds and protect the soil from erosion. The video discusses which trees are best for shading the coffee and illustrates harvesting and drying of the crop and sorting by quality. The coffee producers use simple, traditional farming equipment—machete, digging stick, hoe, and tumpline for carrying loads—together with horticultural techniques, some customary and others not (e.g., mulching). The organic production exemplifies how traditional farming techniques can both serve and be modified in Zapatista practice, while at the same time involving all family members, women and children as well as men, validating their contribution to production.

Mut Vitz organized formally as a commercial cooperative and obtained an official coffee export permit in 1998. The cooperative has a governing board whose members serve for three-year terms. When I visited the cooperative in July 2004, the board members told me that they are responsible for contracting for organic certification, supplied by CERTIMEX, a Mexican firm that inspects members' plots annually to assure compliance to organic standards. The governing council also arranges for shipping the export-quality coffee, first to Chiapa de Corzo for hulling and cleaning as green coffee, then to Veracruz for export. They arrange for customs, insurance, and other documentation needed for export, including certification for anti-bioterrorism now being required by the United States Food and Drug Administration for imports. They ship the lesser-quality coffee to San Cristóbal de Las Casas and Mexico City for sale in Mut Vitz stores, packaged in small cloth bags made by women in members' families.

Mut Vitz is notable not only for its agroecological organic production but also for its marketing arrangements with international solidarity groups. These groups, upon receiving the coffee, by contract pay a deposit equivalent to the local Chiapas harvest price, plus a premium after sale of the coffee abroad and adjustment for shipping and processing costs. It should be pointed out, however, that the marketing arrangement leaves the cooperative members with all the risks of production, including crop failure or other unforeseen problems. These arrangements are similar to the fair trade that avoids middlemen and benefits certified farmer coops globally, including coffee-producing coops in Chiapas. Yet the Mut Vitz marketing rewards cooperative members with especially favorable prices for their crop, for example, U.S.$0.85 per pound in 1999 as compared to the U.S.$0.56 per pound that other Chiapas producers were receiving (when New York spot prices for coffee were about U.S.$0.99 per pound). At that time, foreign buyers contracted for 500 sacks of "gold"-grade coffee; as of 2003, the contracts had expanded tenfold, yielding U.S.$0.82 per pound as compared to the U.S.$0.35 that

Chiapas producers were receiving from local buyers (when New York spot prices had dropped to about U.S.$0.49 per pound).[21] The foreign buyers have thus not only expanded their market; they have afforded some protection against the fall of coffee prices worldwide as a result of new production from Vietnam. The groups marketing Mut Vitz coffee abroad also provide the cooperative with extraordinary linkages to the global anti-neoliberal cause, compensating for the lack of an uncontested territorial base.

In France, for example, the marketing of Mut Vitz coffee has been undertaken by the Confédération Nationale du Travail (CNT), an anarcho-syndicalist union with long-standing ties to similar labor organizations in Europe, the Americas, and around the world.[22] The CNT embraced Mut Vitz as one of several projects in support of the Chiapas Zapatistas and as part of a broad range of international solidarity activities. Within the CNT, the Chiapas support group regularly visits Chiapas, each year bringing financial and material support to three Zapatista communities. When the Zapatistas marched to Mexico City in February 2001 to press the congress to enact constitutional reforms on behalf of indigenous rights and culture, members of the CNT traveled to Mexico to join the Zapatista caravan. After the congress failed to honor the San Andrés accords, CNT members in Paris protested on May 10, 2001, by unfurling two twenty-five-meter banners from the second level of the Eiffel Tower proclaiming "ZAPATA VIVE!" (ZAPATA LIVES!). Last year (2003), members traveled to Cancún to participate in the Zapatista-endorsed protests of the WTO ministerial summit there. These activities are but some among many other projects that the CNT has undertaken or is planning in international solidarity, for example with unionized workers in Colombia, peasant unions in Bolivia, anti-authoritarian groups in Argentina, and in support of undocumented immigrants—in addition to its primary emphasis on social and economic justice for workers in France and elsewhere in Europe.

Another dimension of the Mut Vitz solidarity story is the video itself, *The Strength of the Indigenous People of Mut Vitz*. The video is one of several distributed by the Chicago-based Chiapas Media Project, which works in collaboration with the Zapatista autonomous communities in different parts of Chiapas to train indigenous people to produce videos of their own, narrated in native language with English subtitles that the distributors add. Some of these videos are also about productive projects, for example *Women United* (*Mujeres Unidas*), depicting women's collective farming in the autonomous municipality of 17th of November. Others deal with cultural projects (e.g., *The Healer in the Indigenous Communities of the Highlands of Chiapas*). *Education in Resistance* (*Te Nop Jun Yu'un Pobrehetic*) documents one community's autonomous elementary education program. The Chiapas Media Project provides video cameras, editing equipment and computers, and the training to use them. Producing their own videos, the Zapatistas are not simply demonstrating autonomy projects to one another. They are empowering themselves, and they are publicizing Zapatista solidarity projects to the world of those sympathetic to their anti-neoliberal alternatives.

Mut Vitz and the Municipio de Trabajo sound like success stories. Indeed, they have many appealing aspects. Yet the projects need to be interpreted with caution. A broader assessment would scrutinize issues of social and economic equity across whole landscapes, not just anecdotal cases. Who participates in each project, and who does not? What about people who are excluded or who drop out? How fair is it to peasant producers generally for politicized groups in Europe and the United States to reward just the Zapatista cultivators with higher than other fair-trade prices as an expression of solidarity? And what about producers who do not have access to those niches? In the case of Mut Vitz, which depends on special marketing niches, how much power do producers have vis-à-vis foreign buyers, however well-intentioned they may be? Finally, can projects such as these, which build upon collective efforts and solidarity, withstand the test of time without suffering from internal frictions? To their credit, the Zapatista Juntas of Good Government have begun to address some of these concerns through regional planning of productive projects and by tithing the aid they receive and the profits they make to benefit other communities that do not have them.

I do not want this discussion of Zapatista productive projects to leave the impression that all are agroecological, or that only the Zapatistas are undertaking such production. Mexican and foreign internationalists have encouraged sustainability, which also resonates with the image of indigenous people living in harmony with nature. ISMAM and other indigenous cooperatives began experimenting with agroecological approaches many years before the Zapatista rebellion (see Chapter Seven). Other non-Zapatista communities are developing agroecological production in collaboration with non-government organizations such as the Chiapas-based Forum for Sustainable Development (FORO).[23] The Zapatistas, many of whom embraced non-agroecological technical inputs for agriculture in the heyday of the Union of Unions and other organizations, are open to varieties of technical intervention and experiment, so long as they minimize vulnerability to unfair markets and involve no aid from a government seen as corrupt. Unfortunately, much indigenous production in Chiapas, by Zapatistas as well as non-Zapatistas, continues to use chemical inputs and to tap the environment unsustainably. In the eastern lowlands of Chiapas, for example, Zapatistas and non-Zapatistas are equally involved in timbering rare caoba and cedar hardwoods, which are reportedly selling like hot cakes. The Zapatista Juntas of Good Government are trying to rein in the timbering.[24]

Whatever Chiapas' Zapatistas manage to accomplish by way of autonomy projects, there seems to be little prospect of Mexico veering from its commitment to restructuring and globalization. Many Mexicans are themselves caught up in the world of neoliberalism and ill-founded hopes of competing in a rigged global economy. Some of those who initially agreed with the Zapatista demands now think the Zapatista refusal to engage the government in any way lessens the movement's relevance to the rest of Mexico. Except for La Jornada, the Mexican press pays hardly any attention to the Zapatista movement now. Bookstores that I visited in Mexico City recently have few if any titles relevant to the rebellion. At this point, the best that the

Zapatistas and their sympathizers can hope for on the local and national scene is that they will be granted the autonomy to shield their homelands from being swamped in the current wave of neoliberalism and illusions of benefits from corporate globalization.

Meanwhile, members of Zapatista communities themselves have begun to migrate into undocumented wage work north of the U.S.–Mexico border, following in the footsteps of hundreds of thousands of peasant and indigenous people from north and central Mexico. Between 1995 and 2003, Chiapas moved from twenty-seventh to eleventh Mexican state in migrants' remittances, which grew from $23 million to $355 million.[25] To date, no research that I know of has documented how this development has involved the Zapatistas. Anecdotal reports suggest that Zapatistas are sending remittances from their work in U.S. tomato and strawberry fields back to Chiapas to support autonomy projects—ironic in that the migrants are simultaneously participating in yet resisting economic globalization.

THE SOCIAL INEQUITIES OF AGRICULTURAL FREE TRADE

For most of the past century, agriculture held special status in international trade regulation, which did not interfere with countries' efforts to support and protect domestic food production by means of subsidies, tariffs, and import restrictions. Agriculture was exempt from the trade agreements developed over the years by the General Agreement on Tariffs and Trade (GATT), even during the 1980s, when the United States and Europe began to push for liberalization of global markets for their agricultural exports. The inclusion of agriculture in free-trade agreements such as NAFTA, and in the 1994 Agreement on Agriculture, negotiated by the World Trade Organization as it evolved out of GATT in the early 1990s, thus marked a historic break from policies of national sovereignty over food-trade policy and farming.

The Zapatistas have repeatedly attacked NAFTA. At their antineoliberal convocations they have argued that "free-trade" agreements, which allow heavily subsidized U.S. corn to enter Mexico, signal the death knell for Mexico's indigenous peasantry. They have underscored that agricultural free trade, together with Mexico's abrogation of agrarian reform and opening of the country-side to foreign investment, surrenders not only *economic* sovereignty but also the country's constitutionally grounded *social* sovereignty— the subordination of economic rights to social rights, as in the treatment of Mexico's peasantry as a "social sector" with the right to agrarian reform.

This emphasis on the social as well as economic costs of agricul-tural globalization is echoed and reinforced in what has become a worldwide movement of rural small farmers and peasant producers to reverse agricultural free-trade policies and to embrace policies of national food sovereignty.[26] As GATT began to consider agricultural free trade, small farmers and peasants from Central America, the Caribbean, Europe, Canada, and the United States met at Managua in 1992, arguing that neoliberal policies damage small farmers around the world. Their "Managua Declaration," which advocated sustain-able agriculture and a bill of rights for rural small producers, was taken up by a broader coalition of small farmers and peasants world-wide, Via Campesina. Via Campesina helped mobilize small producers to protest meetings of GATT in Geneva in 1993 and of the WTO in Geneva in 1998, in Seattle in 1999, and in Cancún in 2003. Pointing out that rural people who still make up half of the world's population depend on agriculture for their livelihoods, Via Campesina advocates the removal of agriculture from the purview of WTO and the achievement of national food sovereignty and small farmers' and peasants' rights to land and natural resources.

One of the accomplishments of the anti-neoliberal critique of agricultural globalization is that some of the planners of economic governance now recognize the social inequities that global economic policy has brought to the developing world. The recognition is reflected in former World Bank economist and Nobel laureate Joseph Stiglitz's critique of global economic policy in *Globalization and Its Discontents*, and in the argument of World Bank chief econo-mist Nicholas Stern that rich-country agricultural subsidies are hypocritical and deeply damaging to the developing world. In 2002, the World Bank and other global planners took a similar position arguing that U.S., European, and Japanese agricultural subsidies totaling $350 billion per year are "crippling Africa's chance to export its way out of poverty."[27]

The essence of this critique is that agricultural "free trade" has proved to be economically unfair and socially inequitable. It is unfair because the terms of trade are unequal, given that developing or emerging economies do not have buying power or bargaining power comparable to that of the transnational firms that dominate agricultural trade. It is also unfair because these countries lack the resources to subsidize agriculture the way Europe and the United States have done for decades, and because the terms of structural adjustment loans for "development" have required countries to remove what limited farm protections and food-price supports they once had. It is also socially inequitable, especially given the heavy yoke of debt that developing countries are continuing to bear under structural adjustment, which saps national budgets and drains social programs of their budgets and promise. Global institutions themselves, such as the World Bank, have proposed some remedies. However, these have been limited to the partial alleviation of foreign debt for some countries and reduction or elimination of first-world subsidies. In other words, they are calling for "fairer" global agricultural policies, but do not advocate a retreat from the liberalization of agricultural markets, nor do they support local self-sufficiency.

First-world agricultural subsidies became a major issue of contention in G-8 (Group of Eight) summit conferences of the leading industrial nations and at the WTO ministerial conference at Cancún in September 2003. At the Cancún meeting, opposition to first-world agricultural subsidies was taken up *within* the WTO by representatives of twenty-one developing countries whose economies depend substantially on agricultural exports. For example, countries producing cotton cannot compete with U.S. growers who receive direct government payments to compensate for the low prices at which transnational companies buy cotton for export. Outside the conference, Mexican and international antiglobalization activists mobilized by Via Campesina and other anti-neoliberal groups protested, joined by a delegation of grassroots Zapatistas who greeted the protestors with messages of support from Comandantes Esther and David and Subcomandante Marcos.[28] The meeting ended with the collapse of efforts to negotiate new international tariff reductions as terms of free trade.

Was collapse of the WTO Cancún talks a triumph or a pyrrhic victory for anti-neoliberal forces? Via Campesina claimed the outcome as a victory, but also recognized that the arguments for fairer trade do not necessarily undermine the tenets of free trade. Fairer terms for agricultural exports from developing countries do not mitigate the inherent risk for rural societies of economies that rely on cash crops sold into global markets. One has only to reflect upon how many rural producers of Chiapas and coffee-growing regions worldwide have suffered from the collapse of coffee markets since 1989 to see the limits of "development" strategies that depend on primary-commodity exports. Nonetheless, viewed through the lens of the collaborative alliances fighting for cotton exporters' rights to demand fair first-world tariffs, the outcome must be seen as a success for the pluralistic resistance to the inequities of globalization that the Zapatistas decried and resisted. On the other hand, the WTO seems to be moving forward with agricultural trade liberalization, having worked out a framework for reducing some first-world agricultural subsidies at talks completed in Geneva in July 2004. Thus, while WTO negotiators managed to revive the negotiations, at least symbolically, it remains to be seen whether subsidies will indeed be eliminated, whether this will end the various government supports that now allow U.S. and EU commodities to be dumped (sold at less than the cost of production) on world markets, and whether the strategy of seeking fairer markets for their exports will benefit smaller growers, or only elites, in developing countries.[29]

It is perhaps best to consider the outcome at Cancún in tactical terms as a successful alliance of the relatively weak against the relatively powerful within the emerging global order. At the very minimum, the opponents of agricultural globalization have mobilized criticism that has begun to be echoed in the concerns of some planners of globalization. It remains to be seen whether the indigenous peoples of Chiapas can forge durable alliances with groups elsewhere to negotiate in global markets over forests and agrarian resources and over cultural and intellectual property rights—and above all to secure social equity for themselves.

CHALLENGES FOR GLOBAL RESISTANCE MOVEMENTS

Observers of the Mexican scene are beginning to reassess the role of civil society nongovernment organizations (CSOs or NGOs) within the anti-neoliberal movement. In a recent critique of *altermundismo* (the movement for an alternative world) from a Mexican perspective, Luis Hernández Navarro writes that the movement has failed to persuade the large number of Mexicans who are unhappy with the country's policies to mobilize against free trade. While protestors helped halt the WTO trade talks at Cancún, Hernández notes that Cancún had few broader repercussions within Mexican society. One of the reasons, he argues, is that although NGOs play a significant role in alternmundismo, they are an equivocal force for generalizing the movement. NGOs may have impressive credentials and infrastructure for assessment of public policy and multilateral institutions, but most lack a grassroots base or broad membership and thus have limited capacity—especially in Mexico, but also elsewhere—to organize social protest. They are "colonels without troops" *(coroneles sin tropa)* who claim greater capacity to represent civil society than they deserve.[30]

Nongovernment and civil society organizations such as Greenpeace, Global Exchange, the Institute for Food and Development Policy (Food First), Oxfam, and many others have generally developed as autonomous actors voicing their own concerns— human rights, the environment, women's empowerment, economic and social justice—often through highly intelligent and well-informed analysis of public policy issues. When issues intersect with those of grassroots organizations, CSOs and NGOs sometimes act as the intellectual arm of grassroots movements. Some of these NGOs "accompany" grassroots movements by way of active support (e.g., Global Exchange helped establish peace camps in Chiapas). Others provide technical assistance for sustainable food production. Still others support economic projects such as organic coffee growing and marketing, or send in-kind donations of clothes or school supplies. Many work to amplify the voices of the grassroots and sharpen the critique of neoliberalism and the analysis of alternative options.

The tension between "acting in their own right" and "accompanying" opens CSOs and NGOs to concerns about accountability on the part of grassroots groups. For example, there is a growing sense that some organizations are not directly necessary to grassroots organizations of the anti-neoliberal movement because the latter have developed the capacity to act on their own to develop alternatives to economic globalization—without the sponsorship of NGOs or civil society institutions to "represent" them, as in the past. If NGOs played a central role in the world's "activism beyond borders" of recent decades (Keck and Sikkink 1998), the grassroots groups they have been representing have now begun to author activism themselves.

This change marks a general shift in power relationships within solidarity networks from the twentieth to the twenty-first centuries. Initially, solidarity flowed primarily from first-world groups with economic resources and some political clout that took the lead in helping the third-world oppressed and needy. As economic restructuring drained social programs, developing countries' civil societies joined first-world groups in extending solidarity to the marginalized. The more recent anti-neoliberal movement generally has practiced a more balanced "global solidarity"[31] in which the parties involved listen to and learn from one another as they build more reciprocal relationships between providers and recipients of support. Now, marginalized groups are beginning to insist upon solidarity relationships on their own terms.

For example, the charter for the Zapatista regional Juntas of Good Government, announced in August 2003, asserts just such control over solidarity relationships. According to Marcos, the Juntas must act to prevent misguided if well-intentioned solidarity efforts that have sent the Zapatistas old and nonfunctional computers, used clothing not suitable for rural Chiapas, and outdated medicines; or that have set up libraries in communities that more urgently need safe drinking water; or that establish herb gardens where schools are needed. The problem with NGOs and international organizations that have (mis)guided such aid is that "they decide on what's needed without even consulting our communities, imposing not only specific projects but their schedule and manner of implementation."[32] The Zapatista leadership has declared that Zapatista communities will no longer accept aid, assessment, or collaboration in research except at the initiative of the Juntas, which have (among other things) the responsibility to:

> receive and guide national and international civil society access to communities [for] setting up productive projects, installing peace camps, undertaking research (note: which must benefit communities), or for any other activity permitted in rebel communities....
>
> National and international civil society donations and aid to particular persons, communities, or autonomous municipalities will no longer be allowed. The Junta of Good Government will determine where assistance should go, based on evaluation of community needs.[33]

Another, more troubling aspect of the displacement of NGOs within the global solidarity movement is a growing perception that NGOs are beholden to the very institutions, practices, and ideology of neoliberalism that they are supposed to help marginalized groups resist. Some radical critics even argue that neoliberal planners, as they effected structural adjustment, have used and even funded NGOs to help mitigate the unrest caused by the loss of social programs—making NGOs the "community face" of neoliberalism. Thus some conservation organizations (World Wildlife Fund, the Nature Conservancy, and Conservation International) have been criticized as beholden to the corporations, governments, and institutions that fund them to the extent of neglecting the indigenous peoples whose territories they are supposed to protect. In Chiapas, Zapatista sympathizers have accused Conservation International (CI) of collaborating with USAID and the Inter-American Development Bank in ecotourism in the Montes Azules Bioreserve while advocating that nearby Zapatista communities be dislodged from the reserve, allegations that CI denies.[34]

Other analysts, who have more understanding of the structural positioning of NGOs between powerful institutions and less powerful people, have pointed out that NGOs helping marginalized groups resist economic globalization inevitably have to represent the very forces they are resisting, even as they "represent" those they attempt to aid. This is a dilemma of civil society in solidarity relationships more generally. For example, as church groups sponsored Central American refugees for sanctuary in the United States during the Reagan years, the sponsors not only had to develop expertise in immigration law; they had to "represent" the law by advising refugees how to fight deportation and by selecting which deportation orders to litigate. The sanctuary activists helped refugees win important court protections of their status, but their activities inevitably involved them in gatekeeping litigation and, ironically, in "enforcing" the very immigration laws they were contesting. In effect, NGOs end up working as much to reform as they do to resist.[35]

The jeopardy to global solidarity movements of condemning NGOs as two-faced is the risk of breaking down the collaboration across groups of very different positioning in the global order that has worked so well since the Zapatista rebellion. There will always be tension between reformers and rebels, between those who try to modify the dominant system to make it more equitable and those who want to replace the system altogether. Additionally, even those first-world NGOs that want systemic change, not mere reform, must often speak in terms understood in their own societies, such as the liberal discourse of human rights, in order to give effective political support against the repression of grassroots movements. The Zapatistas themselves began with demands for Mexico's reform and have only recently taken their current position of intransigent resistance. My personal view is that more equitable globalization will advance further if reformers and more radical critics of neoliberalism work together, in Mexico and elsewhere, to bring the public into the middle of their cause—as they quite successfully did when mobilizing people around the world on February 15, 2003, to protest the onset of the U.S. war on Iraq.

Another challenge for global solidarity movements is the growth of exclusionary religious movements around the globe. Religious organizations (along with NGOs and other institutions of civil society) have in general gained influence by providing the social services that neoliberal structural adjustment has prevented states from undertaking. We see this in the United States where faith-based social programs are on the rise. We see it in Egypt and other states of the Islamic world where religious groups are providing schooling, clinics, and a wide variety of social assistance and political leadership no longer adequately provided by state institutions or authorities. Faith-based programs threaten the fundamental secular principle that social rights should be available to all, regardless of religious affiliation. They thus undermine the social justice to which the anti-neoliberal movement aspires. To their credit, the Zapatistas have been steadfastly secular and inclusive in their vision and action, standing above religious difference in building their movement at the grass roots and through transnational networking.

The most serious challenge for the global resistance movements is the scope and power of neoliberal globalization, which, as I have pointed out, benefits from regionalism and the ability to shop in a diverse world for the lowest labor and transaction costs. Neoliberalism thrives on the ideology of individual free choice, which translates into freedom for corporate "individuals" to seek profits unfettered by restrictions to free trade. At the same time, neoliberal ideology fosters the illusion that we are, as individuals, all free to choose the consumption that suits our individual values and identities, notwithstanding the reality that many people cannot afford even basic necessities.

There are some within the antiglobalization movement who argue, as many have argued at times of crisis in the past, that impoverishment brought by transnational corporate expansion is undermining the world's capacity to consume the products of capitalist production. They argue that capitalism is reaching a crisis under neoliberal expansion—and that social protest is growing to a critical mass. Yet faced with social unrest in states weakened by economic restructuring, neoliberal planners have proved adept at promoting "democracy" and "human rights" to bolster states' legitimacy, while pressing states to adhere to the "rule of law" in transnational capital exchange.

If mainstream Mexico has proven difficult for *altermundistas* to mobilize against global economic liberalism, this is in part because neoliberal planners can claim to have shepherded the country into an era of free elections and principles of rights. Although Mexican economic globalization has brought deepening poverty for many, it has brought conspicuous wealth for some, along with the incredible emporium of world goods that have flooded into spreading transnational malls, Wal-Marts, Sam's Clubs, and fast-food chains, holding much of the public in its thrall. The lure of consumerism deeply affects rural communities, where villagers often overstretch their means to buy televisions, VCRs, refrigerators, blenders, stylish clothing, and sneakers.

Capitalism promises much, but in its neoliberal form is not delivering. In pursuit of the bottom line for transnational corporations, neoliberalism continues to search for the bottom in the wages paid to workers and in taxes and public programs. To their credit, some global planners have begun to consider the need for alleviating third-world debt, for taxing offshore financial transactions to tap revenues for the public good, and for arresting the erosion of social services. But these steps seem designed to treat the symptoms rather than the causes of growing world inequities, which really require redressing the overwhelming economic power of transnational corporations and the political power of neoliberal ideology.

Today, everyone wants a life with health care, education, food, a decent job, and the ability to work without migrating, and a system of just governance that is representative of ordinary people and responsive to their needs. These are at their foundation the goals that the Zapatistas are seeking in their efforts to build an alternative to neoliberalism for themselves and for the world.

NOTES

INTRODUCTION

1 The survey was conducted by Lourdes Arizpe and her colleagues (Arizpe, Paz, and Velázquez, 1993).

2 From *Declaración de la Selva Lacandona* emitted by the Comandancia General del EZLN from the Selva Lacandona, Chiapas, Mexico, on December 31, 1993.

3 e.g., Arvide (1994); Guillén (1994); Méndez and Cano (1994); Romero (1994).

4 Indigenous people generally speak one of the native American languages as their first tongue, though many also learn some Spanish. Many indigenous people identify themselves as members of ethnic communities that were classified as "Indian" rather than "Spanish" or mestizo (mixed race) under the period of colonial rule. There are also indigenous people who lack such links to specific communities because they have been diasporic throughout history. Indigenous people often experience discrimination and subordination at the hands of non-indigenous Mexicans.

5 See Williams (1986) on Central American radical movements as responding to peasants' displacement into marginal lands by developing commercial agriculture and ranching oriented to exports.

CHAPTER ONE: CHIAPAS AND MEXICO

1 *Tiempo*, February 4, 1992, pg. 2.

2 Benjamin (1989).

3 See Pick, et al. (1989) for a convenient compilation of census and statistical data for Mexico in 1980.

4 The statistical maps in this book use Mexican population and agrarian census data for townships in Chiapas and in some instances for townships in Tabasco and adjacent areas of the states of Oaxaca and Veracruz.

5 Nations (1994).

6 Ruz (1985).

7 Nations (1994); de Vos (1980, 1988).

8 MacLeod (1973); Wasserstrom (1983).

9 Helms (1975).

10 See also Ruz (1992) for characterization of colonial-era ranches in eastern Chiapas.

11 Gosner (1992); Viqueira (1993).

12 Bricker (1981:60).

13 Chiapas continued to have significant linkages to Guatemala after Independence. See Fábregas, et al. (1985), for one of a series of studies of Mexico's *frontera sur* in relation to linkages of economy, migration, politics, and culture.

14 See Wolf and Hansen (1972) for an insightful discussion of the export enclaves and their impact in Latin America.

15 de Vos (1988).

16 These coffee plantations, which still produce as much as 30 percent of Mexico's coffee exports, in turn stimulated the development of Chiapas' central Grijalva River valley as a breadbasket for the Soconusco, while drawing Indians from the central highlands to work as laborers (Helbig 1964; Taller Tzotzil 1990). The Soconusco area coffee plantations were essentially similar to those in Guatemala documented by the photographer Eadweard Muybridge near the turn of the century; see Burns (1986).

17 Jan Rus (1983, 1989).

18 Wasserstrom (1983).

19 Jan Rus (1994:268–272); Taller Tzotzil (1988).

20 Benjamin (1989:55ff).

21 Wolf (1969) provides a useful overview of the different revolutionary groups, their goals, and their relationships to the regionally different histories of development in Mexico.

22 Merryman (1969).

23 In light of the current uprising, it is also worth noting that the 1917 Constitution embodied no special provisions for Indians until 1992,

when Article 4 was modified to refer to Indians. Mexican and other Latin American thinkers of the time conceived of the mestizo as the quintessential national citizen. Mexico's philosopher/educator José Vasconcelos argued that the mestizo combined the best features of the Iberian and the Indian into a superior race, Vasconcelos's *La Raza Cósmica* (1948). Arguing that Indians should be educated and assimilated, Vasconcelos launched an ambitious rural literacy crusade when he became Minister of Education in the 1920s. Other thinkers, notably Manuel Gamio in *Forjando Patria* (*Forging a Nation*), argued that Mexico's many distinct indigenous heritages were mini-nationalities whose cultural assets should be acknowledged and brought, along with Indians, into the post-revolutionary national project. Diego de Rivera and other public works muralists of the 1920s gave expression to this willingness to embrace the Indian as a contributor of culture to Mexican national society—as did the federal Indianist programs of later decades.

24 Benjamin (1989:119ff); Jan Rus (n.d.).

25 García de León (1991); Benjamin (1989:123ff).

26 García de León (1985); Burguete, in a talk she gave at Stanford in spring 1994; Nigh (1994). García de León, writing about the control that Chiapas oligarchs have held virtually until the present day, sees the reactionary Mapaches as merely part of a continuous succession of power holders that have governed Chiapas in the interest of the land-holding families, including that of ex-governor Absalón Castellanos Domínguez, whom the EZLN kidnapped on January 1, 1994.

27 Spenser (1988).

28 See Wilkie (1970) for an overview of the Mexican agrarian reform from the Revolution through the middle of the twentieth century.

29 See Sanderson (1986:241–250) for an overview of Mexican agrarian policy in the post-war period.

30 Collier (1975, 1987a); Jan Rus (1976:23–26); Wasserstrom (1983:162–167). Most of the land given over to peasants was marginal, yet suitable for peasant milpa cultivation. In the Soconusco, peasants received coffee-producing lands in agrarian reform; see Ascencio (1994) for a discussion of the relations between peasant coffee production in the Soconusco and its relation to production on larger estates.

31 Warman (1980) was one of the first in calling attention to the intensification of peasant production spurred by Mexican fiscal policies.

32 Aguirre Beltrán (1955); de la Fuente (1953). See Pineda (1993) for an interesting analysis of how INI bilingual schoolteachers and promoters gained positions of power in their communities as a result of their work.

CHAPTER TWO: EASTERN CHIAPAS: LAND

1 At conquest, the inhabitants of this region were known as the Lacandón. All of the original Lacandón died out or were removed in slaving expeditions. Later, the region was repopulated by indigenous refugees from other areas. Many have mistakenly taken them to be descendants of the Lacandón of conquest times. For the story of the original Lacandón, see de Vos (1980).

2 Cancian and Brown (1994).

3 Iribarren (1987:16).

4 See Parra (1989, 1993) on the dilemmas of highland Chiapas production on what are for many people tiny plots of land.

5 Earle (1994); Pohlenz (1985:70).

6 See Ascencio and Lleyva's Table 4 (1992:207–208); see also Arizpe, et al., (1993:81) for data on colonists from other states in eastern Chiapas.

7 Ascencio and Leyva (1992:181, fn. 9).

8 Nations (1984:38); see Nigh and Nations (1980) on the multicropping potentials of tropical forest cultivation.

9 See Garza, Paz, Ruiz, and Calvo (1993) for indigenous women's accounts of the settling of this community.

10 Pohlenz (1985).

11 Ascencio and Leyva (1992:194).

12 Leyva and Ascencio (1993); see also Earle (1994) for a discussion of enterprises taken up in the colony of Nuevo Chamula.

13 Cornelius (1992) gives a concise yet thorough summary of the changes made in Article 27 and the Agrarian Code.

14 Gossen (1994:20).

15 *Tiempo*, January 20, 1994, pg. 3.

16 *New York Times*, February 27, 1994, pg. 6.

17 Reyes Ramos (1992:101–102).

18 In Las Margaritas and Ocosingo, claims were resolved in 5.6 years and 5.79 years respectively, on average, as compared to 7.36 years for Chiapas as a whole, according to Reyes Ramos (1992:150–151).

19 Reyes Ramos (1992:93–95).

20 Benjamin (1989:232).

21 Pohlenz (1985:72).

22 The Montes Azules Bioreserve was granted 330,312 hectares, according to Nations (1984:39).

23 The relocation centers were Palestina (later renamed Velasco Suárez) for the Tzeltal-speaking colonists, Corozal (later renamed Echeverría) for the Chol speakers, and Lacanjá Chan Sayab, Mensabak, and Najá for the 400 Lacandón Indians (Nations 1994:32).

24 Iribarren (1988:30).

25 The most important independent organizations were the Union of Unions (UU), the Emiliano Zapata Peasant Organization (OCEZ), and the Independent Confederation of Agricultural Workers and Peasants (CIOAC). The PRA largely bypassed their peasant affiliates (Reyes Ramos 1992:113–118).

CHAPTER THREE: EASTERN CHIAPAS: THE BUILDING OF SOCIAL MOVEMENTS

1 e.g., *Tiempo*, January 5, 1994, pg. 5.

2 *Proceso*, June 7, 1993, pp. 18–21; *La Jornada*, August 2, 1993, pp. 1 and 10; *Proceso*, September 13, 1993, pp. 12–13, 15.

3 Fox 1994a; Harvey 1994.

4 *New York Times*, February 21, 1994, pg. A7.

5 See Bastian (1983, 1990) on the history of Protestantism in Mexico and Latin America; see Hernández Castillo (1993) for a review of the literature on Protestantism in Chiapas.

6 Gossen (1989, 1994).

7 Comisión Nacional de Derechos Humanos (1992).

8 The debates over the conflict between exiles and "traditionalists" take place in the context of the evolving debate as to whether and how to grant autonomy and cultural rights to indigenous communities. See Díaz Polanco (1991, 1992) for a discussion of the Salinas government's proposed revisions of Article 4 of the Constitution to grant indigenous autonomy. See also Chapter Eight's discussion of indigenous rights and culture. On the conflict over exiles, see the special issue of *Cuadernos de la Gaceta* (Vol. 1, No. 1, 1993) concerning "Derechos de los pueblos indígenas."

9 Giménez Montiel (1988).

10 Hernández Castillo (1989).

11 Cancian (1965).

12 Hernández Castillo (1994).

13 *Tiempo*, February 1, 1994, pg. 3.

14 *Tiempo*, February 6, 1994, pg. 4.

15 See the Bibliographical Note at the end of this book for evaluation of what we have learned.

16 Morales Bermúdez (1992:314–348, passim).

17 I myself have witnessed the corrupt sale of quack medicines by a public health nurse in a rural community in Chiapas who also charged patients the equivalent of a rural dayworker's wage for doses of medicines that health authorities had provided her for free distribution.

18 *Tiempo*, March 5, 6, 1994, passim.

19 Morales Bermúdez (1992:259–263). See also Leyva's (1994) discussion of the galvanizing effect of Catholic evangelizing on the peasant organizing in the Cañadas region of Las Margaritas.

20 *Tiempo*, February 5, 1994, pg. 5.

21 *Tiempo*, January 12, 1994, pg. 3.

22 *Tiempo*, January 19, 1994, pg. 3.

23 e.g., Roger Bartra (1974, 1975, 1978, 1982). See Hewitt de Alcántara (1984) for an incisive analysis of the Mexican debate on the peasantry,

and my discussion of the debate with reference to analysis of highland Chiapas (George Collier, 1992).

24 e.g., Armando Bartra (1979); note that Roger Bartra and Armando Bartra hold opposing positions with regard to the peasantry.

25 Flores, Paré, and Sarmiento (1988:66–80).

26 Hernández Navarro (1994).

27 Armando Bartra (1985); Encinas and Rascón (1983:203ff); Flores, Paré, and Sarmiento (1988:80–89); Harvey (1988); Taller de Análisis de las Cuestiones Agrarias (1988); Varese (1992).

28 Paré (1988).

29 Alvarez (1988); Brown (1993:183–196); Marion (1984); Pérez Castro (1989); Sánchez and Ovalle (1986); Taller de Análisis de las Cuestiones Agrarias (1988); Toledo Tello (1996).

30 Oswald, Rodríguez, and Flores (1986)

31 *Proceso*, September 13, 1993, pp. 12–13.

32 Ibid., pg. 15.

33 Harvey (1994); Taller de Análisis de las Cuestiones Agrarias (1988:57–58).

34 Harvey (1994); Leyva (1994); Taller de Análisis de las Cuestiones Agrarias (1988).

35 Unión Tierra Tzotzil (1990); Jan Rus, personal communication.

36 Marcos to CEOIC, the Chiapas State Indigenous Peasant Council, a state-level federation of peasant and indigenous organizations, *Tiempo*, February 8, 1994, pg. 3.

37 *Tiempo*, May 27, 1994, pg. 1.

38 Taller de Análisis de las Cuestiones Agrarias (1988:22); Brown (1993:157); Encinas and Rascón (1983:32); Burguete (1987:xvi).

39 Taller de Análisis de las Cuestiones Agrarias (1988:2).

40 Americas Watch (1990); Minnesota Advocates for Human Rights (1993).

41 *Tiempo*, March 4, 1994, pg. 5.

42 *Resumen Informativo* 25:26. This monthly was published by the Centro de Información y Análisis de Chiapas (CIACH), San Cristóbal de las

Casas, until just before the EZLN uprising. A partial run is available in the Stanford University Libraries.

43 *Tiempo*, February 5, 1994, pg. 6; February 6, 1994, pg. 3.

44 EZLN leaders to journalists, *Tiempo*, February 5, 1994, pg. 6.

45 Marcos, to *Tiempo*, January 18, 1994, pg. 4.

46 Gordillo (1992).

47 Marion (1994:20).

48 *El Sureste*, March 19, 1994, pg. 1.

49 *Tiempo*, February 9, 1994, pg. 2.

50 *Tiempo*, February 9, 1994, pg. 2; February 10, 1994, pg. 3.

51 *Proceso*, September 13, 1993, pp. 13 and 15.

52 *Tiempo*, February 6, 1994, pg. 2.

53 *Tiempo*, February 11, 1994, pg. 3 (through a printer's error, this issue is dated February 10).

54 Ibid.

55 Ibid., pp. 3–4.

56 *Tiempo*, February 6, 1994, pg. 3.

57 Ibid.

58 Ibid.

CHAPTER FOUR: OIL AND THE CRISIS IN MEXICAN AGRICULTURE

1 Cancian (1989:165).

2 Taller Tzotzil (1988, 1990).

3 See Pietri and Stern (1985) on the impact of oil development on Mexico's southeast; Karl (1997) compares Mexican oil development to that of other oil-exporting countries after OPEC; Hirschman (1981) also discusses the impact of Mexican oil-led development. This discussion draws upon Collier, Mountjoy, and Nigh (1994).

4 See Corden (1984) for a review and overview of development economists' concept of "Dutch disease." Scherr (1985) discusses the mixed impact of the "oil syndrome" on the agriculture of Tabasco.

5 Sanderson (1986:241); Spalding (1984).

6 See Armando Bartra (1979); Esteva (1983); and Barkin and Suárez (1985), or Barkin (1987).

7 Based on Collier, Mountjoy, and Nigh (1994) Figure 2, and data from Karl (1997).

8 Hewitt de Alcántara (1992), for example, assembled analyses of Mexican maize pricing policy to help assess what the impact on peasants would be of removing price guarantees for maize.

9 See George Collier (1989, 1990, 1994a); Collier and Mountjoy (1988). Burbach (1994) has drawn on this work in his interpretation of the Zapatista rebellion. For general background on Zinacantán, see Vogt (1969) and Cancian (1965, 1972, 1989, 1992).

10 Cancian (1992); George Collier (1990).

11 George Collier (1990); Flood (1994).

12 Dewey (1981).

13 Scherr (1985).

14 Collier and Mountjoy (1988).

15 Grindle (1988) finds similar diversification of livelihoods in other parts of Mexico.

16 Alvarez and Collier (1994) discuss the Zinacanteco trucking and flower enterprises and compare them to trucking and produce businesses in northern Mexico. Nigh (1992) discusses the small business collectives or "corporative associations" that Mexican peasants are developing in many arenas of production and marketing.

17 Rosenbaum (1993:121); Diane Rus (1990); Jan Rus (personal communication).

18 Loyola (1988).

19 *San Francisco Chronicle*, June 13, 1994, pg. A6.

20 Pohlenz (1985).

21 Ibid.

22 Harvey (1994:9–11) has a particularly useful summary of the deterioration in pricing of various crops critical to peasant market-oriented production.

CHAPTER FIVE: THE TOLL OF RESTRUCTURING ON LIVES AND COMMUNITIES

1 Nash (1994) reviews this problem in global perspective and notes the parallels among the plights of urban and rural poor in the context of restructuring on a global scale.

2 Rosenbaum (1993). Chamula has greater extremes of poverty and wealth than most indigenous communities in Chiapas, and it has received far more governmental attention. See Rus and Collier (2003) for an extended comparison of the experiences of agrarian crisis in Chamula and Zinacantán.

3 Diane Rus (1988, 1990).

4 See Cancian (1965, 1972); George Collier (1975) on Zinacanteco farming strategies and technology.

5 Diane Rus, 1988. See George Collier (1989, 1990) for the Zinacanteco case.

6 Diane Rus (1988); see also Eber and Rosenbaum (1993) and Flood (1994) on women's weaving as a response to economic crisis in highland Chiapas, and Nash (1993) on similar responses in other parts of the world.

7 Jan Rus (1994).

8 Cancian's (1965) study of the Zinacanteco *cargo* system of civil and religious posts showed how Zinacantecos converted their wealth into prestige and community-wide reputation.

9 Nash and Sullivan (1992).

10 The revised Article 27 and Agrarian Code are conveniently available in Gaceta de Solidaridad (1992) and have been summarized and assessed in Cornelius (1992) and DeWalt and Rees (1994). See Gaceta de Solidaridad (1992) and Gordillo (1992) on positive changes intended by reformulation of Article 27 and the Agrarian Code. See also my assessment of the probable impact of the changes on peasant tenure in highland Chiapas (George Collier, 1994c). Studies of the agrarian situation in Chiapas since 1994 (e.g., Villafuerte Solís, et al. 2002) show that the problems I have described still persist.

CHAPTER SIX: EXCLUSION: THE NEW POLITICS

1 The first three sections of this chapter are based on George Collier (1994b) by permission of Kluwer Academic Publishers.

2 See my article on Zinacanteco politics (George Collier 1994b) for a more extended discussion of the new politics of exclusion.

3 The revisions to the penal code appear in *Periódico Oficial* (Tuxtla Gutiérrez, Chiapas) 99(1):31–36 [1988].

4 Minnesota Advocates for Human Rights (1993:ix, 48).

5 See Jane Collier (1973) on Zinacanteco customary law and its relation to Mexican national law.

6 Cancian (1992:46–47, 127–150).

7 *Tiempo*, April 8, 1989, pg. 1.

8 See Jane Collier (1977, 1979) for a comparison of Zinacantán and San Felipe in terms of different styles of litigation, and for a discussion of the changes taking place in Zinacanteco litigation.

9 For expulsions in 1989 from Oxchuc, see *Tiempo*, May 10, 1989; for Mitontic, *Tiempo* June 29, June 30, and July 1, 1989; for Amatenango del Valle, *Tiempo*, August 8, 1989; for Chenalhó, *Tiempo*, November 7, November 9, November 11, and November 14, 1989. See Morquecho (1992) for an overview of the independent organizing that brought many of the exiled groups together in the Indigenous Organization of Highland Chiapas (ORIACH).

10 e.g., Cornelius, Gentleman, and Smith (1989).

11 Russell (1994:66–69, 143–145).

12 Dresser (1991:6–7); Lustig (1994:88).

13 With emphasis as translated in Cornelius, Craig, and Fox (1994:7).

14 García and Pontigo (1993); Hernández Navarro and Célis (1994); Villafuerte (1993).

15 Hernández Navarro and Célis (1994:229).

16 Fox (1994b).

17 *La Jornada*, March 21, 1992, pg. 13.

18 Harvey (1994:20).

19 *Tiempo*, February 25, 1994, pg. 1.

20 e.g., Burguete (1987).

CHAPTER SEVEN: TRANSITIONS

1 *Proceso*, June 20, 1994, pg. 12.

2 *Tiempo*, June 14, 1994 supplement, pg. 6.

3 *Tiempo*, June 16, 1994, pp. 2–3.

4 *Tiempo*, July 5, 1994, pg. 2; *La Jornada*, July 10, 1994, pg. 12; *San Francisco Chronicle*, August 11, 1994, pg. 1.

5 *Proceso*, July 18, 1994, pg. 34.

6 See Collier, Mountjoy, and Nigh (1994) for an analysis of the impact of Zinacanteco off-farm enterprise on the use of purchased inputs in farming

7 See Toledo (1994) on the potentials of peasant multicropping microenterprise; Cortina (1993) and ISMAM (1990) on organic coffee production and organizations in the Soconusco; Brown (1993:237) on the Pantelhó honey cooperative.

8 See de Janvry, Sadoulet, and Gordillo (1994:11) on the needs of infrastructure to facilitate restructuring in peasant production.

9 On overvaluation of the peso in 1994, see interview with economist Paul Krugman in *El Financiero*, June 19, 1994, pg. 4; and discussion, *El Financiero*, June 22, 1994, pg. 5.

CHAPTER EIGHT: THE NEW
INDIGENOUS MOVEMENT

1 See Eber (1997, 1999), Hernández Castillo (1994, 1997), Rojas (1995), and Rovira (1997) on issues of gender. La Botz (1995) and Montemayor (1997) discuss the Zapatista impact on Mexico as a whole.

2 See Womack (1969) and Warman (1980) on Zapata and his popular legacy for the peasants of central Mexico.

3 After 1994, the government removed Zapata's portrait from the ten-peso bill in Mexican currency, perhaps so as to mute attention to the Zapatistas in Chiapas.

4 See Hernández Navarro (1998:11ff) on the "redimensioning" of peasant and indigenous organizations within the framework of what he characterizes as the *nueva lucha india*.

5 Castells (1997) discusses the emergence of identity in the new global order.

6 Keck and Sikkink (1998) provide a fascinating discussion of the development of the human rights movement in Mexico to illustrate a broader analysis of how nongovernmental organizations have come to have so much leverage over contemporary nations' internal affairs.

7 See Amnesty International (1986).

8 See Collier (2001) for analysis of the trajectory of human rights and indigenous rights activism in Chiapas through 1993.

9 See Modiano (1973) on INI bilingual education. See Varese (1983) on the native language programs in Oaxaca. See Warren (1998) on the Maya nationalists in Guatemala and Bonfil (1990) on the call for pluriculturalism. The presence of several thousand Guatemalan indigenous refugees in camps along the Chiapas border and the involvement of the United Nations High Commission on Refugees, the Dioceses of San Cristóbal de Las Casas, and the Mexican government on behalf of refugees and their rights in the 1980s also contributed to concern for indigenous rights. See Kovic (1997) for discussion of the reception of human rights discourse among indigenous refugees resettled near San Cristóbal de Las Casas.

10 A Forum for Rights of Indigenous Peoples was convoked in Matías Romero (Oaxaca) in 1989 and was the first occasion on which indigenous representatives from Oaxaca, Guerrero, Puebla, Veracruz, and other states as far away as Baja California, Chihuahua, and Sonora gathered to discuss their experiences of inequality before the law and violation of their rights (Hernández and Vera 1998:36).

11 Ruiz Hernández and Burguete (1998) provide background on the indigenous organizing of the 1970s and 1980s and its relation to the Zapatista movement. Rigoberta Menchú's winning of the Nobel Peace award and the UN's declaration of 1993 as the International Year of Indigenous Peoples also contributed to these developments.

12 See pages 148–149 for discussion of the Zapatistas' first Aguascalientes convention. The government destroyed this convention center in 1995,

but the Zapatistas simply moved their Aguascalientes to other locations, such as in Oventic (near Simojovel), La Realidad (in the Selva Lacandona), three other locations in Zapatista territory, and even in the San Francisco Bay area. Aguascalientes has become a symbolic location that can move from place to place as a forum for meeting with civilians, much as with "town hall" meetings in the U.S.

13 The role of FIPI, CEOIC, and other organizations in bringing autonomy to the center of the Zapatista agenda is discussed by Ruiz Hernández and Burguete (1998).

14 Autonomy had been an important goal of the 1991 Second Continental Meeting of Indigenous, Black, and Popular Resistance, in Quetzaltenango, Guatemala, involving representatives of fifty-one ethnic groups from all over the Americas (Warren 1998:33).

15 The San Andrés agreements arose from negotiation and dialogue between the representatives of the federal government, mediated by the National Mediation Commission (CONAI) headed by Bishop Samuel Ruiz, and observed by the Commission for Peace and Concord in the State of Chiapas (COCOPA). The federal congress legislated this framework for dialogue after many national and international groups protested a failed government effort, begun on February 9, 1995, to capture and arrest the Zapatista leadership. The negotiation at San Andrés on the theme of indigenous rights and culture was to be the first of several rounds of negotiation on additional issues, such as land and indigenous territories. While the San Andrés accords laid the framework for discussion of further issues, these later negotiations have never begun. The most useful discussion of the San Andrés accords, their background, and their significance is to be found in Hernández Navarro and Vera (1998), together with the text of the accords themselves. See also Hernández Navarro (1998).

16 Burguete (1998b, 1999b), Díaz Polanco (1991, 1997), and Leyva (1999) discuss autonomy and its implementation, the debates regarding the level at which autonomy should function, and the challenges to autonomy that come from internal dissension.

17 See my (1997b) discussion of this shift in Zinacantán, which came about after the Zinacantecos ousted their most villainous PRI caciques in 1994. The ousted caciques switched to the PRD. Meanwhile, the PRI

"reformed" itself to become more inclusive, whereas the PRD splintered into factions fueled by fights over external resources and by divisions in state-level party organization. In 1995 municipal elections, most former PRD affiliates in Apas and other hamlets became "new" PRI affiliates under a municipal president who appropriated Zapatista rhetoric of inclusion. He later proved quite effective in leading his municipal authorities to act through consensus rather than through factionalism and exclusion.

18 Cancian (1992).

19 Gledhill (1998) offers a very interesting analysis of the resurgence of regional elites and the increasing ungovernability of the Mexican countryside. Schultz (1997) offers the best discussion I know of the increasing role and risks of militarization in Mexico. He also discusses the rise and impact of drug trafficking.

Militarization in Chiapas focused initially on containment of the Zapatistas. Through 1994, 1995, and even into 1996, local governments seemed unable or unwilling to control bank assaults, pirate taxi and transport operations, market takeovers, and roadblocks in rural areas and towns such as Teopisca and San Cristóbal de Las Casas, where local groups, inspired by the initial successes of the Zapatistas, took action on their own behalf, sometimes in the name of the Zapatistas.

20 Some of the ungovernability arose from the Zapatista rebellion, for example after transit authorities stopped policing the highways in many areas of rural Chiapas, leading to the collapse of transport monopolies and the rise of pirate transport organizations making use of stolen vehicles (see Collier 1997a:19–20). The government has also sometimes abetted ungovernability as a strategy for controlling groups by opposing them to one another.

21 Before the 1994 rebellion, ranchers' hired guns were the most prominent paramilitaries in Chiapas. After 1994, paramilitaries came to include indigenous social groups as well, for example Paz y Justicia as well as the PRI-aligned Chinchulines of Chilón who took up arms against the PRD-istas of their municipality (see Bobrow-Strain 2004).

22 See also the Centro de Derechos Humanos "Fray Bartolomé de Las Casas" 1998 publication on the "legality of injustice."

23 Castells (1997:79), his emphasis. Cleaver (1998) discusses Zapatista use of the Internet. Cleaver has authored several working papers on Zapatista communication strategies, many of which can be viewed on his web site, which is located at www.eco.utexas.edu/faculty/ Cleaver/hmchtmlpapers.html. Ronfeldt, et al. (1998:9) argue that the Zapatista rebellion exemplifies a new kind of "social netwar," made possible by the information revolution, using "network forms of organization" to communicate across dispersed groups while conducting campaigns in an "internetted manner" rather than through conventional military or guerrilla means. See also Keck and Sikkink's (1998) discussion of how such networking circumvents the efforts of nation-states to control information about what is happening internally.

24 Leyva Solano (2003) underscores the depth of polarization that has followed upon the rebellion even in one of its heartlands, Las Cañadas.

25 Hernández Castillo (1998) provides a timely discussion of the Acteal massacre and its background. The conflict in the municipio of Chenalhó grows out of struggles and episodic violence between in-groups affiliated with the government and opponents over the past two decades.

26 Global Exchange (1999) argues that the expulsion of foreigners violates the legal guarantees that the Mexican Constitution grants foreigners. Morquecho (1999) discusses the lobbying of rights advocates to put pressure through the European Union to delay the signing of commercial treaties with Mexico.

27 On April 7, 1999, Albores Guillén disbanded the autonomous center at San Andrés Sacamch'en, the site of the San Andrés accords. Two days later, some 3,000 Zapatistas and sympathizers reclaimed the autonomous center.

28 The state generally dealt with land claimants on the condition that they bring *all* their claims "to the table" at once, under the legal concept of *finiquites* (binding negotiation). This is the principal mechanism that has been used in Chiapas since 1994 to address the *rezago agrario*, the backlog of land claims that had built up over the years.

29 Bobrow-Strain (2004) is the most current source on land invasions, the 1996 Agrarian Accords, the government's use of trusts to facilitate peasant land purchased in Chiapas, and recipients' abandonment of land they received. Villafuerte Solís, et al. (2002) and Reyes Ramos, Moguel,

and van der Haar (1998) review the ongoing conflicts over land in Chiapas as well as the negotiated settlements based on the Agrarian Accords.

30 See my article and others in the Collier and Stephen (1997) collection assessing the Chiapas realities in the wake of the Zapatista rebellion. For analysis of how the new realities are penetrating individual lives, see Collier, Farías, Pérez, and White (2000).

31 The Zapatista refusal to accept government aid dates from the experience of repeated co-optation of peasant and indigenous groups, as in the case of the ARIC Union of Unions (see page 79). The Zapatistas would not allow the victims of Acteal to accept government (as opposed to nongovernment or international) food or medical assistance after the massacre. The policy reflects a strong stance against co-optation and corruption. See Viqueira (1999) and Viqueira and Sonnleitner (2000) on elections and Zapatista abstensionism as responsible for recent PRI gains.

32 See Servicios de Apoyo Intercultural, A.C. (1999) for a compilation of the comprehensive changes in Oaxaca's political constitution and legal codes in recognition of indigenous rights, which are discussed in Gómez (1998). See also the comparisons of Chiapas and Oaxaca indigenous rights in de León Pasquel (2001).

33 Montemayor (1997:174–175).

34 Burguete (1999a) discusses the challenges of reconciliation in the exercise of customary law. See Jane Collier (1999) for analysis of the Indigenous Court of Peace and Reconciliation in Zinacantán. The court functions effectively even though indigenous understandings of reconciliation are very different from those who frame the concept under Mexican positive law in terms of application of indigenous norms. For indigenous reconciliation, the most important consideration is reaching an outcome in which litigants can go on living together in peace.

35 See Warren (1998) for a full discussion of the pan-Maya activism in Guatemala.

36 See www.ciepac.org, "Plan Puebla Panamá," Boletín "Chiapas al día" Nos. 233 and 234, of March 7 and May 16, 2001.

CHAPTER NINE: CONNECTING THE LOCAL TO THE NATIONAL AND THE GLOBAL

1 Rosset (1994) and Burbach (1994) made the first arguments for the Zapatistas as postmodern. Ronfeldt, et al. (1998:9) assert that the Zapatista rebellion involved a new kind of "social netwar," facilitated by the information revolution, using "network forms of organization" to mobilize support from dispersed groups in an "internetted manner" rather than by conventional military or guerilla means. Martínez Torres (2001) describes the Internet as a tool for civil society and Zapatista antiglobalization movements. Castells (1997) discusses the Zapatista rebellion as the emergence of a postmodern identity in the global order.

2 I was one of countless people who received a forwarded e-mail on the day of the army attempt to capture Marcos, to the effect that San Cristóbal de Las Casas was surrounded by tanks and that the hospital in Comitán was being filled with casualties. I had spoken with a colleague in the Comitán hospital that day and knew that the message was false, but the message had the desired effect of mobilizing people all over the world against the government advance. Three days later I received a fax of a handwritten letter from Zapatistas who had fled the army advance, calling for recipients to protest the military incursions to President Zedillo.

3 See Mattiace's (2003) discussion of Tojolobal experiments with regional governance in eastern Chiapas prior to the rebellion as contributing to the different views, within the indigenous movement, as to the level at which to seek autonomy in the San Andrés accords.

4 Rank and file Zapatistas understand their circumstances in less abstract terms than the leadership's global vision of neoliberalism, and more in terms of the locally based effects of globalization on prices they receive for their corn, the differentials between wages they can earn in Chiapas vs. the United States, and the cutbacks in government supports. Many of them nonetheless understand that their efforts to better their world locally are part of a more general struggle.

5 Dezalay and Garth (2002) provide one of the best analyses and interpretations of the broad changes leading to economic restructuring in the last half of the twentieth century.

6 Oxfam argues that tax havens are a major obstacle to reducing poverty in developing countries, which have lost billions of dollars annually in potential tax revenues to offshore financial activities (see www.oxfam.org.uk/what_we_do/issues/debt_aid/tax_havens.htm).

7 See Harvey (1989) on industrial reorganization and Bello (1994) on the economic and social injustices accompanying globalization. The 1986 PBS documentary film *The Global Assembly Line* (available from New Day Films) illustrated both the advantages to manufacturers and the negative impacts for workers of the globalization of manufacturing in economies opened up to capital and financial flows by free trade in the 1980s.

8 See Oleson (2004a) on the roots of the Zapatista solidarity networks.

9 See *We Are Everywhere: The Irresistible Rise of Global Anticapitalism,* Notes from Nowhere, ed. (2003).

10 ATTAC was founded in France in 1998 and spread as an internationally linked but uncentered network of national organizations focusing on bringing social accountability to the finance industry. See "Campaign for a 'Robin Hood Tax' for Foreign Exchange Markets," by Diego Muro, in John Clark, ed. (2003).

11 See "The Age of Protest: Internet-Based 'Dot Causes' and the 'Anti-Globalization Movement'" by John Clark and Nuno Themudo, in John Clark, ed. (2003).

12 The Zapatistas are offering language education—for foreigners—in Spanish as well as indigenous languages at Oventic. Foreign students are expected to "contribute" the equivalent of three times the legal minimum daily wage in their country of origin, per day, for their lessons. The students also pay for food and lodging in the facilities that the Zapatistas built at Oventic for their first anti-neoliberal convention. The language training for foreigners generates considerable revenue for the Oventic Junta of Good Government.

13 The first Zapatista autonomous regional jurisdiction was Tierra y Libertad, established in April 1998 after it became apparent that the Zedillo government was not going to enact the San Andrés accords. See Burguete (2003) for description and analysis of the new autonomous jurisdictions that indigenous people have established since the rebellion, without state authority. Burguete also discusses the

new jurisdictions that the government has set up under remunicipalization, often in response to local initiatives.

14 In April 2004, the Junta of Good Government of Oventic arrived in force, several hundred strong, together with foreign supporters in Zinacantán to support Zapatistas in the hamlets of Paste and Elanvo who have been in conflict with their neighbors and with Zinacantán's elected municipal authorities of the PRD. Outsiders have interpreted the Zapatistas as having intervened justly to protect Zinacanteco Zapatistas. However, many Zinacantecos I spoke to in July 2004 saw the Junta's intervention as meddling in their internal affairs and violating their own municipal autonomy.

15 I thank Peter Rosset for sharing this account of the Municipio de Trabajo autonomy projects with me. Rosset served among the outside evaluators invited by the community to learn about its initiatives and to share advice. My account also draws on a visit my wife and I made to this agroecology project in July 2004.

16 Illegal drugs and undocumented migrant workers pass through Chiapas from Central America, and some indigenous people of Chiapas have been caught up in trafficking drugs or migrants to the north. During the late 1990s, car theft rings sprang up in some of the highland Chiapas indigenous communities. Some youth have learned of gang culture from migration to northwest Mexico and the United States, and gangs have formed in rural Chiapas.

17 The term *promotor* was first used in the 1950s by the Mexican government's National Indian Institute (INI) to refer to agents of change drawn from within indigenous communities to promote INI initiatives. The Zapatistas have had technical experts help train grassroots promotores of health, education, and production. In appointing people as promotores, the Zapatistas invoke a vocabulary that is intended to be more egalitarian than would be the use of titles such as *maestro* (teacher), *profesor* (professor), or *ingeniero* (engineer or technical expert).

18 Visit the Enlace Civil web site at www.enlacecivil.org.mx/ for more information on this civil society network.

19 The agronomists also recommended that the agroecology promotores experiment with natural pesticides, following the example of Cubans

who have advanced such techniques under the conditions of the embargo they are experiencing.

20 Information about Mut Vitz can be found at www.cooperative coffees.com/producers/mexico/mutvitz.html. The first foreigner to contract for Mut Vitz coffee was Kerry Appel, who markets the product in the United States through The Human Bean Co., www.thehuman bean.com. See Martínez Torres (2003) for an analysis of Mut Vitz and other Chiapas small coffee producers and organizations.

21 Martínez Torres (2003:113) reports the 1999 prices. Prices for 2003 were reported to me in interviews with the Mut Vitz directorate in July 2004. New York spot prices are for Brazilian Arabica coffee as reported by the Horticultural and Tropical Products Division, FAS/USDA.

22 Jane Collier and I visited the CNT offices in April 2004 to learn about the organization's international solidarity activities.

23 See www.laneta.apc.org/forods for information on Foro para el Desarrollo Sustentable, A.C.

24 The Juntas' "Law Concerning the Care of Trees" is described by Subcomandante Marcos in his September 2004 communiqué, "Reading a Video, Part Five: Five Decisions of Good Government," available at www.ezlnaldf.org/comunica/040823video5-eng.html. The same communiqué describes provisions to prevent trafficking in drugs, undocumented migrants, and stolen vehicles in and through Zapatista territory.

25 See Banco de México's *Examen de la Situación Económica de México* 80:940 (April 2004).

26 "Food sovereignty" is defined by Food First (www252.pair.com/prontoii/progs/) as "the right of communities and countries to produce for their own needs, determine their own farming and food-security policies, and decide what to import and export without strong-arm interference by powerful countries or companies."

27 A statement attributed to James Wolfensohn, World Bank president, in a July 5, 2002, *New York Times* article entitled "Subsidies That Kill" by Nicholas D. Kristof.

28 See "Words of Insurgente Sub-Comandante Marcos, Zapatista Army of National Liberation, September 2003," at www.foodfirst.org/wto/reports/ezln3eng.php.

29 See "U.S. Will Cut Farm Subsidies in Trade Deal," *New York Times*, July 31, 2004, pp. B1, 3.

30 See "El altermundismo mexicano" by Luis Hernández Navarro in *La Jornada*, March 8, 2004.

31 See Olesen (2004b) on the emergence of a more egalitarian "global solidarity" after the Chiapas rebellion.

32 My translation, see "Marcos to NGOs: Zapatistas Don't Want Charity, but Respect," August 6, 2003, available at www.narconews.com/Issue31/article833.html.

33 My translation, excerpted from Marcos' announcement of the Juntas of Good Government, in *CHIAPAS: LA TRECEAVA ESTELA. Sexta parte: Un buen gobierno*. Subcomandante Insurgente Marcos, Mexico, July 2003.

34 On NGOs as the community face of neoliberalism, see James Petras, "Imperialism and NGOs in Latin America," December 1997, available at www.rebelion.org/petras/english/ngo1a170102.htm. See Chapin (2004) for the critique of conservation organizations. See also "Conservation International Responds to *World Watch* Article" at www.conservation.org/xp/news/press_releases/2004/wwresponse.xml. On allegations against Conservational International, in Chiapas, see "The Zapatista Struggle in Montes Azules" at www.indymedia.org.uk/en/2004/04/290083.html.

35 See Coutin (1993, 2000) on the sanctuary movement and its gatekeeping of immigration law.

BIBLIOGRAPHICAL NOTE
TO THE THIRD EDITION

Within the avalanche of writing about the Zapatistas since 1994, there are several contributions to our basic understanding of the origins and antecedents of the rebellion. Carlos Rincón Ramírez's *Relaciones de poder y dominio en el movimiento magisterial Chiapaneco* (1996) studies the alternative teachers' movement in Chiapas, which forged solidarity with peasant and other rural organizing groups and, in turn, fed into their development during the 1980s. Neil Harvey's *The Chiapas Rebellion: The Struggle for Land and Democracy* (1998) is the best source of information about the organization and spread of the OCEZ and CIOAC from the Venustiano Carranza and Simojovel regions. Harvey also describes the Union of Unions in relation to the emergence of the Zapatista movement in eastern Chiapas. Xóchitl Leyva and Manuel Ascencio, who are among the few who undertook field research in eastern Chiapas during the decade before the rebellion, have published a collection of their essays on the region, *Lacandonia al filo del agua* (1996). They write about the new society that formed in colonization of the frontier in eastern Chiapas and about how solidarity built on liberation Catholic ideas and practices in the Cañadas de Las Margaritas, a key region of the Zapatista heartland. María del Carmen Legorreta Díaz's *Religión, política y guerrilla en Las Cañadas de la Selva Lacandona* (1998) is also about the Cañadas region, its history of Catholic catechizing, peasant and indigenous organizing, and the relation of both to emergent Zapatismo.

Two books reconstruct the genealogy of the nonindigenous Zapatista leadership, tracing the movement's development from the National Liberation Forces (FLN) in the 1970s. Carlos Tello Díaz's *La Rebelión de las Cañadas* (1995) appeared shortly after the February 9, 1995, "unmasking" of Subcomandante Marcos as Rafael Santiago Guillén Vicente and evoked a firestorm of criticism from

Zapatista sympathizers who claimed that Tello must have used government intelligence sources and that his work is thus tainted by government propaganda. Bertrand de la Grange and Maite Rico, reporters for the French newspaper *Le Monde* and Spain's *El País*, published *Marcos, La Genial Impostura* (1997) with an account similar to Tello's but with much more detail. The book is equally controversial but is being taken more seriously. Both books emphasize the socialist origins of the EZLN as having held sway in the movement until the late 1980s and early 1990s, when after power struggles and splits within the leadership, the movement opted for its more indigenous guise. Both books implicate Bishop Samuel Ruiz and the Diocese of San Cristóbal de Las Casas as having had substantial knowledge of if not complicity with the EZLN up to 1989. At that time, Samuel Ruiz began to fear Marcos' rivalry in control over eastern Chiapas. But in emphasizing the nonindigenous leadership of the EZLN, neither book succeeds in explaining how the movement built up such a powerful indigenous base. Carlos A. Montemayor, in his *Chiapas, La rebelión indígena de México* (1997), places the Zapatista rebellion much more effectively than Tello or de la Grange and Rico in the historical context of movements of the Latin American Left, drawing upon his own contact with native writers in Chiapas to explain indigenous participation. Montemayor also discusses the developments in Chiapas and Mexico through 1996.

Countless publications based on interviews with Marcos attempt to explain the Zapatistas commitment to indigenous concerns. The most respected of these is Yvon Le Bot's *Subcomandante Marcos: El sueño zapatista* (1997). This and similar works are important for representing Marcos' version of how the movement developed but tend to accept that version uncritically. For Zapatista communiqués, including many from Marcos, see Clarke and Ross (1994) and EZLN *Documentos y Comunicados* (1995). *Our Word Is Our Weapon* (Marcos 2001) is an excellent selection of the Subcomandante's enigmatic writings.

The work of Luis Hernández Navarro, on the San Andrés accords (written in collaboration with Ramón Vera Herrera, 1998) and in a series of essays that Hernández compiled in *Chiapas, La nueva lucha india* (1998), helps us understand how progressive Mexicans are thinking about the new indigenous movement. Hernández developed intimate knowledge of peasant movements and alliances with the independent teachers movement and had written thoughtfully before the rebellion, together with other progressive Mexicans, about the capacity of peasant and indigenous people to protagonize their own history. Many intellectuals doubted that capacity, but the Zapatista rebellion forced them to rethink their views. Hernández argues that the current indigenous movement is in many respects an original reconfiguration of earlier indigenous initiatives and consciousness.

It may be many years before we can fully understand from indigenous insiders how the Zapatista movement developed. Muñoz Ramírez's (2003) *EZLN 20 y 10: El fuego y la palabra*, prefaced by Subcomandante Marcos as an authorized history of the rebellion twenty years after the founding of the EZLN, is a start but unfortunately describes the early years as if there were no other indigenous mobilizations than that of the Zapatistas. The best historical work on the region, for example as assembled in Viqueira and Ruz's collection, *Chiapas: Los rumbos de otra historia* (1995), makes clear how important it is to be able to recognize and interpret indigenous genres of history and politics. John Womack's (1999) reader on the historical background of the rebellion conveys the flavor of some of these genres in English-language translations. Most outsiders studying the rebellion do not speak indigenous languages and have little experience of indigenous society and culture. They cannot grasp the rich texture of indigenous understandings of politics and history, local, regional, and national. Low-intensity warfare and polarization make it difficult, even dangerous, for participants to talk frankly about their experiences and perspectives. There are researchers who have been able to continue their long-term work in different areas of Chiapas with indigenous as well as nonindigenous groups (e.g., Burguete, Eber, Hernández Castillo, Leyva), and we are gradually assembling greater knowledge of how the Zapatista movement is being experienced in varying ways in the Chiapas landscape—see Mattiace (2003) and the collections assembled by June Nash (1995a), by myself and Lynn Stephen (1997), and by Jan Rus, et al. (2003). Studies by Moksnes (2003) and Nash (2001) and a collection by Eber and Kovic (2003) have special value for illuminating how Chiapas women are experiencing the quest for autonomy and rights in the era of globalization.

REFERENCES

Aguirre Beltrán, Gonzalo
  1955   A Theory of Regional Integration: The Coordinating Centers.
  América Indígena 15(1):29–42.

Alvarez, Fernando
  1988   Peasant Movements in Chiapas. *Bulletin of Latin American
  Research* 7:277–298.

Alvarez, Robert, and George A. Collier
  1994   The Long Haul in Mexican Trucking: Traversing the
  Borderlands of the North and the South. *American Ethnologist*
  21(3):606–627.

Americas Watch
  1990   *Human Rights in Mexico: A Policy of Impunity.* An Americas
  Watch Report. New York: Human Rights Watch.

Amnesty International
  1986   *Mexico: Human Rights in Rural Areas.* London: Amnesty
  International.

Arizpe, Lourdes, Fernanda Paz, and Margarita Velázquez
  1993   *Cultura y Cambio Global: Percepciones Sociales sobre la
  Deforestación en la Selva Lacandona.* México, DF: UNAM–Centro
  Regional de Investigaciones Multidisciplinarias/Grupo Editorial
  Miguel Angel Porrúa, S.A.

Arvide, Isabel
  1994   *Crónica de una Guerra Anunciada.* México, DF: Grupo Editorial
  Siete, S.A.

Ascencio Franco, Gabriel
  1994   Integración finca-ejido en la cafeticultura del Soconusco, pp.
  66–97 in *El café en la frontera sur*, ed. by Daniel Villafuerte Solís. Tuxtla
  Gutiérrez: Instituto Chiapaneco de Cultura.

244 *BASTA!*

Ascencio Franco, Gabriel, and Xóchitl Leyva Solano
1992 Los municipios de la Selva Chiapaneca, Colonización y dinámica agropecuaria. *Anuario 1991, Instituto Chiapaneco de Cultura,* pp. 176–241.

Barkin, David
1987 The End to Food Self-Sufficiency in Mexico. *Latin American Perspectives* 14(3):271–297.

Barkin, David, and Blanca Suárez
1985 *El fin de la autosuficiencia alimentaria.* México, DF: Centro de Ecodesarrollo/Ediciones Océano, S.A.

Bartra, Armando
1979 *La explotación del trabajo campesino por el capital.* México, DF: Editorial Macehual.
1985 *Los herederos de Zapata: Movimientos campesinos posrevolucionarios en México.* México, DF: Ediciones Era.

Bartra, Roger
1974 *Estructura agraria y clases sociales en México.* México, DF: Editorial Era.
1975 Peasants and Political Power in Mexico: A Theoretical Approach. *Latin American Perspectives* 2(2).
1978 *El poder despótico burgués.* México, DF: Editorial Era.
1982 Capitalism and the Peasantry in Mexico. *Latin American Perspectives* 9(1).

Bastian, Jean-Pierre
1983 *Protestantismo y Sociedad en México.* México, DF: Casa Unida de Publicaciones, S.A. (CUPSA).
1990 *Historia del Protestantismo en América Latina.* México, DF: Centro de Comunicación Cultural CUPSA, A.C.

Bello, Walden
1994 *Dark Victory: The United States, Structural Adjustment, and Global Poverty.* Oakland: Food First Books.

Benjamin, Thomas
1989   *A Rich Land, a Poor People: Politics and Society in Modern Chiapas.* Albuquerque: University of New Mexico Press.

Bobrow-Strain, Aaron
2004   (Dis)accords: The Politics of Market-Assisted Land Reform in Chiapas, México. *World Development* 32(6):887–903.

Bonfil Batalla, Guillermo
1990   *México profundo: una civilización negada.* México, DF: Grijalbo.

la Botz, Dan
1995   *Democracy in Mexico: Peasant Rebellion and Political Reform.* Boston: South End Press.

Bricker, Victoria Reifler
1981   *The Indian Christ, the Indian King: The Historical Substrate of Maya Myth and Ritual.* Austin: University of Texas Press.

Brown, Pete
1993   *The Creation of Community: Class and Ethnic Struggle in Pantelhó, Chiapas, Mexico.* Ph.D. dissertation, Division of Social Science, University of California, Irvine.

Burbach, Roger
1994   Roots of the Postmodern Rebellion in Chiapas. *New Left Review* 205:113–124.

Burguete Cal y Mayor, Aracely
1987   *Chiapas: Cronología de un etnocidio reciente (Represión política a los indios 1974–1987).* Unpublished manuscript, Academia Mexicana de Derechos Humanos, A.C.

1998a   Remunicipalización en Chiapas: los retos. *CEMOS Memoria* 114:14–25.

1998b   Chiapas: autonomías indígenas. La construcción de los sujetos autonómicos. *Quórum* 60:117–159.

1999a   Entre la tradición y la costumbre. Los retos de la reconciliación y la tolerancia indígena en los Altos de Chiapas. *El Cotidiano* 15(93):19–30.

1999b   *México: Experiencias de Autonomía Indígena.* Coordinada por Aracely Burguete. Copenhagen: IWGIA and Guatemala: Ediciones Cholsamaj.

2003   The de Facto Autonomous Process: New Jurisdictions and Parallel Governments in Rebellion, pp. 191–218 in Rus, et al., eds., *Mayan Lives, Mayan Utopias,* Lanham, Md.: Rowman & Littlefield.

Burns, E. Bradford
1986   *Eadweard Muybridge in Guatemala, 1875: The Photographer as Social Recorder.* Berkeley: University of California Press.

Cancian, Frank
1965   *Economics and Prestige in a Maya Community.* Stanford: Stanford University Press.

1972   *Change and Uncertainty in a Peasant Economy: The Maya Corn Farmers of Zinacantan.* Stanford: Stanford University Press.

1989   Economic Behavior in Peasant Communities, pp. 127–170 in *Economic Anthropology,* Stuart Plattner, ed. Stanford: Stanford University Press.

1992   *The Decline of Community in Zinacantan: Economy, Public Life, and Social Stratification, 1960–1987.* Stanford: Stanford University Press.

Cancian, Frank, and Peter Brown
1994   Who Is Rebelling in Chiapas? *Cultural Survival Quarterly* 18(1):22–25.

Castellanos, Rosario
1992   *The Nine Guardians.* Columbia, La. and London: Readers International, Inc. First published in Spanish as *Balún Canán* in 1957 by the Fondo de Cultura Económica, México, DF.

Castells, Manuel
1997   *The Power of Identity.* Vol. 2 of *The Information Age: Economy, Society and Culture.* Oxford: Blackwell Publishers Ltd.

Centro de Derechos Humanos "Fray Bartolomé de Las Casas"
1998   *La legalidad de la injusticia.* San Cristóbal de Las Casas: CDHFBLC.

Chapin, Mac

2004 A Challenge to Conservationists. *World Watch* November/December 2004:17-31.

Chiapas Media Project 2000

2000a *Education in Resistance: Autonomous Education in Chiapas.* Video.

2000b *The Strength of the Indigenous People of Mut Vitz: Producing Fair Trade Organic Coffee in the Highlands of Chiapas.* Video.

2000c *Women United.* Video.

Chiapaslink

2000 *The Zapatistas: A Rouge Guide.* London: Calverts Press.

Clark, John, ed.

2003 *Globalizing Civic Engagement: Civil Society and Transnational Action.* London and Sterling, Va.: Earthscan Publications, Ltd.

Clarke, Ben, and Clifton Ross, eds.

1994 *Communiqués and Interviews from the Zapatista National Liberation Army.* Berkeley: New Earth Publications.

Cleaver, Harry

1998 The Zapatista Effect: The Internet and the Rise of an Alternative Political Fabric. *Journal of International Affairs* 51(2):621-640.

Collier, George A.

1975 *Fields of the Tzotzil: The Ecological Bases of Tradition in Highland Chiapas.* Austin: University of Texas Press.

1987a Peasant Politics and the Mexican State: Indigenous Compliance in Highland Chiapas. *Mexican Studies/Estudios Mexicanos,* 3:71-98.

1987b *Socialists of Rural Andalusia: Unacknowledged Revolutionaries of the Second Republic.* Stanford: Stanford University Press.

1989 Changing Inequality in Zinacantan: The Generations of 1918 and 1942, pp. 111-124 in Victoria R. Bricker and Gary H. Gossen, eds., *Ethnographic Encounters in Southern Mesoamerica: Essays in Honor of Evon Zartman Vogt, Jr. Studies on Culture and Society,* Volume 3,

Institute for Mesoamerican Studies, the University at Albany, State University of New York.

1990 *Seeking Food and Seeking Money: Changing Productive Relations in a Highland Mexican Community.* Discussion Paper 10, United Nations Research Institute for Social Development, Geneva.

1992 Los Zinacantecos en su mundo contemporáneo, pp. 189–215 in *Antropología Mesoamericana: Homenaje a Alfonso Villa Rojas*, ed. by Victor Manuel Esponda, Sophia Pincemin, and Mauricio Rosas. Tuxtla Gutiérrez: Instituto Chiapaneco de Cultura.

1994a Roots of the Rebellion in Chiapas. *Cultural Survival Quarterly* 18(1):14–18.

1994b The New Politics of Exclusion: Antecedents to the Rebellion in Mexico. *Dialectical Anthropology* 19(1):1–44.

1994c Reforms of Mexico's Agrarian Code: Impacts on the Peasantry. *Research in Economic Anthropology* 15:105–127.

1994d The Rebellion in Chiapas and the Legacy of Energy Development. *Mexican Studies/Estudios Mexicanos* 10(2):371–382.

1995 *The Restructuring of Ethnicity in Chiapas and the World. Indigenous Affairs* 3:22–27.

1997a Reaction and Retrenchment in the Highlands of Chiapas. In Collier and Stephen, eds., *Ethnicity, Identity, and Citizenship in the Wake of the Zapatista Rebellion. Special issue of Journal of Latin American Anthropology* (3:1):14–31.

1997b The Zapatista Rebellion in Chiapas. *Encyclopedia of Mexico: History, Society, and Culture*, ed. by Michael S. Werner, Vol II, pp. 1635–1638. Chicago: Fitzroy Dearborn Publishers.

2001 Identidades emergentes en Chiapas, 1986–1993, pp. 245–270 in *Costumbres, Leyes, y Movimiento Indio en Oaxaca y Chiapas*, Lourdes de León Pasquel, compiladora. México, D.F.: CIESAS/Porrúa.

Collier, George A., Pablo J. Farías Campero, John E. Pérez, and Victor P. White

2000 Socio-Economic Change and Emotional Illness among the Highland Maya of Chiapas, Mexico. *Ethos* 28(1):20–53.

Collier, George A., and Daniel C. Mountjoy

1988   *Adaptándose a la crisis de los Ochenta: Cambios socio-económicos en Apás, Zinacantán.* Documento 035–II/88. San Cristóbal de Las Casas: Instituto de Asesoría Antropológica para la Region Maya, A.C.

Collier, George A., Daniel Mountjoy, and Ronald B. Nigh

1994   Peasant Agriculture and Global Change: A Maya Response to Energy Development in Southeastern Mexico. *BioScience* 44:398–407.

Collier, George A., and Jane F. Collier

2003   The Zapatista Rebellion in the Context of Globalization, pp. 242–252 in *The Future of Revolutions*, John Foran, ed. London and New York: Zed Books.

Collier, George A., and Lynn Stephen, eds.

1997   *Ethnicity, Identity, and Citizenship in the Wake of the Zapatista Rebellion. Special issue of Journal of Latin American Anthropology* (3:1).

Collier, Jane F.

1973   *Law and Social Change in Zinacantan.* Stanford: Stanford University Press.

1977   Political Leadership and Legal Change in Zinacantan. *Law and Society Review* 11(1):131–163.

1979   Stratification and Dispute Handling in Two Highland Chiapas Communities. *American Ethnologist* 6:305–327.

1999   Models of Indigenous Justice in Chiapas, Mexico: A Comparison of State and Zinacanteco Versions. *PoLAR* 22(1):94–100.

Comisión Nacional de Derechos Humanos

1992   *Informe sobre el problema de las expulsiones en las comunidades indígenas de los altos de Chiapas y los derechos humanos.* México, DF: CNDH.

Corden, Werner Max

1984   Booming Sector and Dutch Disease Economics: Survey and Consolidation. *Oxford Economic Papers* 36:359–380.

Cornelius, Wayne A.

1992   The Politics and Economics of Reforming the Ejido Sector in Mexico: An Overview and Research Agenda. *LASA Forum* 23(3):3–10.

Cornelius, Wayne A., Ann L. Craig, and Jonathan Fox

1994   *Transforming State-Society Relations in Mexico: The National Solidarity Strategy.* La Jolla: Center for U.S.–Mexican Studies, University of California, San Diego.

Cornelius, Wayne A., Judith Gentleman, and Peter H. Smith, eds.

1989   *Mexico's Alternative Political Futures.* La Jolla: University of California, San Diego.

Cortina Villar, Sergio

1993   Sistemas de cultivo de café en el Soconusco, pp. 52–65 in *El café en la frontera sur: La producción y los productores del Soconusco, Chiapas,* ed. by Daniel Villafuerte Solís. Tuxtla Gutiérrez: Instituto Chiapaneco de Cultura.

Coutin, Susan Bibler

1993   *The Culture of Protest: Religious Activism and the U.S. Sanctuary Movement.* Boulder: Westview Press

2000   *Legalizing Moves: Salvadoran Immigrants' Struggle for U.S. Residency.* Ann Arbor: University of Michigan Press.

Dewalt, Billie R., and Martha W. Rees

1994   *The End of the Agrarian Reform in Mexico: Past Lessons, Future Prospects.* Transformation of Rural Mexico Series, No. 3. La Jolla: Center for U.S.–Mexican Studies, University of California, San Diego.

Dewey, K. G.

1981   Nutritional Consequences of the Transformation from Subsistence to Commercial Agriculture in Tabasco, Mexico. *Human Ecology* 9:151–187.

Dezalay, Yves, and Bryant G. Garth

2002   *The Internationalization of Palace Wars: Lawyers, Economists, and the Contest to Transform Latin American States.* Chicago: University of Chicago Press.

Díaz Polanco, Héctor

1991 *Autonomía regional: La autodeterminación de los pueblos indios.* México, DF: Siglo Veintiuno Editores.

1992 Derecho Nacional y derecho indígena (Reflexiones en torno a la ley reglamentaria del artículo 40. constitucional). Working paper. México, DF.

1997 *La rebelión zapatista y la autonomía.* México, DF: Siglo Veintiuno Editores.

Dresser, Denise

1991 *Neopopulist Solutions to Neoliberal Problems.* Current Issue Brief No. 3, Center for U.S.–Mexican Studies. La Jolla: University of California, San Diego.

Earle, Duncan

1994 Indigenous Identity at the Margin: Zapatismo and Nationalism. *Cultural Survival Quarterly* 18(1):26–29.

Eber, Christine, and Christine Kovic, eds.

2003 *Women of Chiapas: Making History in Times of Struggle and Hope.* New York and London: Routledge.

Eber, Christine, and Brenda Rosenbaum

1993 "That We May Serve Beneath Your Hands and Feet": Women Weavers in Highland Chiapas, Mexico, pp. 155–182 in *Impact of Global Exchange on Middle American Artisans.* June Nash, ed. Albany: SUNY Press.

1997 Communiqúe on Violence Toward Women in Chiapas. *Latin American Perspectives* 23(4):6–8.

1999 Seeking Our Own Food: Indigenous Women's Power and Autonomy in San Pedro Chenalhó, 1980–1998. *Latin American Perspectives* 26(3):6–36.

Encinas R., Alejandro, and Fernando Rascón F.

1983 *Reporte y Cronología del Movimiento Campesino e Indígena,* No. 3–4, July-December 1982. México, DF: Universidad Autónoma Chapingo.

Esteva, Gustavo
1983   *The Struggle for Rural Mexico.* South Hadley, Mass.: Bergin & Garvey Publishers, Inc.

EZLN
1995   *Documentos y Comunicados, 15 de agosto de 1994/29 de septiembre de 1995.* Vol. I. México, DF: Ediciones Era.

1996   *Crónicas Intergalácticas EZLN: Primer Encuentro Intercontinental por la Humanidad y contra el Neoliberalismo.* México, DF: Montañas del Sureste Mexicano, Planeta Tierra.

Fábregas Puig, Andrés, Juan Pohlenz, Mariano Baez, and Gabriel Macías
1985   *La formación histórica de la frontera sur.* Cuadernos de La Casa Chata 124. México, DF: Centro de Investigaciones y Estudios Superiores en Antropología Social.

Flood, Merielle
1994   Changing Patterns of Interdependence: The Effects of Increasing Monetization on Gender Relations in Zinacantan, Mexico. *Research in Economic Anthropology* 15:145–173.

Flores Lúa, Graciela, Luisa Paré, and Sergio Sarmiento Silva
1988   *Las voces del campo: Movimiento campesino y política agraria, 1976–1984.* México, DF: Siglo Veintiuno Editores.

Fox, Jonathan
1994a   The Roots of Chiapas. *Boston Review* 19(2):24–27.

1994b   Targeting the Poorest: The Role of the National Indigenous Institute in Mexico's Solidarity Program, pp. 179–216 in *Transforming State-Society Relations in Mexico: The National Solidarity Strategy*, ed. by Wayne A. Cornelius, Ann L. Craig, and Jonathan Fox. La Jolla: Center for U.S.–Mexican Studies, University of California, San Diego.

Frank, André Gunder
1967   *Capitalism and Underdevelopment in Latin America.* New York: Monthly Review Press.

de la Fuente, Julio
1953   El Centro Coordinador Tzeltal-Tzotzil: Una realización del México de hoy. *América Indígena* 13(1):55–64.

Gaceta de Solidaridad
1992   *Nueva legislación agraria: Articulo 27 constitucional, Ley Agraria, Ley Orgánica de los Tribunales Agrarios.* México, DF: Gaceta de Solidaridad.

Gamio, Manuel
1960   *Forjando patria.* México, DF: Editorial Porrúa.

García Aguilar, María del Carmen, and José Luis Pontigo Sánchez
1993   La política cafetalera y sus efectos en las organizaciones de productores del sector social del Soconusco, pp. 121–135 in *El café en la frontera sur: La producción y los productores del Soconusco, Chiapas*, ed. by Daniel Villafuerte Solís. Tuxtla Gutiérrez: Instituto Chiapaneco de Cultura.

Garza Caligaris, Anna María, María Fernanda Paz Salinas, Juana María Ruiz Ortiz, and Angelino Calvo Sánchez
1993   *Sk'op Antzetik: Una historia de mujeres en la selva de Chiapas.* Tuxtla Gutiérrez, Chiapas: Universidad Autónoma de Chiapas.

García de León, Antonio
1985   *Resistencia y utopía: Memorial de agravios y crónica de revueltas y profecías acaecidas en la provincia de Chiapas durante los últimos quinientos años de su historia.* 2 vols. México, DF: Ediciones Era.

1991   *Ejército de ciegos: Testimonios de la guerra chiapaneca entre Carrancistas y rebeldes, 1914–1920.* México, DF: Ediciones Toledo.

Giménez Montiel, Gilberto
1988   *Sectas Religiosas en el Sureste: Aspectos Sociográficos y Estadísticos.* Cuadernos de La Casa Chata 161. México, DF: Centro de Investigaciones y Estudios Superiores en Antropología Social.

Gledhill, John
1998   Neoliberalism and Ungovernability: Caciquismo, Militarization and Popular Mobilization in Zedillo's Mexico. In *Encuentros Antropológicos: Power, Identity and Mobility in Mexican Society*, Valentina Napolitano and Xóchitl Leyva Solano, eds., pp. 9–28. London: Institute of Latin American Studies, University of London.

Global Exchange, et al.

1999   *Foreigners of Conscience: The Mexican Government's Campaign against International Human Rights Observers in Chiapas.* San Francisco: Global Exchange.

Gómez, Magdalena

1998   El Derecho indígena en Oaxaca, las nuevas iniciativas constitucionales y legales. *Quórum* 7(60):45–54.

Gordillo de Anda, Gustavo

1992   *Más allá de Zapata: Por una reforma campesina.* México, DF: Cal y Arena.

Gosner, Kevin

1992   *Soldiers of the Virgin: The Moral Economy of a Colonial Maya Rebellion.* Tucson: University of Arizona Press.

Gossen, Gary H.

1989   Life, Death, and Apotheosis of a Chamula Protestant Leader, pp. 217–229 in *Ethnographic Encounters in Southern Mesoamerica: Essays in Honor of Evon Zartman Vogt, Jr.,* Victoria R. Bricker and Gary H. Gossen, eds. Albany: Institute of Mesoamerican Studies, SUNY.

1994   Comments on the Zapatista Movement. *Cultural Survival Quarterly* 18(1):19–21.

de la Grange, Bertrand, and Maite Rico

1997   *Marcos, La Genial Impostura.* Paris: PLON et IFRANE.

Grindle, Merilee Serrill

1988   *Searching for Rural Development: Labor Migration and Employment in Mexico.* Ithaca, N.Y.: Cornell University Press.

Guillén Trujillo, Julio Cesar

1994   *¿La guerra o la paz?* Tuxtla Gutiérrez: Editorial Diálogo.

Harvey, David

1989   *The Condition of Postmodernity: An Enquiry into the Origins of Cultural Change.* Oxford and New York: Blackwell.

Harvey, Neil
 1988 Personal Networks and Strategic Choices in the Formation of an Independent Peasant Organization: The OCEZ of Chiapas, Mexico. *Bulletin of Latin American Research*, 7:299–312.
 1994 *Rebellion in Chiapas: Rural Reforms, Campesino Radicalism, and the Limits to Salinismo.* Transformation of Rural Mexico Series, No. 5. La Jolla: Center for U.S.–Mexican Studies, University of California at San Diego.
 1998 *The Chiapas Rebellion: The Struggle for Land and Democracy.* Durham: Duke University Press.

Helbig, Carlos
 1964 *El Soconusco y su zona cafetalera en Chiapas.* Tuxtla Gutiérrez: Instituto de Ciencias y Artes de Chiapas.

Helms, Mary
 1975 *Middle America: A Culture History of Heartland and Frontiers.* Englewood Cliffs, N.J.: Prentice Hall.

Hernández Castillo, Rosalva Aída
 1989 Del Tzolkin a la Atalaya: Los cambios en la religiosidad en una comunidad Chuj-K'anhobal de Chiapas, pp. 123–224 in *Religión y Sociedad en el Sureste de México*, Vol. 2, ed. by Andrés Fábregas, et al. Cuadernos de La Casa Chata 162. México, DF: Centro de Investigaciones y Estudios Superiores en Antropología Social.
 1993 Entre la victimización y la resistencia étnica: revisión crítica de la bibliografía sobre protestantismo en Chiapas. *Anuario 1992, Instituto Chiapaneco de Cultura*, pp. 165–186.
 1994 La "fuerza extraña" es mujer. *Ojarasca* 30:36–37.
 1997 Between Hope and Adversity: The Struggle of Organized Women in Chiapas Since the Zapatista Rebellion. In Collier and Stephen, eds., *Ethnicity, Identity and Citizenship in the Wake of the Zapatista Rebellion.* Special issue of *Journal of Latin American Anthropology* (3:1):102–120.
 1998 *La otra palabra: Mujeres y violencia en Chiapas, antes y después de Acteal.* Ed. by Rosalva Aída Hernández Castillo. México, DF: CIESAS.

Hernández Navarro, Luis
  1994   The Chiapas Uprising, pp. 44–56 in *Rebellion in Chiapas*, ed. by
  Neil Harvey. Transformation of Rural Mexico Series, No. 5. La Jolla:
  Center for U.S.–Mexican Studies, University of California at San
  Diego.
  1998   *Chiapas: La nueva lucha india.* Madrid: Talasa.

Hernández Navarro, Luis, and Fernando Célis Callejas
  1994   Solidarity and the New Campesino Movements: The Case of
  Coffee Production, pp. 217–231 in *Transforming State-Society Relations
  in Mexico: The National Solidarity Strategy,* ed. by Wayne A. Cornelius,
  Ann L. Craig, and Jonathan Fox. La Jolla: Center for U.S.–Mexican
  Studies, University of California, San Diego.

Hernández Navarro, Luis, and Ramón Vera Herrera, eds.
  1998   *Acuerdos de San Andrés.* México, DF: Ediciones Era.

Hewitt de Alcántara, Cynthia
  1984   *Anthropological Perspectives on Rural Mexico.* London:
  Routledge & Kegan Paul.
  1992   *Reestructuración económica y subsistencia rural: El maíz y la crisis
  de los ochenta.* Edited by Cynthia Hewitt de Alcántara. México, DF: El
  Colegio de México.

Hirschman, Albert O.
  1981   *Essays in Trespassing: Economics to Politics and Beyond.*
  Cambridge: Cambridge University Press.

Iribarren Pascal, Fr. Pablo
  1987   *Visita pastoral a la zona de Ocosingo.* Typed ms.
  1988   *Visita pastoral a la zona de Miramar.* Typed ms.

ISMAM
  1990   *Manual práctico del cultivo biológico del café orgánico.* Indígenas
  de la Sierra Madre de Motozintla, San Isidro Labrador. Motozintla,
  Chiapas: S.O.S. Werelhandel.

de Janvry, Alain
  1981   *The Agrarian Question and Reformism in Latin America.*
  Baltimore: Johns Hopkins University Press.

de Janvry, Alain, Elisabeth Sadoulet, and Gustavo Gordillo de Anda
  1994   NAFTA and Mexico's Corn Producers. Paper presented at the XVIII Latin American Studies Association International Congress, March 10–12, 1994, in Atlanta, Georgia.

Karl, Terry L.
  1997   *The Paradox of Plenty: Oil Booms and Petro-States.* Berkeley: University of California Press.

Keck, Margaret E., and Kathryn Sikkink
  1998   *Activists Beyond Borders.* Ithaca: Cornell University Press.

Kovic, Christine
  1997   *Walking with One Heart: Human Rights and the Catholic Church among the Maya of Highland Chiapas.* Ph.D. dissertation, City University of New York.

Le Bot, Yvon
  1997   *Subcomandante Marcos: El sueño zapatista.* México, DF: Plaza & Janés.

Legorreta Díaz, María del Carmen
  1998   *Religión, política y guerrilla en Las Cañadas de la Selva Lacandona.* México, DF: Cal y Arena.

de León Pasquel, Lourdes, coord.
  2001   *Costumbres, leyes y movimiento indio en Oaxaca y Chiapas.* México, DF: Centro de Investigaciones y Estudios Superiores en Antropología Social.

Leyva Solano, Xóchitl
  1994   Militancia político-religiosa e identidad en la Lacandona. Working paper. San Cristóbal de Las Casas: CIESAS Sureste.
  1999   Chiapas es México: autonomías indígenas y luchas políticas con una gramática moral. El Cotidiano 15(93):5–18.
  2003   Regional, Communal, and Organizational Transformations in Las Cañadas, pp. 161–184 in Rus, et al., eds., *Mayan Lives, Mayan Utopias,* Lanham, Md.: Rowman & Littlefield.

Leyva Solano, Xóchitl, and Gabriel Ascencio Franco
1993 Apuntes para el estudio de la ganaderización en la Selva Lacandona. *Anuario 1992, Instituto Chiapaneco de Cultura*, pp. 262–284.
1996 *Lacandonia al filo del agua*. México, DF: Fondo de Cultura Económica.

Leyva, Xóchitl, Mercedes Olivera, and Aracely Burguete
1999 Los pasos atrás en la Ley Albores, pp. 8–9 in supplement to *La Jornada*, Domingo, March 28, 1999.

Loyola, Luis J.
1988 *Brokerage, Capital Accumulation and Development: Transporters in the Process of Economic and Political Change in Chiapas, Mexico.* Doctoral dissertation, Graduate Faculty of Anthropology, City University of New York.

Lustig, Nora
1994 Solidarity as a Strategy of Poverty Alleviation, pp. 79–96 in *Transforming State-Society Relations in Mexico: The National Solidarity Strategy*, ed. by Wayne A. Cornelius, Ann L. Craig, and Jonathan Fox. La Jolla: Center for U.S.–Mexican Studies, University of California, San Diego.

MacLeod, Murdo J.
1973 *Spanish Central America: A Socioeconomic History, 1520–1720.* Berkeley: University of California Press.

Mattiace, Shannan L.
2003 *To See with Two Eyes: Peasant Activism and Indian Autonomy in Chiapas, Mexico.* Albuquerque: University of New Mexico Press.

Marcos, Subcomandante
2001 *Our Word Is Our Weapon: Selected Writings*, Juana Ponce de León, ed. New York: Seven Stories Press.

Marion Singer, Marie-Odile
1984 *El movimeinto campesino en Chiapas, 1983*. México, DF: Centro de Estudios Históricos del Agrarismo en México.
1989 *Las organizaciones campesinas autónomas: un reto a la producción.* México, DF: Instituto Nacional de Antropología e Historia.

1994   Crónica de un desastre evitable. *Asuntos Indígenas* 1:18–20.

Martínez Torres, María Elena
2001   Civil Society, the Internet, and the Zapatistas. *Peace Review* 13(2):347–355.
2003   *Sustainable Development, Campesino Organizations and Technological Change among Small Coffee Producers in Chiapas, México.* Doctoral dissertation, Latin American Studies, University of California at Berkeley.

Mattiace, Shannon L.
2003   *To See with Two Eyes: Peasant Activism and Indian Autonomy in Chiapas, México.* Albuquerque: University of New Mexico Press.

Méndez Asensio, Luis, and Antonio Cano Gimeno
1994   *La guerra contra el tiempo: Viaje a la selva alzada.* México, DF: Espasa Calpa Mexicana, S.A.

Merryman, John
1969   *The Civil Law Tradition: An Introduction to the Legal Systems of Western Europe and Latin America.* Stanford: Stanford University Press.

Minnesota Advocates for Human Rights
1993   *Civilians at Risk: Military and Police Abuses in the Mexican Countryside.* Minneapolis: Minnesota Advocates for Human Rights.

Modiano, Nancy
1973   *Indian Education in the Chiapas Highlands.* New York: Holt, Rinehart and Winston.

Moksnes, Heidi
2003   *Mayan Suffering, Mayan Rights: Faith and Citizenship among Catholic Tzotziles in Highland Chiapas, Mexico.* Göteborg: Göteborg University.

Montemayor, Carlos A.
1997   *Chiapas, la rebelión indígena de México.* México, DF: Editorial Joaquín Mortiz, Grupo Editorial Planeta.

Morales Bermúdez, Jesús

1992 El Congreso Indígena de Chiapas: Un Testimonio. *Anuario 1991, Instituto Chiapaneco de Cultura*, pp. 242–370.

Morquecho Escamilla, Gaspar

1992 *Los Indios en un Proceso de Organización: La Organización Indígena de los Altos de Chiapas.* ORIACH. San Cristóbal de Las Casas: Universidad Autónoma de Chiapas.

1999 La caminata por los derechos humanos en Chiapas. El centro de Derechos Humanos "Fray Bartolomé de Las Casas" 1989–1998. *El Cotidiano* 15(93):40–48.

Muñoz Ramírez, Gloria

2003 *EZLN 20 y 10: el fuego y la palabra.* México, D.F: La Jornada Ediciones.

Nash, June

1993 *Crafts in the World Market: The Impact of International Exchange on Middle American Artisans.* Ed. by June Nash. Albany: SUNY Press.

1994 Global Integration and Subsistence Insecurity. *American Anthropologist* 96:7–30.

1995a *La explosión de comunidades en Chiapas.* Ed. by June Nash. Documento IWGIA 16. Copenhagen: IWGIA.

1995b The Reassertion of Indigenous Identity: Mayan Responses to State Intervention in Chiapas. *Latin American Research Review* 30(3):7–41.

2001 *Mayan Visions: The Quest for Autonomy in an Age of Globalization.* New York and London: Routledge.

Nash, June, and Kathleen Sullivan

1992 Return to Porfirismo: The Views from the Southern Frontier. *Cultural Survival Quarterly* 16(2):13–17.

Nations, James D.

1984 The Lacandones, Gertrude Blom, and the Selva Lacandona, pp. 26–41 in *Gertrude Blom: Bearing Witness*, Alex Harris and Margaret Sartor, eds. Chapel Hill: University of North Carolina Press.

1994 The Ecology of the Zapatista Revolt. *Cultural Survival Quarterly* 18(1):31–33.

Nigh, Ronald B.
1992   La agricultura orgánica y el nuevo movimiento campesino en México. *Antropológicas, Nueva Epoca* 3:39–50.
1994   Zapata Rose in 1994: The Indian Rebellion in Chiapas. *Cultural Survival Quarterly* 18(1):9–13.

Nigh, Ronald B., and James D. Nations
1980   Tropical Rainforests. *The Bulletin of the Atomic Scientists* March 1980, pp. 12–19.

Notes from Nowhere, ed.
2003   *We Are Everywhere: The Irresistible Rise of Global Anticapitalism.* London and New York: Verso.

Olesen, Thomas
2004a   *International Zapatismo: The Construction of Solidarity in the Age of Globalization.* London and New York: Zed Books.
2004b   Globalizing the Zapatistas: From Third World Solidarity to Global Solidarity. *Third World Quarterly* 25:255–267.

Oswald, Ursula, Rafael Rodríguez, and Antonio Flores
1986   *Campesinos protagonistas de su historia. (La coalición de los Ejidos Colectivos de los Valles del Yaqui y Mayo: una salida a la cultura de la pobreza).* México, DF: Universidad Autónoma Metropolitana, Unidad Xochimilco.

Paré, Luisa
1988   *El proletariado agrícola en México:¿ campesinos sin tierra o proletarios agrícolas?* Revised edition. México, D.F: Siglo Veintiuno Editores.

Parra Vázquez, Manuel (compiler)
1989   *El subdesarrollo agrícola en los altos de Chiapas.* Serie Agronomía 18, Colección Cuadernos Universitarios. México, DF: Universidad Autónoma Chapingo.
1993   *Estructura económico y desarrollo campesino en la region Altos de Chiapas.* Ph.D. dissertation, Facultad de Economía, UNAM. México, DF: Universidad Nacional Autónoma de México.

Pérez Castro, Ana Bella
1989 *Entre montañas y cafetales: Luchas agrarias en el norte de Chiapas.*
Instituto de Investigaciones Antropológicas, Serie Antropológica 85.
México, DF: Universidad Nacional Autónoma de México.

Pick, James B., Edgar W. Butler, and Elizabeth L. Lanzer
1989 *Atlas of Mexico.* Boulder: Westview Press.

Pietri, Rene, and Claudio Stern
1985 *Petróleo, agricultura y población en el sureste de México.* México,
DF: El Colegio de México.

Pineda, Luz Olivia
1993 *Caciques Culturales: El case de los maestros bilingues en los Altos de
Chiapas.* Puebla: Altres Costa-Amic.

Pohlenz, Juan C.
1985 La conformación de la frontera entre México y Guatemala: El
caso de Nuevo Huixtán en la selva Chiapaneca, part I, pp. 21–30 in *La
formación histórica de la frontera sur,* Andrés Fábregas, Juan Pohlenz,
Mariano Báez, and Gabriel Macías, eds. Cuadernos de la casa chata
124. México, DF: Centro de Investigaciones y Estudios Superiores en
Antropología Social.

Reyes Ramos, María Eugenia
1992 *El reparto de tierras y la política agraria en Chiapas, 1914–1988.*
México, DF: Universidad Nacional Autónoma de México.

Reyes Ramos, María Eugenia, Reyna Moguel Viveros, and
Gemma van der Haar
1998 *Transformaciones rurales en Chiapas.* México, DF: Universidad
Autónoma Metropolitana and San Cristóbal de Las Casas: El Colegio
de la Frontera Sur.

Rincón Ramírez, Carlos
1996 *Relaciones de poder y dominio en el movimiento magisterial
Chiapaneco.* Tuxtla Gutiérrez: Universidad Autónoma de Chiapas,
Facultad de Humanidades.

Rojas, Rosa
1995 *Chiapas ¿y las mujeres qué?* 2 vols. México, DF: La Correa
Feminista.

Romero, César
1994 *Marcos: ¿Un profesional de la esperanza?* México, DF: Grupo Editorial Planeta.

Ronfeldt, David F., et al.
1998 *The Zapatista "Social Netwar" in Mexico.* Santa Monica, Calif.: Rand.

Rosaldo, Renato
1989 *Culture & Truth: The Remaking of Social Analysis.* Boston: Beacon Press.

Rosenbaum, Brenda
1993 *With Our Heads Bowed: The Dynamics of Gender in a Maya Community.* Albany: SUNY Press.

Rosset, Peter
1994 Insurgent Mexico and the Global South: A New Kind of Guerilla Movement? Institute for Food and Development Policy, *Food First News & Views,* Spring, pp. 1 and 4.

Rovira, Guiomar
1997 *Mujeres de maíz: La voz de las indígenas de Chiapas y la rebelión zapatista.* México, DF: Ediciones Era.

Ruiz Hernández, Margarito, and Araceli Burguete Cal y Mayor
1998 Chiapas: Organización y lucha indígena al final del milenio (1974–1998). *Asuntos Indígenas* No. 3.

Rus, Diane
1988 Responding to the Crisis: Changing Economic Roles of Indigenous Women in the Chiapas Highlands. Working paper. San Cristóbal de Las Casas: INAREMAC.

1990 La crisis económica y la mujer indígena: El caso de Chamula, Chiapas. Document 038-VIII-90. San Cristóbal de Las Casas: INAREMAC.

Rus, Jan
1976 Managing Mexico's Indians: The Historical Context and Consequences of Indigenismo. Manuscript prepared for Department of Anthropology, Harvard University.

1983   Whose Caste War? Indians, Ladinos, and the Chiapas "Caste War" of 1869, pp. 127–168 in *Spaniards and Indians in Southern Mesoamerica*, Murdo J. MacLeod and Robert Wasserstrom, eds. Lincoln: University of Nebraska Press.

1989   The "Caste War" of 1869 from the Indian's Perspective: A Challenge for Ethnohistory, pp. 1033–1047 in *Memorias, Coloquio Internacional de Mayistas*, Vol. II. México, DF: Universidad Nacional Autónoma de México/Centro de Estudios Mayas.

1994   The "Comunidad Revolucionaria Institucional": The Subversion of Native Government in Highland Chiapas, 1936–1968, pp. 265–300 in *Everyday Forms of State Formation: Revolution and the Negotiation of Rule in Modern Mexico*, eds. Gilbert M. Joseph and Daniel Nugent. Durham: Duke University Press.

n.d.   Contained Revolutions: Indians and the Struggle for Control of Highland Chiapas, 1910–1925. Forthcoming, *Mexican Studies/Estudios Mexicanos*.

Rus, Jan, Rosalva Aída Hernández del Castillo, and Shannan Mattiace, eds.
2003   *Mayan Lives, Mayan Utopias: The Indigenous People of Chiapas and the Zapatista Rebellion*. Lanham, Md.: Rowman & Littlefield.

Rus, Jan, and George A. Collier
2003   A Generation of Crisis in the Central Highlands of Chiapas: The Cases of Chamula and Zinacantán, 1974-2000, pp. 33-61 in *Mayan Lives, Mayan Utopias*, Rus, Hernández, and Mattiace, eds., Lanham, Md.: Rowman & Littlefield.

Russell, Philip L.
1994   *Mexico under Salinas*. Austin: Mexico Resource Center.

Ruz, Mario Humberto
1985   *Copanaguastla en un espejo: un pueblo Tzeltal en el virreinato*. Tuxtla Gutiérrez: Universidad Autónoma de Chiapas.

1992   *Savia India, Xoración Ladina: Apuntes para una historia de las fincas comitecas* (siglos XVIII y XIX). México, DF: Consejo Nacional para la Cultura y las Artes.

Sánchez, Pontigo, and José Luis Ovalle Muñoz
1986   Lucha laboral y sindicalismo en Simojovel y Huitiupán, Chiapas, pp. 153–160 in *Asalariados agrícolas y sindicalismo en el campo mexicano,* ed. by Hubert C. de Grammont. México, DF: Joan Pablos Editor, S.A./Instituto de Investigaciones Sociales, UNAM.

Sanderson, Steven E.
1986   *The Transformation of Mexican Agriculture: International Structure and the Politics of Rural Change.* Princeton: Princeton University Press.

Scherr, Sara J.
1985   *The Oil Syndrome and Agricultural Development: Lessons from Tabasco, Mexico.* New York: Praeger Publishers.

Schulz, Donald E.
1997   Between a Rock and a Hard Place: The United State, Mexico, and the Challenge of National Security. *Low Intensity Conflict & Law Enforcement* 6(3): 1–40.

Servicios de Apoyo Intercultural, A.C. (SAIAC)
1999   *Los derechos de los indígenas, y de los pueblos y comunidades indígenas en la legislación Oaxaqueña.* Taller sobre Derecho Indígena, March 26, 27, and 28, 1999, Ciudad de Oaxaca, Oaxaca. México, DF: SAIAC.

Silko, Leslie Marmon
1991   *Almanac of the Dead: A Novel.* New York: Penguin Books.

Spalding, Rose J.
1984   *The Mexican Food Crisis: An Analysis of the SAM.* Research Report Series, 33. La Jolla: Center for U.S.–Mexican Studies, University of California, San Diego.

Speed, Shannon, and Jane F. Collier
2000   Limiting Indigenous Autonomy in Chiapas, Mexico: The State Government's Use of Human Rights. *Human Rights Quarterly* 22:877–905.

Spenser, Daniela
1988   *El Partido Socialista Chiapaneco: rescate y reconstrucción de su historia.* Ediciones de la Casa Chata 29. México, DF: Centro de Investigaciones y Estudios Superiores en Antropología Social.

Stavenhagen, Rodolfo
1975   *Social Classes in Agrarian Societies.* Translated by J.A. Hellman. Garden City, N.Y.: Anchor Books.

Stephen, Lynn
2002   *Zapata Lives! Histories and Cultural Politics in Southern México.* Berkeley and Los Angeles: University of California Press.

Taller de Análisis de las Cuestiones Agrarias
1988   *Los Zapatistas de Chiapas.* San Cristóbal de Las Casas: Taller de Análisis de las Cuestiones Agrarias.

Taller Tzotzil
1988   *Buch'u la smeltzan Jobel?/Quien hizo San Cristóbal.* Comp. and trans. by Jan Rus, José González and Diane Rus. San Cristóbal de Las Casas: INAREMAC.
1990   *Abtel ta pinka/Trabajo en las fincas.* Ed. and trans. by Jan Rus, José Hernández, and Diane Rus. San Cristóbal de Las Casas: INAREMAC.

Tello Díaz, Carlos
1995   *La rebelión de las Cañadas.* México, DF: Cal y Arena.

Toledo, Victor M.
1994   La vía ecológico-campesina de desarrollo: Una alternativa para la selva de Chiapas. *La Jornada del Campo* 2(23):4–6.

Toledo Tello, Sonia
1996   *Historia del Movimiento Indígena en Simojovel.* Serie Monografías 6, Instituto de Estudios Indígenas. Tuxtla Gutiérrez: Universidad Autónoma de Chiapas.

Union Tierra Tzotzil
1990   *Kipaltik, lo'il sventa k'u cha'al la jmantkutik jpinkakutik/La historia de como compamos nuestra finca.* Ed. and trans. by Salvador Guzmán and Jan Rus. San Cristóbal de Las Casas: INAREMAC.

Varese, Stefano
1983 *Proyectos étnicos y proyectos nacionales.* México, DF: Fondo de Cultura Económica.
1992 Grupos No Gubermentales y Organizaciones de Base. Manuscript, Chapter 8, for *Agricultural Sector Reform and the Peasantry in Mexico,* for Special Programming Mission to Mexico, International Fund for Agricultural Development. Rome: United Nations.

Vasconcelos, José
1948 *La raza cósmica: Misión de la raza Iberoamericana, Argentina y Brazil.* México, DF: Espasa-Calpa Mexicana.

Villafuerte Solís, Daniel, ed.
1993 *El café en la frontera sur: La producción y los productores del Soconusco, Chiapas.* Tuxtla Gutiérrez: Instituto Chiapaneco de Cultura.

Villafuerte Solís, Daniel, et al.
2002 *La tierra en Chiapas: Viejos problemas nuevos.* México, DF: Fondo de Cultura Económica.

Viqueira Albán, Juan Pedro
1993 *María de la Candelaria: India natural de Cancuc.* México, DF: Fondo de Cultura Económica.
1999 Los peligros del Chiapas imaginario. *Letras Libres* 1(1):20–28, 96–97.

Viqueira Albán, Juan Pedro, and Mario H. Ruz, eds.
1995 *Chiapas: Los rumbos de otra historia.* México, DF: Universidad Nacional Autónoma de México.

Viqueira Albán, Juan Pedro and Willibald Sonnleitner, coords.
2000 *Democracia en tierras indígenas: Las elecciones en Los Altos de Chiapas (1991–1998).* México, D.F.: Centro de Investigaciones y Estudios Superiores en Antropología Social, El Colegio de México, and Instituto Federal Electoral.

Vogt, Evon Z.
1969 *Zinacantán: A Maya Community in the Highlands of Chiapas.* Cambridge: Harvard University Press.

de Vos, Jan

1980   *La paz de Dios y del Rey: La conquista de la Selva Lacandona por los españoles, 1525–1821.* México, DF: Gobierno del Estado de Chiapas.

1988   *Oro verde: La conquista de la Selva Lacandona por los madereros tabasqueños, 1822–1949.* México, DF: Fondo de Cultura Económica.

Warman, Arturo

1980   *"We Come to Object": The Peasants of Morelos and the National State.* Trans. by Stephen K. Ault. Baltimore: Johns Hopkins University Press.

Warren, Kay B.

1998   *Indigenous Movements and their Critics: Pan-Maya Activism in Guatemala.* Princeton: Princeton University Press.

Wasserstrom, Robert

1983   *Class and Society in Central Chiapas.* Berkeley and Los Angeles: University of California Press.

Wilkie, James W.

1970   *The Mexican Revolution: Federal Expenditure and Social Change since 1910.* Berkeley and Los Angeles: University of California Press.

Williams, Robert G.

1986   *Export Agriculture and the Crisis in Central America.* Chapel Hill: University of North Carolina Press.

Wolf, Eric R.

1969   *Peasant Wars of the Twentieth Century.* New York: Harper & Row.

Wolf, Eric R., and Edward C. Hansen

1972   *The Human Condition in Latin America.* New York: Oxford University Press.

Womack, John, Jr.

1969   *Zapata and the Mexican Revolution.* New York: Alfred Knopf.

1999   *Rebellion in Chiapas: An Historical Reader.* New York: New Press.

INDEX

About the Authors

George A. Collier obtained a Ph.D. in Social Anthropology from Harvard University. He is Professor of Anthropology Emeritus at Stanford University, where he has also served as Chair of Anthropology and Director of the Center for Latin America Studies. Dr. Collier began his studies of agrarian politics and agrarian change in Chipapas, Mexico, in the 1960s. He is the author of *Fields of the Tzotzil: The Ecological Bases of Tradition in Highland Chiapas* (University of Texas Press, 1975); *The Inca and Aztec States: Anthropology and History, 1400–1800* (Academic Press, 1982, co-edited with Renato Rosaldo and John Wirth); *Socialists of Rural Andalusia: Unacknowledged Revolutionaries of the Second Republic* (Stanford University Press, 1987) and numerous journal articles.

Elizabeth Lowery Quaratiello, a graduate of Wheaton College, is a freelance journalist with interest in anthropology, food, and economics. A former crime reporter, she is married and has one child.

FOOD FIRST BOOKS OF RELATED INTEREST

To Inherit the Earth: The Landless Movement and the Struggle for a New Brazil
Angus Wright and Wendy Wolford
The story of one of the world's most successful contemporary grassroots movements, Brazil's Landless Workers Movement (MST). The authors put the movement in its historical, political, and environmental context, trace its growth and organization, sum up its accomplishments and setbacks, and analyze the issues the MST faces going forward.
Paperback, $15.95
ISBN: 0-935028-90-0

Benedita da Silva: An Afro-Brazilian Woman's Story of Politics and Love
As told to Medea Benjamin and Maisa Mendonça
Foreword by Jesse Jackson
The inspiring memoir of a woman who overcame poverty and tragedy to become one of the most prominent policians in Brazil. Benedita da Silva shares the story of her life as an advocate for the rights of women, people of color, and the poor, and argues persuasively for economic and social human rights in Brazil and everywhere.
Paperback, $15.95
ISBN: 0-935028-70-6

The Future in the Balance: Essays on Globalization and Resistance
Walden Bello
Edited with a preface by Anuradha Mittal
A new collection of essays by Third World activist and scholar Walden Bello on the myths of development as prescribed by the World Trade Organization and other institutions, and the possibility of another world based on fairness and justice.
Paperback, $13.95
ISBN: 0-935028-84-6

Views from the South: The Effects of Globalization and the WTO on Third World Countries
Foreword by Jerry Mander
Afterword by Anuradha Mittal
Edited by Sarah Anderson
This rare collection of essays by Third World activists and scholars describes in pointed detail the effects of the WTO and other Bretton Woods institutions.
Paperback, $12.95
ISBN: 0-935028-82-x

Call our distributor, CDS, at (800) 343-4499 to place book orders.
All orders must be pre-paid.

ABOUT FOOD FIRST

Food First, also known as the Institute for Food and Development Policy, is a nonprofit research and education-for-action center working to expose the root causes of hunger in a world of plenty. It was founded in 1975 by Dr. Joseph Collins and Frances Moore Lappé, author of the best selling *Diet for a Small Planet*. Food First research has revealed that hunger is created by concentrated economic and political power, not by scarcity. Resources and decision-making are in the hands of wealthy few, depriving the majority of land, jobs, and therefore food.

Hailed by the *New York Times* as "one of the most established food think tanks in the country," Food First has grown to profoundly shape the debate about hunger and development. Through books, reports, videos, media appearances, and speaking engagements, Food First experts reveal the often hidden roots of hunger, and show how individuals can get involved in ending the problem. Food First inspires action by bringing to light the courageous efforts of people around the world who are creating faming and food systems that truly meet people's needs.

BECOME A MEMBER OF FOOD FIRST

Individual member contributions provide more than half of the funds for Food First's work. Because Food First is not tied to government, corporate, or university funding, we can speak with a strong, independent voice. The success of our program depends on dedicated volunteers and staff, as well as financial support from our activist donors. Your gift will help strengthen our effort to improve the lives of hungry people around the world.

I would like to become a Food First member! Enclosed is my tax-deductible contribution of:

☐ $35 ☐ $40 ☐ $50* ☐ $100* ☐ $500* ☐ $1,000* ☐ Other: $____
All gifts are tax-deductible.

METHOD OF PAYMENT

☐ Check or money order enclosed. ☐ Visa ☐ MC ☐ AmEx

All foreign orders must be in US funds. Make checks out to Food First. Send to: 398 – 60th Street, Oakland, CA 94618, (510) 654-4400, FAX (510) 654-4551, www.foodfirst.org.

NAME ON CARD

CARD NUMBER   EXPIRATION DATE

NAME

ADDRESS

CITY   STATE   ZIP

TEL: (DAY)   TEL: (EVE)

*A donation of $50 or more includes a FREE one-year subscription to the *New Internationalist*.